Marko Bojcun

TOWARDS A POLITICAL ECONOMY OF UKRAINE

Selected Essays 1990–2015

With a foreword by John-Paul Himka

UKRAINIAN VOICES

Collected by Andreas Umland

The book series "Ukrainian Voices" publishes English- and German-language monographs, edited volumes, document collections and anthologies of articles authored and composed by Ukrainian politicians, intellectuals, activists, officials, researchers, and diplomats. The series' aim is to introduce Western and other audiences to Ukrainian explorations, deliberations and interpretations of historic and current, domestic and international affairs. The purpose of these books is to make non-Ukrainian readers familiar with how some prominent Ukrainians approach, view and assess their country's development and position in the world. The series was founded and the volumes are collected by Andreas Umland, Dr. phil. (FU Berlin), Ph. D. (Cambridge), Senior Research Fellow at the Institute for Euro-Atlantic Cooperation in Kyiv.

Marko Bojcun

TOWARDS A POLITICAL ECONOMY OF UKRAINE

Selected Essays 1990–2015

With a foreword by John-Paul Himka

Bibliografische Information der Deutschen Nationalbibliothek

Die Deutsche Nationalbibliothek verzeichnet diese Publikation in der Deutschen Nationalbibliografie; detaillierte bibliografische Daten sind im Internet über http://dnb.d-nb.de abrufbar.

Bibliographic information published by the Deutsche Nationalbibliothek

Die Deutsche Nationalbibliothek lists this publication in the Deutsche Nationalbibliografie; detailed bibliographic data are available in the Internet at http://dnb.d-nb.de.

Cover picture:
ID 67923934 © Naumenkoaleksandr | Dreamstime.com
ID 109272599 © Cherokee4 | Dreamstime.com

ISBN-13: 978-3-8382-1368-2
© *ibidem*-Verlag, Stuttgart 2020
Alle Rechte vorbehalten

Printed in the EU

Contents

List of Tables

Acknowledgements

I would like to thank all the people who supported and encouraged me, who shared their ideas and research with me and who gave me the opportunity to present my work at their seminars and conferences and in their journals and books. Here I would like to mention those who made an especially important contribution in the past thirty years to help shape, sharpen and sustain my contribution to the study of contemporary Ukraine:

Peter Gowan, with whom I discussed more than with anyone else the epochal changes of our days.

Anatoli Artemenko and Yarko Koshiw, with whom I worked making documentary films in Ukraine at the time of the Soviet Union's collapse.

Halya Kowalsky at Amnesty International.

Chris Ford of Workers' Liberty and the Ukraine Solidarity Campaign in London, England.

Roman Senkus at the Journal of Ukrainian Studies.

Bohdan Krawchenko and John-Paul Himka at the Canadian Institute of Ukrainian Studies.

Mike Newman and Yaroslav Mudryi at London Metropolitan University.

Olena Bekh, Jim Dingley and Peter Duncan at the School of Slavonic and East European Studies, University of London.

Gareth Dale at Brunel University, London.

Hiillel Ticktin and Stephen White at the University of Glasgow.

Neil Robinson at the University of Limerick.

Andrew Kilminster at Debatte: Journal of Contemporary Central and Eastern Europe.

Tatiana Zhurzhenko at V. Karazin Kharkiv National University and the Institute for Human Sciences in Vienna.

Olha Briukhovetska at the University of Kyiv Mohyla Academy.

Volodymyr Ishchenko at Kyiv Polytechnic Institute and the journal *Spil'ne*.

Zakhar Popovych at the Kyiv Centre for Social and Labour Research.

Andreas Umland at the Institute of Euro-Atlantic Co-operation in Kyiv who invited me to submit this selection of essays for publication.

I would like to thank Halya Kowalsky for her careful proofreading of the draft manuscript.

Finally, I owe this book to my partner Jane Greenwood, with whom I built a family, a home and a circle of good friends in Britain, where I resettled in the 1980s.

Abbreviations

bcm — billion cubic metres
bn — billion
BRIC — Brazil, Russia, India, China
CBMMO — Capacity Building in Migration Management Programme
CIA — Central Intelligence Agency of the United States of America
CIS — Commonwealth of Independent States
cm — cubic metres
Comecon — Council for Mutual Economic Assistance; after 1991 renamed Organisation for International Economic Co-operation
CPSU — Communist Party of the Soviet Union
CPU — Communist Party of Ukraine
EU — European Union
FDI — Foreign Direct Investment
FSB — Federal Security Service of the Russian Federation
FSU — Former Soviet Union
G7 — Group of Seven (USA, Canada, Japan, Germany, United Kingdom, France, Italy)
G8 — Group of Eight (USA, Canada, Japan, Germany, United Kingdom, France, Italy, Russian Federation)
GATT — General Agreement on Tariffs and Trade
GDP — Gross Domestic Product
GUUAM — Georgia, Ukraine, Uzbekistan, Azerbaijan, Moldova
ha — hectares
IMF — International Monetary Fund
IOM — International Organisation for Migration
KGB — Committee for State Security of the Soviet Union
kwh — kilowatt hours
m — million
mcm — million cubic metres
mt — million tons
NATO — North Atlantic Treaty Organisation
NBU — National Bank of Ukraine
ODI — Overseas Direct Investment

PCA—Partnership and Co-operation Agreement
PHARE—Poland and Hungary Assistance for the Restructuring of the Economy
Rukh—People's Movement of Ukraine for Restructuring
SAWS—Seasonal Agricultural Workers Programme, United Kingdom
SBS—Sector Based Scheme, United Kingdom
SBU—Security Service of Ukraine
SPU—Socialist Party of Ukraine
TACIS—Technical Assistance to the Commonwealth of Independent States
tr—trillion
t—ton
UHU—Ukrainian Helsinki Union
UN—United Nations
UPR—Ukrainian People's Republic
USSR—Union of Soviet Socialist Republics
VAT—Value Added Tax

Foreword

Anyone who wants to understand how Ukraine functions (and also malfunctions) should study the essays that Marko Bojcun has collected here in a single volume. The essays date from various years, starting in 1990, shortly before Ukraine became an independent country. Reading and rereading them, even after so many years, I am struck by their clarity of explanation and the untarnished validity of their content. Even though they were all written close to the events they analyse, somehow they have managed to avoid becoming superseded or even stale and remain valuable sources to the history of contemporary Ukraine. I ascribe their longevity to Marko's approach, which is unique in the field of Ukrainian studies.

Marko likes to focus on the nexus between politics and economics. Although Marx is not cited or even mentioned so much as once in this collection, his spirit hovers over it. All the essays look at the economic underpinnings of certain political results, although never in a simplistic base-and-superstructure fashion. Almost half the book analyses the 1990s, when the transition from the Soviet planned economy to a market economy took place. This period laid the track for the future course of Ukraine's development and deserves the detailed treatment that Marko devotes to it.

Another aspect of Marko's approach that distinguishes it from much of the literature on the Ukrainian transition is the conceptual distance he maintains from capitalism. Marko keeps the reader aware that the transition has not been from the clunky planned economy into some kind of putative normalcy, into some natural and rational culmination of economic evolution, but from one specific, historically-formed type of economic system into another, from Soviet-style socialism into Western-dominated capitalism. He is aware of the features of the latter, both positive and negative for Ukraine, and this awareness gives him a vantage point in analysis that committed free-marketers have difficulty reaching.

Workers and workers' movements find extensive treatment in Marko's texts, especially those of the Donbas. After 2014 and the outbreak of war and separatism in the eastern part of that region, it is particularly interesting to be reminded of all the workers' activism that emerged there in 1978, 1989–90, and 1992–93. Those moments are infrequently cited in analyses of the current conflictual situation. Could anyone back then have guessed the direction things would take?

Actually, Marko had a clear sense of the possible problem already in 1990. Considering the larger historical context, he wrote: "The main weakness of previous bids for Ukraine's independence — in 1917 and during World War II — lay in the historic division between Western Ukrainian nationalism and the Eastern Ukrainian proletariat. The former saw national unification and independence as a panacea without considering fully the political and social egalitarian aspirations of workers in such a movement for a new state. The latter, a multinational working class with a sizeable Russian component in the most industrialized part of Ukraine, was radical in social and political demands, but not quite sure whether its region should belong to Ukraine or to Russia." Throughout the essays in this volume, Marko has kept an eye on regionalism, particularly the east-west divide in Ukraine. Again, the strong sense of a regionally divided Ukraine has by no means been shared by all analysts. Many have not wanted to see the divisions and have constructed in their imaginations a united Ukrainian people with a single will and a cohesive Ukrainian state to which it pledged loyalty. But the reality kept exposing itself, with every election and with every revolutionary moment on Kyiv's Maidan.

The essays are sensitive to Ukraine's delicate geopolitical situation between Russia and the West. Marko's position again stands out among analysts. Most analysts writing in English concentrate on Russia's designs on Ukraine, which have been more apparent since the crisis on 2014. Analysis of Western relations with Ukraine has been, by contrast, relatively neglected. This is similar to the case of Marko's approach to the economic formations in the transition; more or less everyone else agreed about the need for Ukraine to move away from the Soviet planned economy, but they paid little attention to the nature of the goal for which Ukraine was naturally expected to strive: the free market economy, aka capitalism. Just as

Marko looked critically at capitalism's role in Ukraine, so too he looks critically at the West as well as Russia. He illuminates, but not with soft lighting, Ukrainians' labour emigration to Western Europe and the EU's blatant toying with Ukraine. In Marko's view, one has to factor into the analysis the "rivalry between Russian and European imperialisms to incorporate Ukraine into their respective transnational strategies." And as he points out, neither of the two vectors was willing to acknowledge how they had complicated the environment of the new born state: "The fact that [Ukraine's] economy was closely tied to both the Russian and EU markets, asymmetrically but nevertheless in equally strong measure — through debt to the West, energy supplies from the East, and trade with both — was simply ignored by Russian and EU leaders."

Marko also takes an expertly aimed shot at Western hubris towards post-Soviet Ukraine. In the 1994 parliamentary elections in Ukraine, some candidates distributed goody bags to boost support, a practice condemned by the Western democracies. But Marko is absolutely correct to observe: "While these were certainly violations of Ukraine's electoral law, one may well ask what is a more serious distortion of the democratic process — the delivery of food packets to pensioners containing condensed milk, barley, sugar and a leaflet from the donor candidate, or the undisclosed donation by a large corporation of millions of pounds/dollars to the election campaign fund of a political party?" He wrote this in 1995, and a quarter of a century later the goody bags have disappeared from Ukrainian politics, but the corporate distortion of elections in the West has only increased.

Marko brings a highly intelligent leftist perspective to his analysis of Ukraine's politics and economy. Some American, British, and German leftists, so opposed to Western policies and particularly those of the United States, have sought to justify the policies of anti-Western forces such as the Islamists or Russia. In the latter case, this has led to some anti-Ukraine and anti-Ukrainian rhetoric marked by essentialism and prejudice. Marko is certainly not one of this kind of leftist. He stands on the left, but he also stands for deeper democracy and for Ukraine. How did he arrive at this standpoint?

Here I will say a bit about one station on Marko's journey to become the insightful, original analyst that he became. We were both involved in a particular milieu in Canada in the 1970s and 1980s, the Ukrainian Canadian anti-Soviet left. We had our own journals. One was *Meta*, which came out mainly in English in 1975–79. Marko was a member of the editorial collective, which was based in Toronto, where he then lived. The journal described itself on its cover as "a forum for left wing analysis and discussion on the Ukrainian question, Eastern Europe and related international issues." Marko was also a member of the editorial board of *Diialoh*, which came out entirely in Ukrainian from 1977 to 1987. The politics of this journal was well captured by the motto it bore on its cover: "For socialism and democracy in an independent Ukraine." The audience the journal was aimed at was Ukrainians in Poland, Czechoslovakia, and the USSR. Emissaries from the group travelled into Eastern Europe with copies of the journal. To be honest, its greatest impact was not on Ukrainians in the communist states, but on the young people that put it together in Canada. Most of the work on the journal—typing, layout, reproduction—was done in Edmonton, Alberta, about 3500 kilometres west of Toronto, where Marko lived, but the collective held regular conferences that Marko attended. Marko also penned two long analyses in 1981, under his pseudonym Taras Lehkyi, one on the situation in Poland in that year, the year of the Gdańsk strikes and rise of Solidarity, and the other on the Soviet invasion of Afghanistan that had begun two years earlier. The latter article can be found on the internet, reprinted by the leftist Ukrainian site *Vpered* in February 2019.

The leftism in our milieu varied from orthodox Marxist to more vaguely progressive, with strong feminist elements. Many of the members of the *Meta* and *Diialoh* collectives had been active in organizations of the Fourth International, including Marko. These Trotskyists preferred the terminology "anti-Stalinist" to "anti-Soviet," since the latter term in the cold war era conjured up right-wing reaction. The moment of our greatest enthusiasm was 1981, when the workers in Poland rose up against the communist regime, supported by dissident, left-leaning intellectuals like Adam Michnik and the late Jacek Kuron. This was our vision: that the Soviet proletariat would rise up against the regime and insist on installing genuine and democratic socialism. And we felt that Ukraine would be the vanguard of this revolution, since its population suffered from both social and national oppression. It turned out we were wrong about this, and Marko's essays in this volume document his recalibration to the actual results of the historical process.

During the 1970s and 1980s we all believed in the need for Ukraine to become an independent country. And when it happened, when Ukraine declared independence and the Soviet Union collapsed in 1991, the cohesion among us became fissiparous. I often recall the words attributed to the Polish statesman, Józef Piłsudski: "Comrades, I took the red tram of socialism to the stop called independence, and that's where I got off." Some of us went off to Ukraine to help build the state. Some of us remained in the West and tried to make sense of the new situation. Some of us dropped out.

Marko, by then living in London, charted his own course. The essays that follow constitute the logbook.

John-Paul Himka
Professor Emeritus, University of Alberta

Ukraine: The Issue of National Self-determination[*]

The Ukrainian Soviet Socialist Republic was established by the Bolsheviks after the 1917 Revolution and Civil War. It had a population of approximately 30 million people on a territory of 443,000 square kilometres, encompassing present-day Central and Eastern Ukraine. Western Ukraine came under control of the newly established states of Poland, Czechoslovakia and Romania. In December 1922 the Ukrainian SSR formally joined the USSR on the basis of the Treaty of Union. It was further enlarged during World War II with the annexation by the Soviet Army of Galicia and Volyn from Poland in 1939, northern Bukovyna and sections of Bessarabia from Romania in 1940, and Transcarpathia from Czechoslovakia in 1945. With the transfer of Crimea in 1954 from the Russian SFSR to the Ukrainian SSR, the republic further grew to its present size of 603,700 square kilometres.

With the collapse of Czarism in 1917, political control of the Ukrainian provinces of the Russian Empire was contested by the Provisional Government based in Petrograd, the Central Rada based in Kyiv and the workers parties (mainly Mensheviks and Bolsheviks) based in the urban soviets. The Rada emerged the strongest contender in October 1917. It took power with the overwhelming support of peasants on the land and in the army and with a growing base among workers, especially in the northern provinces. In November the Rada declared the formation of the Ukrainian People's Republic (UPR).

Although the Bolsheviks entered the 1917 Revolution largely convinced that new nation states were an anachronism, their branches in Ukraine supported the Rada against the Provisional Government in October and then sought a place in the leadership of the Ukrainian People's Republic. Having failed to find agree-

---

[*] First published in: *The Times Guide to Eastern Europe: Inside the other Europe*, ed. Keith Sword (London: Times Book:, 1990), 224–236.

21

ment on their proportional representation, the Bolsheviks withdrew and established a competing Ukrainian People's Republic government in December 1917, with headquarters in Kharkiv based mainly on the urban soviets of the Donbas region in southeastern Ukraine. The Kharkiv-based UPR became the Russian Bolsheviks' fig leaf for their military intervention against the Kyiv-based UPR in January 1918 which led the latter to declare independence from Soviet Russia in January 1918 and to seek military support from the Austro-Hungarian armies.

After three years of civil war, foreign interventions by Axis, Entente, White and Red armies, and no less than 14 separate governments, the Bolsheviks finally took power in Ukraine with the military and economic backing of Soviet Russia. They consolidated power here during the 1920s by conceding the New Economic Policy to the peasantry, which gave them a chance to prosper as individual producers, and by admitting left wing sections of the patriotic intelligentsia to the Communist Party, to government office, the educational system, mass media and the trade unions. Through such institutions the Ukrainian intelligentsia set out in the 1920s to make Ukrainian the language of civic life, education and economic activity, and to strengthen the republic's rights vis-a-vis Moscow.

The first post-revolutionary decade is considered a golden era of national rebirth. The second decade leading up to World War saw a brutal collectivization of agriculture, the death of approximately seven million peasants in the famine of 1932–3, the extermination by Stalin's secret police of an entire generation of Ukraine's political, cultural, scientific and religious leaders, and the crash industrialisation programme with which Stalin prepared his country for war.

World War II, which brought about the unification of practically all Ukrainian territories into the Ukrainian SSR, also cost the republic six million lives, or 30 percent of the USSR's total human losses, and the destruction of much housing, industry and communications, amounting to 47 percent of the USSR's material losses. These were compounded by the outbreak of famine in Ukraine in 1946, the continuing campaign by Soviet units in Western Ukraine against the guerrilla Ukrainian Insurgent Army and the mass deportations to Siberia and the Far East of this region's villagers on suspicion of nationalism and disloyalty to the Soviet regime. 'When the casualties of the civil war, collectivisation, the purges and the Second World War are combined, more than half the male and a quarter of the female population perished'.[1]

The status quo in Ukraine was challenged in the latter half of the 1950s and 1960s (the period of de-Stalinization throughout the USSR) by the opposition or dissident movement. Unlike its counterpart in Russia, the Ukrainian opposition movement was supported actively by workers, both in membership of its various organizations and participation in meetings, petitions, etc., particularly in its early years. This movement had as its primary objectives the restitution of civil rights and national self-determination for the republic. It gained support within the Communist Party of Ukraine and a number of key republican state institutions, in response to which the central Communist leadership under Leonid Brezhnev ordered the movement to be crushed. A wave of arrests of prominent oppositionists swept the republic in January 1972 and many were subsequently incarcerated to long terms in labour camps, psychiatric prison hospitals and internal exile. The Communist Party of Ukraine was purged of its patriotically inclined members and its First Secretary, Petro Shelest, was removed from office.

Volodymyr Shcherbytsky, Brezhnev's faithful ally, replaced Shelest in 1973. He ruled the republic until 1989 when he retired from office and died soon afterwards in February 1990. By the end of his term in office Shcherbytsky had discredited himself publicly by his iron rule, subservience to Moscow and his cover up of the immediate and long term effects of the 1986 Chernobyl disaster. His failure to cope with the July 1989 miners' strike in Donbas or the emergence of the Popular Movement of Ukraine for Restructuring (Rukh) made him appear out of step with the times and a liability for the Party. In September 1989, after careful preparation in Moscow by the CPSU Politburo, a plenum of the CPU Central Committee

---

1   Bohdan Krawchenko, *Social Change and National Consciousness in Twentieth-century Ukraine* (London: Macmillan, 1985), 171.

in Kyiv elected Volodymyr Ivashko as the Party's new republican First Secretary. At 57 years of age and a Party member since 1960, Ivashko was described by Mikhail Gorbachev as 'intelligent, cultured and simply very accessible'[2]. His task was to steer the republic through an impending storm of political change, which was already blowing in adjacent Eastern Europe, and to keep the Party in office.

The political terrain

Three key political forces were evident in Ukraine at the beginning of 1990: the Communist Party, Rukh and an array of independent workers' organizations, principally among the miners. Also, several new political parties were about to formally constitute themselves and seek office within a multi-party electoral system. The signal for such a system was given in February 1990 by the CPSU's declaration that it would give up its monopoly of power. The Ukrainian republican elections in March came too soon for a genuine multi-party contest here, but their outcome showed clearly that the CPU was destined to share power or to become a minor party in opposition.

The Communist Party of Ukraine claimed 3.3 million members at the beginning of 1989, one-sixth of the CPSU's total. However, it was losing both members and authority within society at large, because its leadership under Shcherbytsky was associated with the Brezhnev era. It was failing to improve the economic situation or to make any concessions to popular demands for change in linguistic and cultural policy, nuclear energy, environmental protection and political reform.

Through its control of electoral commissions the Party prevented the nomination of all but a few Rukh candidates to stand in the first all-Union elections in March and April 1989 to the Congress of People's Deputies. The electorate responded with a boycott of many single candidate constituency elections, thus defeating unpopular nominees of the CPU apparatus. On the other hand, reform-

---

2   *Moscow Radio*, 28 September 1989.

minded Communists in other constituencies who had publicly declared support for Rukh's programme were elected to the Congress.

Ivashko's first months in office saw the Party leadership steering several progressive pieces of legislation through the Ukrainian Verkhovna Rada (parliament): on improving the status of the Ukrainian language in the republic; making its electoral law more democratic; and declaring the need to close the Chernobyl nuclear power station for good. Such measures were intended to improve the CPU's image and to convince the population that Ivashko's elevation signalled a major turn to responsible and accountable government in the republic. But they did not arrest the flow of resignations from the Party. More alarming still, a wave of mass protest against oblast Party leaders on charges of corruption and patronage swept the republic in the first three months of 1990, forcing their resignation in five of the 25 oblasts. Ivashko acknowledged in March 1990 that it was no longer easy to attract professionals and people of standing in the community to the Party and spoke of his previous career as a college lecturer as "the better years of my life".[3]

Rukh has its origins in 1988 when attempts were made in various cities to launch popular front organizations on the model of those in the Baltic states. The most active participants in such attempts were former political prisoners just released from labour camps and exile, radical students and members of the Ukrainian Writers' Union. Many of the last were also members of the Communist Party. However, all these attempts were crushed by the authorities until November 1988, when an initiative committee composed of prominent Kyivan writers and other intellectuals was formed in Kyiv. The committee wrote Rukh's draft programme, which was published in February 1989 in *Literaturna Ukraina*, the writers' union newspaper. Local Rukh branches sprang up in all 25 oblasts, the strongest centres being Kyiv, Lviv and the towns of Central and Western Ukraine.

Despite intense pressure applied by the CPU leadership against its own members in Rukh, as well as a continuous campaign

---

3   Interview with Marko Bojcun for *HTV Wales*, 1 March 1990, *Ukraine Today*, No. 2, August 1990, 19–23.

of slander and abuse against the organization in the state controlled media, Rukh prepared and convened its first national congress in Kyiv on 8–10 September 1989. Of the 1,158 delegates in attendance representing 280,000 Rukh members, almost a quarter were CPU members. Engineers, teachers, industrial and cultural workers were well represented. Ukrainians made up a majority of those in attendance, followed by Russians and Jews. Among the informal groups whose members were active also in Rukh, the Ukrainian Helsinki Union was the best organized and most prominent.

The founding congress adopted a new programme that deleted all previous acknowledgements of the 'leading role' of the Communist Party and declared 'humanism, democracy, openness, pluralism, social justice and internationalism' as its guiding principles. It elected Ivan Drach, a well-known writer, as its head and Mykhailo Horyn of the Ukrainian Helsinki Union as chairman of its ten-member Secretariat. It declared its intention to issue a national newspaper, establish permanent headquarters in Kyiv and run its candidates in future election campaigns.

The retirement of Shcherbytsky and his replacement by Ivashko soon after Rukh's first national congress was interpreted by many political observers as the Party's attempt to stem defections from its ranks to Rukh. Some in the CPU leadership like Leonid Kravchuk, Ideological Secretary in the Politburo and its emissary to the Rukh Congress, saw that a clear split in the CPU's ranks might result from the rapidly changing political conjuncture, and entertained the idea of a "Hungarian evolution": a split between the old conservative wing and the younger reform Communists, but with the latter seeking to draw the more moderate and federalist wing of Rukh into a new formation with them.

As noted above, the CPU leadership also launched a number of legislative initiatives to improve its image. Finally, it skilfully dragged out negotiations with Rukh over the latter's access to printing facilities for a national newspaper and its legal registration. Both questions were critical to Rukh's participation in the March elections. In the end, Rukh was not registered until mid-February 1990, after nominations of election candidates were closed, and so its candidates were forced to seek nomination by other, registered organizations or on the basis of place of residence or occupation (as permitted in the new electoral law). Rukh managed to produce the first issue of its newspaper, *Narodna hazeta*, at the end of February, too late to have a significant impact on the first round of elections on 4 March. Yet it was still ascendant in the first months of 1990, with a membership surpassing half a million and an ability to organize, for example a 300-mile human chain across the republic on 21 January to mark the anniversary of Ukrainian independence in 1918.

The third important political force to consider in Ukraine is the independent workers' movement, centred in 1989 and 1990 around Donbas mining communities. This movement was triggered by the July 1989 miners' strike, which spread from the Russian Republic into Ukraine and encompassed all of Donbas and the Galician-Volynian coalfield. As in other parts of the Soviet Union, Ukrainian miners established strike committees to lead them, negotiate with the government and maintain order in the towns. The strike committees evolved into workers' control committees in August, after negotiations were concluded, which were charged with monitoring implementation of the agreement. The control committees united into a regional organization in August and set out in September to found the Donbas Union of Workers, an independent union encompassing workers in all industries.

The workers' movement first emerged in Donbas for several reasons. Ukrainian miners have a long tradition of struggle, even in the most difficult years. The Association of Free Trade Unions, established in 1978 by Vladimir Klebanov and suppressed mainly by psychiatric abuse of its leading members, was based here. Problems of housing, food supply and working conditions became worse in the 1970s and 1980s as the central government shifted capital investment away from Donbas into Western Siberian open cut mining. The accident rate soared. In 1987, in the midst of a spate of fatalities in the pits, the Ukrainian republic's coal ministry was abolished and control of the industry was recentralized in Moscow even more. By 1989 the situation here was clearly coming to a breaking point: in the first three months there were eleven strikes. A lull followed, and the twelfth strike on 17 July brought Donbas into the country-wide miners' strike.

The strikers did not limit themselves to economic demands, although these were clearly of paramount immediate importance. The miners wanted a form of enterprise autonomy and regional cost accounting that gave their own organizations control of capital investments, the wage fund, management appointments, domestic wholesale trade and a part in international trade of their coal as well. They demanded the removal of unpopular trade union, government and police officials; the Chervonohrad miners in Western Ukraine demanded Shcherbytsky's removal. Most important of all, strike committees in Ukraine and other parts of the Soviet Union demanded the abolition of Article 6 of the Soviet Constitution that guaranteed political power to the Communist Party.

Further evidence of a rapid politicization of miners included: participation of their strike leaders as observers in the September Rukh congress; readiness to mount a general strike if the original CPU draft of the new republic election law was not withdrawn (the original draft reserved a number of uncontested seats for CPU-sponsored organizations); fielding candidates in the March elections; and the mounting of strikes and demonstrations in Donetsk oblast on the eve of the elections to force the oblast CPU leadership to resign.

The miners' strike and its aftermath had a lasting impact upon other groups of Ukrainian wage earners. First, it demonstrated to them how the strike weapon could be applied effectively, without creating pretexts for a violent reaction from the authorities. This led to the formation of strike committees in numerous towns and cities that accepted the strike as a weapon of last resort in the pursuit of all manner of popular demands. Second, the miners impressed upon other workers the value of independent organization, which took form later in the Donbas Union of Workers, the Horlivka Workers' Union and Yednist (Unity), formed in February 1990 in Kharkiv by workers' committees from 16 towns and cities across the republic.

The republican elections

All 450 seats in the Verkhovna Rada, as well as those of municipal and oblast governments, were contested in the March 1990 elections. An average of six to seven candidates vied for each seat in the Verkhovna Rada. Because Rukh was unable to field candidates in its own name, it entered into a Democratic Bloc with other registered and informal organizations that shared its programme and had its candidates nominated by such registered organizations as the Taras Shevchenko Ukrainian Language Society, by work collectives or resident voters' meetings. In a number of constituencies protests were levelled against the Party-controlled electoral commissions for refusing to register Democratic Bloc, Zelenyi Svit (Green World) and other candidates. Demonstrations against the commissions broke out in February in Vynnytsia, Kyiv, Ternopil, Chernivtsi and Poltava.

The election campaign period was marred also by persistent rumours of impending pogroms against Jews and attacks by civilians on Soviet troops stationed in the republic. At rallies and in public appeals to soldiers and civilians, Rukh denounced these rumours as an attempt by conservatives in the Party leadership, KGB and military command to intimidate voters and strengthen their own nominees' chances in the elections.

In the end 129 Democratic Bloc candidates and 72 independents supported by the Bloc stood in the elections. They were well represented in the western oblasts of Lviv, Ternopil and Ivano-Frankivsk, moderately so in the central oblasts, and poorly in the south and east, particularly Odesa, Crimea and Poltava, where they fielded no candidates at all. The Communist Party fielded its candidates in all 450 constituencies, but it was by no means clear that all those elected would remain loyal to the CPU leadership and not defect to the Democratic Bloc. A number of strike committees also managed to field candidates, mainly in the coal, steel and machine building centres of southeastern Ukraine. Many of them were supported by the Democratic Bloc.

In the first round of the elections 120 out of the 450 seats were filled by 71 Communist Party candidates, 36 Democratic Bloc candidates and 13 independents supported by the Bloc. In Western Ukraine, the Bloc did particularly well, taking a large majority of the available seats. In the remaining 330 constituencies, where no candidate had received 50 percent of the vote in the first round and which had to go through to a second round runoff between the two leading contenders, the Democratic Bloc remained in the running in 103 constituencies. It secured another 72 seats in the second round, giving it a total of 108 deputies in the Verkhovna Rada. Supported by independent deputies, the Democratic Bloc commanded up to 170 votes, against 280 behind the CPU leadership.

Such an outcome did not mean, however, that it would be simply consigned to opposition status for the coming five years. It became increasingly clear in the course of the election period and afterwards that the Communist Party of Ukraine was dividing into a reform wing that straddled both the Party and Rukh, and a conservative wing behind First Secretary Ivashko. Some of the most radical reformists were trying to mount a breakaway movement for an independent Ukrainian Communist Party on the Lithuanian model. Furthermore, many Rukh leaders belonging to the Communist Party, including Ivan Drach, Volodymyr Yavorivsky and Dmytro Pavlychko, publicly quit the Party after the elections, as did numerous groups of rank-and-file members, especially in the western oblasts. Therefore, it was within the range of possibilities that the conservative wing of the CPU could be cast into opposition within the Verkhovna Rada by an alliance of Rukh/Democratic Bloc, reform Communists and strike committee leaders.

The fragmentation of the CPU was fostered by the awareness that a multi-party system was only a matter of time. Similarly, while Rukh functioned well in this period as an umbrella organization of various democratic and patriotic political tendencies, the imminence of a multi-party system encouraged such tendencies to prepare for life as fully fledged parties. Thus in the first months of 1990 plans were put in motion to establish the following: a Ukrainian Democratic Party by reform Communists in Rukh, a Ukrainian Social Democratic Party by local groups in six cities, a Ukrainian

Republican Party by the Ukrainian Helsinki Union (UHU), a Ukrainian National Party by a breakaway group from UHU, a Ukrainian Peasant Democratic Party by an initiative committee based in Lviv, and a Green Party by the Green World association.

Volodymyr Ivashko was elected chairman of the Verkhovna Rada, and in June he resigned as CPU First Secretary in the face of Democratic Bloc criticism that his occupation of these two posts was unconstitutional. Second Secretary Stanislav Hurenko replaced Ivashko in the CPU leadership.

The issues

The major issues that shaped the election contest and will continue to dominate the political terrain in the future are: democratisation, the economic crisis, the environment, and the complex and long-term question of national sovereignty.

In view of the Communist Party's declared readiness to relinquish its monopoly on power, the issue of democratisation is now a question of how to end this monopoly and make the transition to a genuine multi-party system. The Communist Party is naturally concerned to retain some role in future governments and not be completely marginalized in the process. Rukh, on the other hand, faces the task of maintaining unity of all the groups under its wing in order to enforce this transition to a multi-party democracy, while at the same time allowing these groups to prepare themselves as competing political parties. A thoroughgoing process of democratisation must also address the delicate issue of the KGB, the Soviet Army and other means of coercion available to the state authority. Without their subordination to a democratically elected government, the process will be incomplete.

Although its economic weight has declined since World War II in relation to the country as a whole, Ukraine remains a crucial economic region of the Soviet Union. Today it produces one quarter of the USSR's food and one fifth of its industrial goods. Donbas provides a quarter of the Soviet Union's annual coal output, while the republic's five nuclear power stations account for 40 percent of the USSR's nuclear generating capacity. Producer goods, which make

up 70 percent of the republic's GNP, include rolled steel, diesel locomotives, coal mining and agricultural machinery.

The republic's economy is characterized by its intense use of
fuels, raw materials and labour, both in the agricultural and industrial branches; by its relatively worn-out, technologically backward
and ecologically harmful capital assets; and by grave disproportions between its base industries, manufacturing, social infrastructural and consumer goods sectors. Soviet Ukrainian economists estimate their economy is in a worse state than those of Russia, Belarus and the Baltic republics. Four years of perestroika have left it
with a less desirable output structure than before (the consumer
goods sector shrinking below 30 percent of GNP), in eleventh place
in the average republican wages table, and below the Soviet average in provision of social services, trade turnover in consumer
goods, per capita housing space and educational levels.[4]

The republic's leaders have been able to do very little until
now to combat shortages, disproportions in output and other problems because economic decision making (investment allocations,
wholesale and retail prices, tariffs, etc.) has been determined in
Moscow and implemented by union ministries. The Ukrainian republic controls only 5 percent of the gross national product created
on its territory. Enterprises run by union ministries control the rest,
and these enterprises deposit into the republic's budget a mere 3.5
percent of their income as payment for labour and infrastructural
costs.[5]

The terms on which Ukraine trades are disadvantageous to its
own interests. Payments for its annual exports to other parts of the
Soviet Union are 1 billion roubles less than the costs calculated to
produce those exports. Its electricity exports to Central and Eastern
Europe are sold at one kopek per kilowatt hour.[6] Although comprehensive analyses of the republic's trade are not yet available, the
general feeling both in Rukh and the Communist Party is that
Ukraine suffers a net outflow of wealth and has practically no say

---

4   *Radians'kyi ekonomist*, 9 October 1989, 2–3; *Ekonomika Radians'koi Ukrainy*, No. 4,
     1989, 60.
5   *Robitnycha hazeta*, 18 April 1989.
6   *Izvestiia*, 9 September 1989.

in the matter. Not surprisingly, insistent calls are now made to re-claim control of economic strategy, domestic production and trade from the central government and its agencies.

Five objectives, first articulated by Rukh but co-opted in large part by the Communist Party leadership, have been set out: repub-lican economic independence exercised by the Verkhovna Rada and its Council of Ministers, with veto power over any centrally initiated project; customs duty, banks and other fiscal instruments under republican control; a new Treaty of Union laying down the division of powers between the union and republican government, with a radical increase in the powers of the latter; independent ac-cess to the world market; and the promotion of a mixed economy with personal, co-operative and state ownership enjoying equality before the law.

Serious differences do exist, however, between Rukh and the Communist Party in their interpretation of these objectives and the procedures needed to realize them. Fundamentally, the differences are as follows. The Party is seeking a new economic arrangement in a renewed Soviet federation, guaranteed and arbitrated by a pow-erful executive presidency, whereas Rukh seeks recognition of full republican economic independence first, to be followed by negoti-ations with Moscow and other republics about trade and co-opera-tion. It is, nevertheless, important to stress that, as in the Baltic re-publics, Ukraine's entire political spectrum now wants a radical in-crease of its power over the economy.

Closely related to the economy, but an important issue in its own right, is the environment. The republic is facing a serious water shortage. Pollution has destroyed many sources of potable water. Irrigation systems covering more than 5 million hectares, various industrial processes and nuclear power stations all impose a heavy burden on available supplies. Attempts to increase agricultural yields by irrigation and the intensive use of phosphate fertilizers have over the years exhausted and then poisoned Ukraine's once fertile black-earth zone and contributed in turn to the further pol-lution of water. Industrial pollutants in the air, water and soil, par-ticularly in the south-east, have pushed up the incidence of disease, genetic defects and infant mortality. A qualitatively new dimension was added by the 1986 Chernobyl disaster, which seriously contaminated 3.7 million hectares of land with its fall-out and damaged the health of still unknown numbers of people.

A growing awareness of the ecological situation, particularly after the Chernobyl disaster, has led to a widespread movement in defence of the environment, of which Green World is the main republic-wide organization. This movement has managed to block all further construction of nuclear power stations in Ukraine, including the abandonment of those close to completion. It will most likely force the complete closure and dismantling of the Chernobyl station, which has operated practically without interruption since the disaster there. The republic's leading scientists and economists are preparing a new energy strategy in the context of a decisive shift in economic strategy overall away from energy and resource intensive technologies and processes.

The question of national sovereignty in a renewed federation or outright independence is the overriding long term political issue. Both Soviet and Western observers accept that without Ukraine the Soviet Union cannot be a superpower. It is conceivable that Moscow will let the Baltic republics go, but to lose even control of Ukraine would greatly accelerate the already evident fragmentation of the Union and embolden all the non-Russian peoples seeking greater national self-determination.

What, then, will determine the outcome of this issue in the long term? The evidence so far suggests that a worsening Soviet economy will generate more urgent demands for political separation, an internal economic reorganization in the direction of self-sufficiency and proportionality within a single national republican market, and the renegotiation of trade terms with other states. Similarly, the deepening political instability across the Soviet Union will strengthen separatist sentiment in Ukraine and weaken the central government's ability to combat it. Young men, for example, do not wish to serve in the Soviet Army if that means they will be sent to the Baltic republics, Transcaucasia or Soviet Central Asia to put down nationalist movements there. On the contrary, the mass demonstrations across Ukraine in late March and April 1990 in support of Lithuania's bid for independence showed that growing numbers of people support such movements elsewhere and the peaceful resolution of their demands.

These are negative features of the all-Union situation that are promoting the idea of Ukraine's separation. The positive feature is, above all, the re-awakening of national pride and dignity among the Ukrainians, which brings with it a confidence that their republic can stand alone if it wishes to and should determine its relations with other republics as equals with them. But the republic will stand alone only if the majority of its population becomes convinced that independence is needed to bring greater freedom, better living standards and greater security than they presently enjoy under Soviet rule.

There was a fairly strong desire within Rukh at the beginning of 1989 to renegotiate the terms of the Treaty of Union with Russia and the other republics. Only after that option had been tried and had proved unsatisfactory was independence going to be considered as a serious alternative. The CPSU leadership and central government in Moscow responded to such a desire here, as in other republics, by drafting new proposals on the national question, on economic independence for the republics and, finally, mechanisms for negotiated disengagement from the Union. However, none of these proposals gave Rukh much hope in a new Treaty of Union. Their actual content showed that the central government was not interested in real concessions to the republics. The April 1989 Tbilisi massacre, the military intervention in Azerbaijan and Armenia, and Gorbachev's response to Lithuania reinforced such a view. Thus Rukh was forced to consider outright independence all the more urgently.

The main weakness of previous bids for Ukraine's independence – in 1917 and during World War II – lay in the historic division between Western Ukrainian nationalism and the Eastern Ukrainian proletariat. The former saw national unification and independence as a panacea without considering fully the political and social egalitarian aspirations of workers in such a movement for a new state. The latter, a multinational working class with a sizeable Russian component in the most industrialized part of Ukraine, was radical in social and political demands, but not quite sure whether its region should belong to Ukraine or to Russia. The conservative wing of the Communist Party of Ukraine is very much aware of this historic division and has worked hard to re-create it, without much success, in the present situation. Of course, the size, location and composition of the working class has changed a great deal since World War II. By 1970 it accounted for more than a half of the total population; it was more evenly spread across the republic and three quarters of its members were Ukrainian. The important question, however, is what political outlook the just emerging workers' movement will take on the issue of national self-determination and whether its leaders will look to Moscow or to Kyiv as their political centre. This still largely unknown factor will have immense relevance for the future course of events in Ukraine.

The Ukrainian Parliamentary Elections in March–April 1994[*]

The Ukrainian electorate went to the polls in March and April 1994 to elect a new parliament—Verkhovna Rada. These were the first general elections since Ukraine became independent in 1991. They were also the first democratically contested general elections since the elections of the All-Russian Constituent Assembly in November 1917. The purpose of this article is to analyse the process of these elections and their results, with several important questions in mind: why were they called; how did they contribute to the ongoing formation of the new political system; what kind of ideological and political cleavages in society did they reveal; and what impact did the elections have on the project of nation building and the legitimacy of the new nation-state?

During their four years in office, the deputies of the Verkhovna Rada elected in March 1990 were under almost continuous pressure from various quarters to resign and call new elections. The 1990 elections had not been democratic on a number of counts. The ruling Communist Party had prevented Rukh, its main opponent, from contesting half the 450 constituencies. Rukh had no access to the mass media and could not even find a state publishing house to print its newspaper until the last weeks of the election campaign. There was widespread intimidation of opposition candidates and their supporters. The highest authorities did nothing to dispel the persistent rumour in Kyiv of impending anti-Jewish pogroms and the imposition of martial law.[1] The opposition claimed that the ballot was rigged in several constituencies, including that of CPU First Secretary Volodymyr lvashko. Foreign observers were refused visas to enter the country.[2] However, the massive political

---

[*]   First published in: *Europe-Asia Studies*, Vol. 47, No. 2, 1995, 229–249.
[1]   Interview with Volodymyr Ivashko, First Secretary, Communist Party of Ukraine, *Ukraine Today*, 2, August 1990, 20–22.
[2]   J.V. Koshiw, "The March 1990 elections in Ukraine," *Ukraine Today*, 2, August 190, 5–8.

awakening of this period overcame these obstacles and the opposition Democratic Bloc, through which Rukh managed to field candidates, captured a quarter of the seats in the legislature. From their newly won platform they could and did argue that the Rada did not represent the real balance of political forces within the electorate.

The extra-parliamentary opposition also continued to make an issue out of the undemocratic conduct of the March elections. In October 1990, when the new Verkhovna Rada was convened, Ukrainian student unions launched a mass hunger strike in Kyiv, demanding its dissolution and the organisation of new elections. They were supported by daily demonstrations of up to 100 000 protestors outside the parliament building and by strike alerts in Kyiv's factories. The students gathered sufficient support to force the Prime Minister, Vitalii Masol, to resign and the Council to pledge to hold a referendum of confidence in itself. The referendum never took place but the action served to strengthen the opposition within the Council.[3]

After the declaration of Ukraine's independence in August 1991 and its affirmation in the 1 December referendum it seemed logical to the opposition forces that the people should now exercise their sovereignty in the democratic, as well as the national, sense by electing a new legislative assembly. The national democratic parties maintained this argument throughout the period between the 1990 and 1994 elections.

A second argument came to the fore in 1992 and 1993 that eventually was decisive in forcing new elections: neither the Verkhovna Rada nor the Cabinet of Ministers approved by it, nor indeed the President seemed able to combat the economic crisis and to lead the country to recovery. As the crisis deepened numerous organised groups began to press for new elections to all levels of government. They disagreed over the causes of the economic crisis, but they concurred that the Verkhovna Rada and the successive

---

3   Marko Bojcun, "Ukraine: the issue of national self-determination," in *The Times Guide to Eastern Europe*, ed. Kieth Sword (London: Times Books, rev. ed. 1991), 246.

governments under Vitold Fokin and Leonid Kuchma had neither the ability nor the confidence of the population to tackle it. More competent leaders with a mandate from the electorate were needed.

The economic crisis took its heaviest toll in the industrialised and militant Donbas, where workers mounted strikes repeatedly in 1992 in an attempt to secure immediate economic demands, a strategic plan for the reconstruction of heavy industry and manufacturing, and a new political leadership in Kyiv. The appointment of Leonid Kuchma, director of the Yuzhmash missile plant in Dnipropetrovsk, as Prime Minister in October 1992 and his assumption of executive powers to deal with the economic crisis was precisely a response to such pressures. Kuchma failed to achieve anything in the face of a conservative Verkhovna Rada and the situation worsened. The resistance of the Verkhovna Rada to its self-dissolution was broken finally in June 1993 when a powerful strike wave swept through the Donbas, its participants demanding a vote of confidence in all the national institutions of power, greater economic and political autonomy for the eastern oblasts and Ukraine's full integration with the Commonwealth of Independent States. Additional support for these demands (some observers even claimed the inspiration itself for them) came from the region's industrial directors and oblast leaders, a development that seemed particularly ominous to the central state leadership in Kyiv, nervous as they already were about the fragility of their new state.[4] The Verkhovna Rada resolved on 17 June 1993 to hold referenda of confidence in itself and President Leonid Kravchuk on 26 September 1993 and to organise elections for either should a majority of the electorate decline to lend its support.[5] However, as the referenda date drew near the Verkhovna Rada overturned its previous decision and resolved to proceed straight to new elections of its deputies on 27 March and presidential elections on 26 June 1994.[6]

---

4   *Narodna hazeta*, 13, 1994, *Ukrains'ka hazeta*, 24 June–7 July 1993.
5   *Demokratychna Ukraina*, 19 June 1993.
6   *UNIAR* news agency report, *Kyiv radio*, 23 September 1993.

The election law

The law "On elections of people's deputies of Ukraine", adopted by the Verkhovna Rada on 18 November 1993, accords every citizen aged eighteen years of age and over the right to elect in a free, equal, direct and secret ballot one of the 450 deputies to the Council, each representing a single member constituency.[7] There is no provision in the law for the election of deputies on the basis of proportional representation of parties, as in Russia, Poland and elsewhere. Candidates for election must be citizens of Ukraine 25 years of age and over, and resident in Ukraine for at least the two preceding years. They are nominated initially in one of three ways: in a declaration signed by at least ten voters in their constituency, by a meeting of their workplace collective, or by a conference of the political party to which they belong. The regulations for nomination by one's political party are by far the most complicated and exacting, requiring the convocation of a regional party conference by at least two thirds of the membership or more than 50 delegated members, and the submission to the district electoral commission of many documents, including a list of the first hundred members of the respective regional party organisation, giving their occupation, address, passport number and signature. A group of voters nominating a candidate must also submit such a list with the same personal details and their signatures to the commission, but that is all. And it is naturally simpler to do so for ten voters than 100 party members, not to mention the additional documentation required from the latter. In the case of a workplace nomination, the commission merely requires a declaration to that effect signed by a representative nominated by the workforce. The district electoral commission subsequently issues blank lists to all nominees and then registers as candidates for deputy those who succeed in gathering the signatures of 300 supporters in their constituency.

A candidate is required under the law to open an election fund account in one of the state banks, in which he/she may accumulate from his/her own sources and from donations up to the equivalent

---

7   The law is published in *Holos Ukrainy*, 27 November 1993.

of 100 minimum monthly incomes (around six million *karbovantsi* at the time of these elections). Cheques are written on this account to pay campaign costs. However, the law requires that the district electoral commission print 2,000 posters for each candidate, with their biographical details, that it ensure the publication of each candidate's platform in a local government or state sponsored newspaper, and secure equal time for all candidates on regional radio and television. The costs are borne by the Central Electoral Fund, managed by the Central Electoral Commission.

The stipulated method of voting is cumbersome, requiring the voter to cross off the ballot paper with a horizontal mark each of the candidates he/she does not support, leaving only one candidate's name, or none at all. Otherwise, a ballot is ruled invalid.[8] It is the same method that was used in the Soviet period when voters came to the polling stations, picked up ballot papers bearing the name of a single Communist Party candidate and threw them unmarked into the ballot urn, bypassing altogether the voting cubicle. It becomes decidedly more complicated and time consuming to vote this way when several candidates appear on the ballot.

Election of each deputy requires that half or more of the registered voters in the constituency cast a valid vote, and that the successful candidate acquires more than half of the votes cast. Should the first condition be met, but not the second, the two candidates with the highest numbers of votes go to a second round run-off, in which at least half the registered voters of the constituency must again take a valid part. One of these two candidates should gain a majority of the votes cast, although this may be denied to both candidates by a sufficient number of invalid (spoiled) ballots and/or valid ballots on which both the candidates' names are crossed off. Should a majority of registered voters fail to appear in the first or second rounds, altogether new elections are to be held, beginning with a fresh call for nomination and registration of candidates.

The law was widely criticised in the months leading up to the elections on several important counts. The leaders of Rukh and other centre-right political parties argued that the electoral system

---

8   *Holos Ukrainy*, 26 March 1994.

adopted did nothing to stimulate the development of political parties because it failed to accord seats in the Verkhovna Rada on a party proportional basis.[9] The greater demands placed upon political party nominees for successful registration as candidates than upon nominees of workplace collectives or groups of voters appeared to add credence to this view. Ihor Tsyliuko, Secretary of the Central Electoral Commission, explained the anomaly by recalling that the law on elections was first drafted with a mixed system of single member constituencies and proportional representation in mind. The exacting demands placed upon registration of political party candidates were meant to ensure that proportional representation was not abused by a plethora of hastily convened or fictitious parties. When, finally, the law was adopted without any provision for proportional representation, Tsyluiko argued, these clauses were not removed. It was simply a hastily composed and clumsy piece of legislation.[10]

Some critics went further and claimed that the existing ex-Communist majority in the Verkhovna Rada and the government ministries had excluded proportional representation quite deliberately so that they would not have to identify themselves openly with the newly reconstituted Communist Party (CPU), the Socialist Party (SPU) or another party identified with the *nomenklatura* or the old regime, and thus lessen their chances of election.

The second important criticism concerned the requirements that more than half the electorate cast votes in the first round or both the first and second rounds, and that additionally one candidate gain more than half of the votes cast for a successful election to take place. Pessimism abounded during the election campaign about the expected turnout. Again, the critics of the "party of power" claimed that the hurdles had been set so high in order to prevent the successful completion of these elections, which would either allow the deputies of the old Verkhovna Rada to stay in their

---

9   *Narodna hazeta*, 13, 1994.
10   Author's interview with Ihor Tsyluiko, Central Election Commission in Kyiv, 18 March 1994.

posts for another year (until the Council's statutory term expired), or would provide President Kravchuk with a pretext to assume extraordinary executive powers.[11]

Third, critics of the law claimed it gave far too much authority to the Central and District Electoral Commissions, appointed respectively by the heads of the Verkhovna Rada and the oblast councils. The commissions registered candidates, printed their campaign literature, acted as gatekeepers of the state-run mass media (in concert with the latter's directors), organised the machinery of voting, counted and validated ballots, and announced the results. They interpreted and implemented the electoral law and were the adjudicators in disputes and claims of illegality brought forward by voters and candidates. The Central Commission could overrule a District Commission, and only the Supreme Court of Ukraine could overrule a decision of the Central Electoral Commission. Unfortunately, the Supreme Court existed largely on paper at the time of the 1994 parliamentary elections because the Verkhovna Rada had failed to agree on a way to elect its members.[12] To some participants in the campaign, the Commission's powers demonstrated the paternalistic embrace of the highest state authorities over a formally democratic decision making process. In the most mistrustful minds, the Central Electoral Commission, headed by Ivan Yemets, was actually working to sabotage the elections altogether by withholding essential information from the voters and making every stage of the electoral process more difficult and confusing than it should have been.[13]

---

11 *Vechirnyi Kyiv*, 25 March 1994; *Ukraina moloda*, 25 March 1994.
12 *Holos Ukrainy*, 11, 12, 18, 20 and 24 February and 3 and 5 March 1993.
13 This charge was made most forcefully by the independent press centre Vybory 94 (Elections 94), whose organisers claimed that the Central Election Commission had violated the law by refusing to provide the electorate, through the mass media, with candidate lists, occupational and party affiliation profiles of the candidates, the names of officials and the addresses of the 450 District Election Commissions. Interviews with Serhii Naboka, 18 March 1994, and with Roman Zvarych, 28 March 1994, at Vybory 94 headquarters in Kyiv. See also *Holos Ukrainy*, 28 January 1994, for a report on the extensive preparations required to train and equip the Election Commissions for this first application of the electoral law.

The contestants

Nomination of candidates closed on 27 January 1994 and their registration by District Commissions ended officially on 17 February. In all, 5,833 candidates were registered, an average of 13 candidates per constituency. The largest concentrations of competing candidates were in the constituencies of Kyiv city, where the highest number in one constituency (31) was also to be found. Political parties had nominated only 11 percent of the candidates, whereas work collectives had nominated 26.7 percent and groups of voters 63.3 percent. The complex requirements of nomination by a political party must have played a part in this pattern, and in fact there were formally independent candidates nominated by groups of voters who actually were political party members and campaigned as such. The Central Electoral Commission estimated that 27.4 percent of all candidates belonged to political parties. After the election was over, even more independent candidates who succeeded were likely to declare an affiliation.

Women accounted for a little over 7 percent of all candidates, a considerably smaller proportion than among Communist deputies in the Verkhovna Rada during the Soviet period. The largest age cohort was 41–50 years, accounting for 39 percent of candidates. This suggested that a generational changing of the guard was underway. The fact that about half the deputies of the Verkhovna Rada elected in 1990 were not seeking re-election seems to reinforce this view. As for nationality, Ukrainians accounted for 78.1 percent of candidates (slightly overrepresented in comparison with their proportion in the population), Russians 18.5 percent and other nationalities 3.4 percent. The level of education among candidates was comparatively high, with engineers, jurists, economists and educators constituting the most prevalent professions. Almost half knew a foreign language (English, German, Polish and French; practically all knew Russian, which is hardly a foreign language in Ukraine).[14]

---

14   "Dovidka pro kil'kisnyi i yakisnyi sklad zareiestrovanykh kandydativ u narodni deputaty Ukrainy" (Information about the numbers and characteristics

The election campaign

Voters faced considerable difficulties in making an informed choice. The entire process was atomised on the constituency level and proved difficult to raise to the level of a nationwide contest. There were many candidates from whom to choose in each constituency. Approximately three-quarters entered the contest as independents, and only after some time did the voters find out what they stood for and who among them was in fact affiliated to a party. Bearing in mind also the underdevelopment of political parties as such in Ukraine, the electorate was not offered a clear choice even between political parties. Rather, it was necessary actively to seek out in one's constituency a candidate one knew, or something in a candidate that one could support.

The mass media bore some responsibility for this state of affairs. Their role is indispensable in modern democracies in presenting the electoral contestants and portraying the struggle between them to a widely dispersed populace for a sustained period of time. The Ukrainian mass media were both misused and underutilized in this respect during the 1994 parliamentary elections. The Central Electoral Commission had ruled that no candidate could appear on the national television channel (UTl) as it was impossible to provide all candidates with equal time on it. However, political party representatives who were not running for parliament were allowed to appear, and the UTl channel broadcast special party political debates during the election campaign. Thus in a double sense these debates did not address the ongoing election campaign and did not help voters much in making up their minds. The oblast state television channels, where they existed, provided candidates with equal time to present themselves, but often at rather inappropriate times. For example, the Kyiv channel broadcast the candidates' presentations between 4pm and 6pm, when most voters were either still at

---

of candidates registered for the election of People's Deputies of Ukraine), Central Electoral Commission circular (n.d.), Kyiv. See also *Holos Ukrainy*, 23 February 1994.

work or on their way home.[15] Furthermore, the capacity of television could not be used to its full extent in Ukraine, because more than two-thirds of the country's viewers regularly watch Ostankino TV, a channel that broadcasts from the Russian Federation and that provided only sporadic coverage of the elections in its news programme. Less than 10 percent of viewers regularly watch the Ukrainian national and regional channels.[16] Radio and the press offered voters more information on a regular basis, and their content is naturally easier to absorb (in various locations, at different times of the day). Still, criticism of the media was widespread, and it was confirmed by surveys that found voters ill-informed in the final days of the election campaign period.[17] Svytlana Vyryha, deputy minister of social security and a candidate in Kyiv's Obolon constituency, said three days before polling day:

> People have practically no detailed information about the candidates and the course of the campaign. One gets the impression that there was one extreme in Russia—a certain political force seized the television screens and rammed its line through to the very end. Here it is the opposite extreme—everyone is silent. Can it be normal that the fourth estate has such little influence on the formation of public opinion during the elections?[18]

Whether by design, incompetence or through sheer inexperience, the election campaigning did not appear to gather momentum, leading to widespread fear among Kyiv's intelligentsia that the elections themselves would fail on the first round as a combined result of voter ignorance, confusion, apathy and outright mistrust of the electoral process as such. In the last weeks of the campaign period the outgoing Verkhovna Rada, the media, trade unions and various citizens' organisations mounted a campaign aimed solely at bringing the electorate out to vote on 27 March.[19] All of these factors help to explain why the election struggle was not waged around a key issue or a set of issues on a pan-national scale. The

---

15   *Vechirnyi Kyiv*, 1 March 1994.
16   SOCIS Index Survey, Kyiv, September 1993.
17   *Vechirnyi Kyiv*, 25 March 1994.
18   *Ukraina moloda*, 25 March 1994.
19   *Holos Ukrainy*, 3 February 1994, *Vechirnyi Kyiv*, 1 March 1994, *Nezavisimost*, 25 March 1994.

problem, quite literally, was to ensure that the battle was joined by contenders with an adequate national presence and that the voters saw it joined inside a single arena.

Yet this did not mean that the electorate did not have key concerns that played some role in focusing their attention on the candidates and helping them make up their minds. According to a state-wide survey conducted by the Kyiv International Institute of Sociology, the most important issues for the voters were the economic crisis, relations with Russia and crime, in that order. These were followed by concern about the security of the Ukrainian state, the status of the Russian language, nuclear weapons in Ukraine, the future of Crimea and the Black Sea Fleet.[20] The first three issues had a strong affinity with each other in the voters' estimation, insofar as the economic situation is seen to have been aggravated particularly by the breakdown of trade with Russia and by the corruption of state officials, mafia operations in domestic and foreign trade, tax evasion and the illegal flight of capital abroad.

Nor should the absence of a sharply focused national struggle waged by the parties involved lead one to conclude that they did not present the voters with alternative policies. They did so, even though the generalities in which they expressed them led the less informed voters (often through no fault of their own) to conclude that there was no real difference between the parties and the independents. It is in the very nature of the transition period in Ukraine (and elsewhere) that political struggles are fought over questions of general orientation in state, social and economic affairs - how to move from one historical societal formation to another — rather than over the functional details of a stable societal formation, which does not yet exist. One can hardly debate the level of personal income tax when state institutions are not yet in place to levy and collect it.

Parties of the left (Communist Party, Socialist Party and Peasant Party) defended a broad range of common positions: the maintenance of a significant level of state ownership in the economy; a preference for the acquisition of denationalised assets by their work collectives, rather than by outside investors; opposition

---

20   *Holos Ukrainy*, 17 February 1994.

to rapid privatisation, macroeconomic "shock therapy" or significant foreign takeovers of Ukraine's key industries; provision of a
social safety net for those worst affected by market economic reforms; Ukraine's close integration with the CIS as an important part
of the solution to the economic crisis. They were prepared to seek
an economic and military union with Russia, although the pace and
depth of union preferred by each of the left parties remained unclear. These parties made the most of the economic crisis, laying the
blame for it upon the Kyiv establishment — the alliance of the "party
of power" and the national democrats — which they identified as
nationalistic, pro-Western and anti-Russian.[21]

The national democrats went into the election campaign together, in a front called Democratic Union Ukraine *(Demokratychne
Obiednannia Ukraina)* with 41 member parties. This, however, was
not a front based upon political agreement but a clearing house
through which the participating members sought not to compete
with one another in the same constituencies. Agreement to that end
was reached in 320 constituencies, according to the organisers.[22]

The most important parties within the Union were Rukh, the
Republican Party, the Democratic Party and the Congress of
Ukrainian Nationalists. The first three parties share the goals of establishing an independent state, a democratic civil society and a
capitalist market economy with an undefined mix of state and private ownership. The more recently formed Congress of Ukrainian
Nationalists is the most "nationalist" in the national democratic
camp, judged by the higher priority it places upon defending
Ukraine's statehood over these other goals. Indeed, the Congress
veered further towards the right during the election campaign.[23] The

---

21   Mykola Tomenko, Viktor Melnychenko and Vasyl Yablonsky, 'Ukraine before
     and after the parliamentary elections: a survey of political forces', *Politicheskaia
     Mysl'*, 1994, 2, 157–158; *Holos Ukrainy*, 26 February 1994; *Demokratychna Ukraina*,
     24 March 1994; *Vechirnyi Kyiv*, 12 March 1994.
22   Interview with Serhii Odarych, Rukh organiser, Kyiv, 18 March 1994. See also
     Vechirnyi Kyiv, 25 March 1994.
23   Interview with Roman Zvarych, Kyiv, 28 March 1994. The American-born libe-
     ral democrat Roman Zvarych, who drafted the original Congress programme,

national democratic camp as a whole sees Ukraine's future within Europe, as opposed to an alliance with Russia, which they fear. This broadly defined set of objectives was their message to the electorate.[24]

However, this camp has been split for some time, with Rukh maintaining a stance of open, "constructive" criticism towards the ruling establishment in Kyiv, demanding new elections and more rapid economic reforms, while the Democratic and Republican parties have been quicker to support the status quo, to take up portfolios of state office offered to their members both at home and abroad, and to emphasise the priority of the Ukrainian state-building project over that of internal political and economic reform, particularly in the face of the challenges to Ukrainian statehood from the east.[25]

Between the left parties and the national democrats stand the centrists, notably the Party of Democratic Renewal, the Social Democratic Party, the Civic Congress, the Party of Labour and others. The centrists have attempted to combine their strength through bloc formations, including the New Ukraine movement in 1993 and the Interregional Bloc for Reforms in 1994, the latter having a high profile in this election campaign. This camp is composed primarily of liberal democrats, federalists (for regional autonomy within Ukraine) and advocates of rapid privatisation and market reforms. Their objective in the long-term transition from the Soviet societal formation has been summarised as "capitalism with a human face". In the course of these elections, the Interregional Bloc for Reforms, led by Volodymyr Hryniov of the Party of Democratic Renewal and ex-Prime Minister Leonid Kuchma, leader of the Congress of Industrialists and Entrepreneurs, sought to expand outward from the centrist camp. Rejecting the "extremism" of the communists and the nationalists, the Interregional Bloc proposed a strategic union with Russia that would help overcome Ukraine's economic crisis and stabilise the geopolitical space left vacant by the collapse of the

---

received death threats during the election campaign, apparently from an organisation/organisations of the far right. He was expelled from the Congress leadership after the elections.

24 *Holos Ukrainy*, 26 February 1994.
25 *Nezavisimost*, 16 March 1994; Tomenko, Melnychenko and Yablonsky, "Ukraine before and after the parliamentary elections", pp. 158–159.

Soviet Union. The Bloc emphasised also regional autonomy and an eventual federal structure for Ukraine. It organised conferences of regional political leaders and businesspersons during the election campaign period in major eastern and southern cities in an attempt to extend its network and cement loyalties. Thus its leaders hoped to capture a significant base in the central, southern and eastern regions where the left parties would otherwise run virtually unchallenged.[26] If successful in capturing key urban constituencies, they could then have exploited them for a new corporatist alliance in Kyiv with the left or right, in which industrialists, businesspersons and regional political leaders could replace the "party of power" as the central power broker.

Those who managed to gain a national perspective on the 1994 elections (a relatively small group of people who had the resources to amalgamate fragmented sources of information) saw it as a contest between these three broad formations of the left, centre and national democrats. It was difficult, however, for the average voter to extrapolate from his/her local situation and to see such a contest unfolding because the national democrats were confined largely to their western stronghold, the left-wing parties to the east, and the centrists were scattered unevenly across the country.

Foreign observers of the elections, totalling over 600 persons from 50 states and 12 international organisations, concluded that they were generally free and democratic, with a high level of civic participation.[27] They noted some violations of the electoral law, as well as its inadequacies, the reports of which the Central Electoral Commission promised to study. A survey of the Ukrainian press in the weeks leading up to the first round of elections on 27 March 1994 points up some of the most prevalent violations. Candidates took advantage of their official position to canvas and win votes, either by promises of improved services after election (such as new roads, bus routes, gas supply to villages, etc.) or by actual delivery

---

26 *Pravda Ukrainy* 1 March 1994; *Holos Ukrainy*, 27 January 1994; *Demokratychna Ukraina*, 24 March 1994.

27 United Nations Office in Ukraine, Press Release, 28 March 1994; *Holos Ukrainy*, 20 April 1994.

of material goods and services to voters during the election campaign period. Viktor Pohorilko, Deputy Head of the Commission, identified this as the most common violation.[28] While these were certainly violations of Ukraine's electoral law, one may well ask what is a more serious distortion of the democratic process — the delivery of food packets to pensioners containing condensed milk, barley, sugar and a leaflet from the donor candidate, or the undisclosed donation by a large corporation of millions of pounds/dollars to the election campaign fund of a political party?

Violence and coercion had its place in these elections, although such incidents were not widely reported in the mass media. The press centre *Vybory 94* recorded alleged acts of violence against 16 candidates and their relatives, including physical assault, burning of their homes and property, the slashing of brake cables of one candidate's car and the attempted murder of another candidate in Ternopil, who required treatment in hospital for a bullet wound in the head.[29] Perhaps the most sensational of these incidents was the disappearance in January of Mykhailo Boichyshyn, head of the Rukh Secretariat and co-chairman of its Election Committee. The Rukh leader, Viacheslav Chornovil, alleged that Boichyshyn had been kidnapped on the orders of the "party of power" for two reasons: he had documents incriminating state officials at the highest levels in massive corruption, which he was to make public in the midst of the election campaign period; and he was the key Rukh fundraiser. After his disappearance, Rukh leaders claimed that many businesspersons who supported the organisation were subjected to searches and interrogations by the Ministry of Internal Affairs. Chornovil believed that the Boichyshyn affair was part of a larger campaign to destroy Rukh's chances in the elections.[30] Boychyshyn's whereabouts remained a mystery throughout the elections.

---

28 See *Vechirnyi Kyiv*, 25 March 1994 and *Vybory 94* press releases Nos 8, 15, 17, 23, 25, 28, 31 (18 February–23 March 1994).
29 *Vybory 94* press releases Nos 6, 8, 12, 13, 14, 15, 17, 18, 21, 23, 24, 25, 27, 29, 31, 33 (16 February–25 March 1994).
30 *Holos Ukrainy*, 4 February 1994; *Vybory 94* press releases Nos 7, 8, 16 (17 February–2 March 1994).

The results

The campaign to bring the voters out continued right up to polling day on 27 March. In true Soviet tradition, the stores and specially erected buffets at the polling stations were stocked with food and drink rarely seen outside the major city centres. In the villages, the beer flowed and free discotheques were staged for young people that evening, all in an effort to entice the populace to the polling stations. That such efforts were undertaken by the authorities, both centrally and at the district level, casts some doubt on the charge that the "party of power" wanted to sabotage the election. More likely, it suggests that, as a coalition of various interests, the state elite was divided in its attitude towards the elections. While for some the unpredictability of change was reason enough to avoid elections, for others the elections offered an avenue for advancement.

The turnout on the first round exceeded the most optimistic prognoses, with 75.6 percent of voters across Ukraine and a majority in each of the 450 constituencies taking part. The turnout was highest in the western oblasts, reaching 90 percent in Ternopil. The industrialised eastern oblasts registered high levels of participation, with 75 percent in Luhansk, 72 percent in Donetsk and 71 percent in Kharkiv. The turnout in Crimea was 61 percent, and in Kyiv a disappointing 56 percent. However, because of the large number of candidates competing in most constituencies, only in 49 of them did a single candidate manage to secure more than 50 percent of the votes cast. In one constituency (No.105, Dnipropetrovsk oblast) where there were only two candidates, but neither secured a majority (it is possible to cast a valid vote rejecting all candidates on the ballot), new elections were required. In the remaining 400 constituencies, a second round of voting was declared for the period 2–10 April. The Central Electoral Commission left it to the discretion of the District Commissions to choose the day for voting within that time period, arguing that rotating power cuts to factories across Ukraine prevented a single suitable day being chosen.[31]

---

31   Press conference of Central Election Commission, Kyiv, 29 March 1994; *Holos Ukrainy*, 8 April 1994.

The greatest number of those elected in the first round were from the westernmost (19) and easternmost (14) oblasts. The left-wing bloc of parties did well in the east, while the national-democratic bloc dominated in the west. This was to be one of the patterns of voting in the second round. Many of the first elected candidates were nationally known political figures, including Ivan Pliushch, Speaker of the Verkhovna Rada, Leonid Kuchma and Viacheslav Chornovil.

The turnout in the second round of voting, which took place on 2, 3, 9 and 10 April, was 66 percent of registered voters across the country. A majority of registered voters turned out in 380 of the 400 constituencies where balloting took place, and in 289 of these a single candidate received a majority of the votes cast. Evidently a large enough proportion of the voters in the 91 other constituencies crossed out the names of both candidates who remained on the ballot (or spoiled their ballot) to give neither a majority.[32] New elections were to be held on 24 July 1994 in 112 constituencies (in one that failed in the first round and 111 in the second round).[33]

Thus by the end of the second round a total of 338 deputies had been elected to the Verkhovna Rada, giving it a constitutional quorum. These deputies are grouped according to party affiliation in Table 1. Twelve women were elected, a far smaller proportion of the total (3.6 percent) than the proportion of women among the original candidates (7 percent). Three-quarters of the elected deputies are between the ages of 25 and 50. Almost three-quarters are Ukrainian by nationality and a fifth are Russian, which corresponds quite closely to their respective shares of the total population.[34]

Analysis of results

A meaningful interpretation of the results requires some reflection on the ongoing political differentiation of Ukrainian society. This process has been very rapid in the past five years, since the formation of Rukh in 1989 broke the monopoly of the Communist

---

32   *Holos Ukrainy*, 27 April 1994.
33   *Holos Ukrainy*, 13 May 1994.
34   *Holos Ukrainy*, 13 May 1994.

Party. Rukh was the cradle of practically all the parties that were formed in 1990 and today occupy the national-democratic space, alongside Rukh itself, and part of the centrist space within the ideological spectrum. The period since 1989 also witnessed the splintering of the Communist Party into pro-independence and pro-union factions, its banning after the failed coup of August 1991 and its restoration in June 1993. The Communist Party initially lost members to Rukh (one-quarter of the latter's membership in 1990) from which they then passed mainly to the centrist parties in 1990 and 1991. After their party was banned Communists went into the Socialist Party, formed in October 1991, and the Peasant Party in December 1991. Some 120,000 returned to the reconstituted Communist Party in 1993 and 1994. The latter three parties and the Communist Party of Crimea occupy the left wing of the ideological spectrum.

The radical or integral nationalist right—notably the Ukrainian National Assembly/Ukrainian People's Self-Defence Organisation, State Independence of Ukraine, Social National Party of Ukraine and the Ukrainian Conservative Republican Party (an offshoot from the Ukrainian Republican Party)—emerged to prominence only in 1992 and 1993 as the economic crisis deepened, regional tensions grew and disappointment set in over the still meagre benefits of independence. The extreme right had its origins in the student movement of western Ukraine and Kyiv and among a minority of former political prisoners (Ivan Kandyba, Yurii Shukhevych,—Hryhoriii Prykhodko and others). By far the most important organisation is the Ukrainian National Assembly and its paramilitary wing, the Ukrainian People's Self-Defence Organisation, which together comprise several thousand members. They have not limited their work to western Ukraine, the heartland of nationalist movements, but have made a serious effort since mid-1993 to extend their influence eastwards into working-class and armed forces communities.[35]

---

35   Bohdan Nahaylo, 'Ukraine', *RFE/RL Research Report* (special issue about extremist movements), 3, 16, 22 April 1994, 42–45.

Table 1:   Results of the Ukrainian parliamentary elections March–April 1994

Left parties	Number elected	Percent
Communist Party	86	25.4
Peasant Party	18	5.3
Socialist Party	14	4.1
Communist Party of Crimea	5	1.5
Centrist parties		
Interregional Bloc for Reforms	15	4.4
Party of Democratic Renewal	4	1.2
Labour Party	4	1.2
Social Democratic Party	2	0.6
Civic Congress	2	0.6
National-democratic parties		
Rukh	25	7.4
Republican Party	11	3.3
Congress of Ukrainian Nationalists	7	2.1
Democratic Party	3	0.9
Christian Democratic Party	1	0.3
Integral nationalist parties		
Ukrainian National Assembly	3	0.9
Conservative Republican Party	2	0.6
Independents	136	40.2
Total elected	338	100
Elections failed in 112 constituencies		

Sources: Holos Ukrainy, 9 and 27 April 1994; UNIAR, 21 May 1994.

Paradoxically, the rapid political differentiation of society has not translated into a strong multiparty system. For although Ukrainian society has become politicised to an unprecedented degree, the widespread mistrust of political parties, equated by many with state instruments of domination and vehicles for personal gain, has kept the new political parties from the centre to the right small in membership and underdeveloped in terms of their infrastructure (press, local organisations, networks, etc.). These have remained largely as parties of the intelligentsia, reflecting its internal divisions, rather than those of society at large. The parties on the left are numerically stronger—their combined membership is estimated at one-quarter of a million—owing to the fact that they are in large measure based in reconstituted allegiances and networks of the once mighty, three million strong ruling party that was only incompletely, even barely, suppressed in August 1991. The numerical strength of the left-wing parties was by no means the sole reason for their strong showing in the 1994 elections, as we see below, but it did make a difference in view of the weakness of the centrist and national democratic parties, whose registered members range in number from a few hundred to a few thousand each.

There is another important reason why many powerful officials of the central state apparatus in particular chose to run as independents in these elections and not as members of political parties. This phenomenon stems from the terms of the historic compromise made between the ruling Communists and the national-democratic opposition when the Ukrainian state was declared independent in August 1991. In a nutshell, the Communist Party leadership agreed to the banning of their party and to support independence in exchange for their individual retention of the key positions they then occupied throughout the state and economy. This has meant that no systemic change has been undertaken since independence, a fact crucial to understanding the present crisis. And it has resulted in the phenomenon called the "party of power", a ruling state elite that has chosen not to identify with any political party, including the Communist Party that it once commanded, and that stakes its fortunes on its present hold on the levers of power and influence. It is grouped around the President and his administration, the government and its ministries, the Secretariat of the Verkhovna Rada, the General Staff of the armed forces, the Ministry of the Interior and the State Security Service. It is essentially an executive power over which legislative and judicial authority have minimal influence. Its members work together through institutional channels and informal networks. In a way, the "party of power" can formulate and impose policy quite independently for as long as it faces no serious organised rivals in the most public institutions of state decision making, notably the legislature. It managed to do so after August 1991 by co-opting the most promising leaders of the opposition national democrats (with the exception of Viacheslav Chornovil) and embracing their ideology of nation-state building, while assuring the leaders of state industry and agriculture that no sudden systemic change (of ownership, for example) would occur. In the 1994 elections, the "party of power" fielded candidates overwhelmingly as independents in an attempt to maintain or even expand its presence within the legislative arm of the state.

The term "party of power" is widely used in Ukrainian political discourse in at least three ways, all of which have some relevance to the analysis of Ukraine's evolving political system. The term was first used to denote a specific coalition built around Leonid Kravchuk as Speaker of the Verkhovna Rada and later as President. Kravchuk managed to unite politicians of quite different persuasions, from communists to nationalists, on the basis of loyalty to an independent state. The network operated without a public profile as a party. In fact, it included persons publicly identified with different political parties, but whose authority stemmed mainly from their membership of the "party of power".

Second, the term is used to suggest that the determination of policy within the Ukrainian state is neither entirely transparent nor primarily in the hands of the legislature, but substantially under the control of members of this elite network without a party face who are entrenched in the executive, security and other state institutions. The lack of policy coherence on the part of the Ukrainian elite should not unduly detract from this proposition. For although its members may disagree on basic issues and fail to act decisively on some of the most pressing ones, they remain united in ensuring that any systemic change in the transition period will not threaten their predominance in the state nor their capacity to use state office to accumulate personal material wealth.[36]

Third, the Ukrainian public makes liberal use of the term "party of power" to express its mistrust of state institutions and its disappointment in the first years of Ukraine's independent statehood. What is most important here is that the public expected transparency of government and accountability of its individual officers under a democratic system. However, a good part of the process of

---

36   Mykola Ryabchuk, "Democracy and the so-called 'Party of Power' in Ukraine", *Political Thought*, No. 3, 1994, 154–59.

government remains a secret affair. So many candidates running in the 1994 parliamentary elections as independents created an impression within the electorate that they had something to hide (in particular their past) and a belief that upon being elected they would not be accountable, not even to the collective discipline of a party.[37]

The left-wing parties emerged from the elections as the largest single bloc. Excluding the Communist Party of Crimea (which merits attention more as a party of regional interests than of left-wing policies), they managed to elect 118 deputies in 34.8 percent of the 338 constituencies. The Communist Party of Ukraine, with 86 deputies, is the largest party in the Verkhovna Rada. The national-democratic bloc captured 47, or 14 percent of the constituencies, with Rukh as the largest single party within this bloc, holding 25 seats. The centrist bloc of parties took 27 seats in the new parliament, or 8 percent of the total number. The Interregional Bloc for Reforms failed to carve out a broad base to the left of centre, claiming only 15 deputies at the end of the second round. The extreme right scored a surprise victory in western Ukraine with the election of three candidates from the Ukrainian National Assembly/Ukrainian People's Self-Defence Organisation. Stepan Khmara, leader of the Ukrainian Conservative Republican Party, defeated Republican Party chief Mykhailo Horyn, gaining one of the two seats taken by his party. The independents came away with 136 constituencies, or just over 40 percent of the total number of elected deputies.

The analysis of the gains of parties and blocs is difficult to undertake with precision for two reasons. First, the official returns published by the Central Electoral Commission (in *Holos Ukrainy*, 9 and 27 April 1994) identified elected deputies as independents if they were so registered as candidates. In fact, a proportion of independents campaigned for election as members of political parties. Therefore, for the purposes of this analysis the official sources are supplemented by information about party affiliation of elected deputies provided by the Ukrainian Independent Information Agency

---

37   Such views and beliefs were expressed to the author of this article by many people of different social backgrounds during the election campaign period.

(UNIAR).[38] Second, the process of public identification and affiliation of candidates with parties and blocs continued after the two rounds of voting, as parliament convened. This analysis, therefore, attempts to identify the strength of parties and blocs at the point of election, and does not investigate the process further, except to understand the complexion of the Verkhovna Rada at this date, 10 April 1994, at the end of the second round.

The geographical distribution of the votes for parties and blocs was striking. The Communist Party of Ukraine took half its seats (43) in the five easternmost oblasts of Kharkiv, Luhansk, Donetsk, Zaporizhzhia and Kherson. It took two-thirds (66.3 percent) of its seats in these five oblasts plus four more neighbouring oblasts of the south-east (Dnipropetrovsk, Mykolaiv, Odesa and Kirovohrad). The three national left-wing parties (Communist, Socialist and Peasant) together took 88, or 67.8 percent of their bloc total of 118, in these same nine oblasts. The left-wing parties took no seats at all in historical western Ukraine, that is the oblasts of Chernivtsi, Zakarpattia, lvano-Frankivsk, Ternopil, Lviv and Rivne.

Rukh, the main party of the national-democratic bloc, took 16 or 64 percent of its seats in historical western Ukraine (even with no seats at all in Zakarpattia). Adding its victories in Kyiv city (4) and Kyiv oblast (2) to those above gave Rukh 22 or 88 percent of its total of 25 seats. The national-democratic bloc (Rukh, Republican, Democratic and Christian Democratic Parties, Congress of Ukrainian Nationalists) swept Rivne oblast and, together with the national-democratic independent bloc Nova Khvylia (New Wave) and the extreme right parties, they also swept Lviv and Ternopil oblasts. The national-democratic parties gained 31 or 66 percent of their total number of 47 seats from the oblasts within historical western Ukraine. With Kyiv city and Kyiv oblast included in the calculation, the bloc had 39 or 83 percent of their total number from these two regions alone. With the exception of the one and only Christian Democrat, elected in Odesa oblast, the national democratic bloc was completely frozen out of the nine eastern and southeastern

---

38   *UNIAR*, 21 May 1994, a list of 338 deputies, detailing constituency, party affiliation and occupation.

oblasts dominated by the left-wing bloc. Thus the division between western Ukrainian nationalism and eastern Ukrainian communism/socialism that has featured so prominently in the country's modern history has been resurrected in the latest general elections.

There were other important regional features in the returns, reflecting both centrifugal and centripetal tendencies at work in border regions, as well as these regions' historical peculiarities of political culture. The President of Crimea, Yurii Meshkov, and the peninsula's most powerful coalition, Blok Rossiia, urged voters to boycott the Ukrainian parliamentary elections (there were simultaneous Crimean parliamentary elections), which resulted in 12 out of 23 seats there being left vacant. No candidates were elected from the four constituencies of Sevastopol. The voters elected five members of the Communist Party of Crimea, five independents and one member of the Interregional Bloc for Reforms.[39] The result confirmed the tendency of Crimea's disengagement from Ukraine that was well underway since the election of Meshkov in January 1994.

Chernivtsi, under Romania in the interwar years, adjacent to Moldova and with strong ethnic minorities (notably Romanian and Jewish), delivered a splintered result. Each of the six constituencies with a successful outcome returned a representative of a different interest: the Democratic Party, the Romanian Society, Bukovinian Accord, New Ukraine, the Peasants Union and Rukh.

Zakarpattia oblast, under Hungary during the interwar years, with strong ethnic minorities (Hungarian, Slovak and the Ruthenian movements) and attached by virtue of its geographical location on the Hungarian Plain to this neighbouring state's economy, shunned all political parties and returned seven independents, four of them members of the President's Administration. This may indicate a deliberate effort by the "party of power" to reinforce its control of Zakarpattia.

---

39   Analysis of results by *UNIAR*, 21 May 1994. Four of the elected independents subsequently joined the IBR. See Dominique Arel and Andrew Wilson, "The Ukrainian Parliamentary Elections", *RFE/RL Research Report*, 3, 36, 1 July 1994, 15; Andrew Wilson, "The Elections in Crimea", *RFE/RL Research Report*, 3, 25, 24 June 1994, 18.

Ivano-Frankivsk is a region of western Ukraine that suffered enormously from political repression, deportations and calculated outmigration after its incorporation into the Soviet Union in 1945. It was a stronghold of the Ukrainian Insurgent Army into the early 1950s. Its populace shows a high level of national political awareness and involvement. Its voters returned ten independents and only two representatives of the national-democratic bloc. The paradoxical result may be explained by the disillusionment being felt by lvano-Frankivsk voters with the parties of the national-democratic bloc, who appear to have failed to influence official Kyiv' s domestic and foreign policies sufficiently to stabilise the new republic and, moreover, to provide tangible benefits to the people in far-off (from Kyiv) lvano-Frankivsk. In contrast to the voters of Rivne, Ternopil and Lviv oblasts, where the national-democratic parties did very well, lvano-Frankivsk voters turned to proven individuals campaigning as independents such as deputies of the previous parliament V. Kostytsky, P. Movchan and V. Pylypchuk, Ye. Proniuk of the Society of the Repressed, and R. Krutsyk, who (campaigning as a member of the Congress of Ukrainian Nationalists) is widely known for his work unearthing the graves of Stalin's victims throughout the region and rehabilitating survivors of the post-war purges.

Volyn oblast, on the border between Orthodoxy and Uniatism, once at the edges of imperial Poland and Russia, under Poland in the interwar years, also displays a particular regional political culture. In the 1920s and 1930s its inhabitants gave support both to the Communist Party of Western Ukraine and the moderate Ukrainian National Democratic Union, and simultaneously to the Ukrainian Insurgent Army and to the Red Partisans in the war against Nazi Germany. Volynian voters generally shunned political parties in these elections, returning five independents and one member of the Congress of Ukrainian Nationalists. Here again, four representatives of the "party of power" were elected.

On the whole, the centrist parties performed poorly. The election of 15 members of the Interregional Bloc for Reforms[40] was a

---

40   According to *UNIAR*, 21 May 1994, they were elected in Chernihiv, Mykolaiv, Dnipropetrovsk, Kherson and Kharkiv oblasts and Crimea.

respectable but disappointing result against the background of well publicised efforts to build the Bloc in the big cities of the south and east during the election campaign period and predictions by its leaders that it would become the power broker between east and west in the new parliament. The IBR co-chairman, Hryniov, claimed right after the election that they had a fraction of 21 deputies,[41] the original 15 presumably augmented from among the "independent" deputies. However, Kuchma and Hryniov did not gain a sufficiently large mandate to allow them to dominate the centre ground, nor even to register a parliamentary fraction (requiring 25 or more members). By the end of May the IBR had around 10 members in the Verkhovna Rada, which means that some of its adherents who were successful in the elections subsequently defected to other parliamentary fractions.[42]

Table 2:   Occupational distribution of 163 elected deputies formally registered as independent candidates

Occupational grouping	Percent
Ministers, deputy ministers, heads and deputy heads of state committees and security organs	12.3
President's representatives and officials of President's Administration	10.6
Oblast, city and local government officials	8.2
People's Deputies, heads and deputy heads of Verkhovna Rada Commissions	7.6
Military officers	4.7
Judges and other officials of judiciary	2.3
Directors, managers, deputies and department heads in state, co-operative and private enterprises and banks	28.8
Academics and academic administrators	11.8
Other professions	12.9
Total	99.2

Source: Holos Ukrainy, 9 and 27 April 1994.

Another centrist fraction of deputies, called "Centre", was launched immediately after the second round by Vasyl Durdynets, deputy speaker of the former Verkhovna Rada. It attracted more

---

41   *Holos Ukrainy,* 11 May 1994.
42   *Holos Ukrainy,* 28 May 1994.

than 50 deputies from the independents within days. The Centre fraction places a priority in its platform on the defence of Ukraine's statehood and territorial integrity, the principal feature that distinguishes it from the IBR.[43] Thus the centre ground in the new Verkhovna Rada, which in large measure will be structured by the organised fractions to which the elected independent deputies choose to adhere, seems destined to be divided (alongside other parameters) over Ukraine's international orientation — strategic union with Russia or cleaving to Europe as the counterweight to Russian influence from the east.

The independents in the new parliament fill a space between the left parties and the national-democratic parties in both a geographical and an ideological sense. Virtually half of the independents (67 out of 136, or 49.2 percent) were elected in 11 oblasts geographically located between the five eastern left-wing and the five western national-democratic/right-wing strongholds (that is, in Cherkasy, Kirovohrad, Chemihiv, Sumy, Vynnytsia, Khmelnytsky, Zhytomyr, Kyiv, Mykolaiv, Odesa, Poltava and Dnipropetrovsk). There were some notable clusters of independents in oblasts where all the political parties did poorly (Vynnytsia, Zhytomyr, Zakarpattia, Volyn, Odesa and Cherkasy). More than a quarter of those elected as independents live in the capital, though only one independent has so far been elected from a Kyiv city constituency. Upon analysing the occupational profile of all elected deputies who were formally registered as independent candidates (163 in all), it becomes clear that they are mainly employed in the higher levels of state institutions and the state-controlled economy, with an admixture of the traditional intelligentsia and the new rich (see Table 2). Therefore, the election of independents may be interpreted in various ways, depending on the specific local situation: as a sign of the underdevelopment of the party political system (in the absence of strong parties) or of the underdevelopment of the electorate's independent political judgement (where local economic and political bosses can buy their way into office) or, for that matter, as a sign of

---

43   *Holos Ukrainy*, 26 and 29 April 1994.

sophisticated political judgement (intimate knowledge of individual candidates' qualifications and platform, disregarding party affiliation). Nevertheless, the "party of power" resides within this category of deputies.

Conclusions

The election of 338 deputies to the Verkhovna Rada in the two rounds of voting in March and April 1994 was a qualified success, both in giving Ukraine a constitutionally legitimate legislature and as the country's first exercise in democratic general elections since independence. In the face of widespread pessimism and fear of failure, three-quarters of the electorate turned out in the first round and two-thirds in the second, a level of participation exceeding that exhibited in the parliamentary election in Hungary in 1990, in Poland in 1991 and in Russia in 1993.[44] To a Western observer, Ukrainians sometimes appeared unduly self-critical and underrated their society's democratic credentials. It was only the stringent requirements of the electoral law, more exacting than in most Western democracies, that prevented these elections from filling all 450 seats in the legislature. There were irregularities and violations of the electoral law, but none so serious or systematic as to invalidate the entire process in the eyes of domestic or foreign observers.[45] Therefore, the first conclusion to be drawn is that the Ukrainian electorate proved capable of exercising its democratic prerogative, despite its scant previous experience of democratic government. How its democratic culture has been sustained deserves investigation in its own right. The democratic nature of the elections gives the new Verkhovna Rada an authoritative mandate to tackle the country's most pressing problems, a mandate the Verkhovna Rada elected in 1990 did not enjoy.

---

44   See Frances Millard, "The Polish parliamentary elections of October 1991", *Soviet Studies*, 44, 5, 1992, 837–855.

45   The allegations of violence perpetrated against candidates warrant further investigation. The practice of buying votes with material inducements and promises of services invites comparison with elections in other wealthy and poor societies.

The elections were successful in another sense as well—they provided an opportunity to move forward towards a multi-party political system. This may not be apparent at first sight, given that 40 percent of those elected are independents. And certainly the unitary majoritarian system of single member constituencies provides no encouragement to fledgling political parties. Yet this impediment did not prove insurmountable in the process. Whereas political parties managed to nominate only 11 percent of the contenders who entered the race, the actual number of declared party members who contested the election was at least a quarter of the total, and the proportion of those who emerged victorious was well over one half. Thus one can discern a process of selection at work in these elections, both in the increasing identification of candidates with a political party and in the voting for them. This process continued after the elections, with more of the elected independents coming out of the closet and adhering to the parliamentary fractions of parties and blocs.[46]

The results point to an evolution of the political cleavages within Ukrainian society along three axes. The first of these, seen in the context of the entire period from 1989 to 1994, is the ongoing differentiation along ideological and programmatic lines. If in the elections of March 1990 there were essentially two contending forces—Rukh and the Communist Party—there were 32 parties contesting the 1994 elections, and 15 of these won seats in the legislature. The entire political spectrum, with the exception of the far left, has now been occupied.

Second, the parties of the left have emerged as the strongest single bloc, reversing their decline, indeed ostracism, before and immediately after independence. Their success on this occasion is undoubtedly the electorate's reaction to the deepening economic crisis, and can be compared with the outcome of the most recent elections in Poland and Hungary. The crisis is attributed in the public's mind to the loss of an ordered economy, regulated by the state, and to the emergence of the new robber barons undertaking the primitive accumulation of their wealth through appropriation of

---

46   *Holos Ukrainy*, 11 May 1994.

state assets ("spontaneous privatisation" or *prykhvatyzatsiia* – privatisation by seizure) and profits from trade. These unrestrained processes and the absence of effective state control are identified with capitalism and the market and are blamed for the socio-economic crisis facing the country. They gave the left-wing parties a broad field for agitation along social-democratic lines and/or along communist lines, that is, "nostalgia for the past".

By the same token the national democrats proved unable to broaden their base because they did not convince the electorate that they had a serious strategy to combat the economic crisis. Their poor showing outside Kyiv and western Ukraine also reflected a certain discrediting of Ukrainian state independence over the past two years by its identification with the economic crisis. The national democrats knew this from their public opinion surveys, which showed a decisive shift in favour of restoring strong ties with Russia, Ukraine's principal trading partner. Yet the threat to independence that the national democrats see coming from Russia prevented them from embracing wholeheartedly a strategic orientation (not union) towards Russia. On the other hand they did not have an explicit strategy for moving forward to privatisation and the market that simultaneously addressed the immediate impact of the economic crisis on people's living standards.

The results and the first moves towards establishing parliamentary fractions indicate that the centre is split into two, possibly more, groupings. The strength of the Interregional Bloc and the Centre fraction, and the extent to which they gravitate towards their respective left and right flanks, may well decide which camp takes the upper hand in the long run, the kind of government the legislature approves and the policies it pursues both in domestic and international affairs. It is not a result that favours the centrist camp as a power broker, however it is reconstructed by parliamentary fractions. The bloc of left parties was in the lead coming out of the elections and consolidated its lead quite quickly once in the new legislature. Oleksandr Moroz, head of the Socialist Party, was elected Speaker of the Verkhovna Rada on 17 May, polling 171 votes against his nearest rival, Vasyl Durdynets, Centre fraction leader, with 103 votes.[47] An estimate of the relationship of forces at the end of May in the parliamentary newspaper *Holos Ukrainy*[48] gave the left bloc more than 110 deputies, the Interregional Bloc for Reforms around 10, representatives of the "party of power" about 70, the national-democratic bloc more than 80, and the extreme right 10. These initial developments suggest that the "party of power" in the Verkhovna Rada is vacillating between the camps, needing specific support from both sides: from the left quite simply because it has been given a powerful mandate from the electorate; and from the national democrats because they are committed unconditionally to the defence of the independent state.

Finally, the geographical split of the vote for the left and national-democratic blocs between the eastern and western oblasts brings to the fore again a division of Ukraine that has deep historical roots. The returns in Crimea, and to a significantly lesser extent in other border regions to the west, are also a cause for concern about the future integrity of the country. The elections have aggravated the centrifugal tendencies at work insofar as the electorate was united across the country only in the fact that it participated in the same elections. The elections did not unify them in a contest between forces present in all its main regions. None of the parties, blocs nor even the independents can claim to have a national presence. There are clearly ideological and policy differences between the parties and blocs; however, these blocs are as much, if not more, the expression of regional identities and interests as they are of ideology and policy.

The east-west split remains one of the main challenges facing the Ukrainian state as it undertakes the nation-building project, with important implications for the strategy needed to rebuild the country's economy, for the country's security and foreign policy orientations, its linguistic and minorities policies, and the division of powers between the central state, regional and local governments. All these policy choices are the substance of the transition from the Soviet societal formation under way in Ukraine, and they will test the capacity of its new legislators to work together for the next five years.

---

47   *Radio Ukraine International*, 17 May 1994.
48   28 May 1994.

Leonid Kuchma's Presidency in Its First Year[*]

In June 1993, in the midst of Leonid Kravchuk's term as the first president of Ukraine after the collapse of the Soviet Union, a powerful strike wave engulfed the eastern industrial oblasts. Driven to strike by a collapsing industrial base, by the break-up of trade ties with Russia upon which the coal, steel, machine building and other sectors of the economy depend, and by the central government's failure to advance a credible strategy of economic recovery, the regional strike organizations demanded a vote of confidence in all the national institutions of power, greater economic and political autonomy for the eastern oblasts and Ukraine's fuller integration with the Commonwealth of Independent States (CIS). The acting prime minister, Leonid Kuchma, was forced to step down in September 1993 after a fruitless year in office, his hands tied by the Verkhovna Rada (parliament) and President Kravchuk. The Rada negotiated an end to the strikes by agreeing to hold referendums of confidence in both state institutions in September. As the moment approached, however, the Rada changed its mind and called new parliamentary and presidential elections for March and June 1994 respectively.

The law governing presidential elections required the winning candidate to amass more than half of the votes cast by more than half of the registered electorate. There were seven candidates in the first round on 26 June 1994 and none managed to meet this requirement. The incumbent, Kravchuk, came in with 37.7 percent, followed by Kuchma with 31.2 percent, Oleksandr Moroz, the head of the Rada, with 13.1 percent, and the liberal market economist Volodymyr Lanovy with 9.4 percent. This result led to a second round run-off between Kravchuk and Kuchma on 10 July, in which 71.6 percent of the registered electorate took part. Kuchma won with 52.1 percent against Kravchuk's 45.1 percent. Whereas Kravchuk's

---

[*]   First published in: *Journal of Ukrainian Studies*, Nos 1–2 Summer–Winter 1995, 177–193.

support came overwhelmingly from the western oblasts (87.4 percent of the vote), Kyiv city (59.7 percent), and the central Right Bank oblasts (54.1 percent), Kuchma's came from the eastern (75.6 percent), southern (72.5 percent), and central Left Bank (65.9 percent).[1]

Kuchma owed his victory mainly to a fundamental change over the previous two years in Ukrainians' attitudes to independence, the economy and relations with Russia and the CIS. Eighteen months of independence under President Kravchuk saw the country sink deeper into economic crisis: the gross domestic product approached half its pre-independence level; inflation ran at 10,000 percent annually (in 1993); debt to the Russian Federation for fuel imports mounted; and relations with Russia worsened owing to disagreements over Crimea, participation in the CIS and other issues. Meanwhile, very little had been offered in the way of credits, loans, or investments by the Western industrial states.

Kravchuk did not make the economic crisis a priority in his election campaign, but focused instead upon a continued defence of Ukraine's statehood through a pro-European orientation in foreign affairs. Kuchma, on the other hand, campaigned on a platform of economic recovery and reform as the best guarantee of continued state independence, and restoration of ties with Russia and other CIS states as a necessary condition of economic recovery. He demanded the establishment of a strong executive authority to carry through domestic reform. He also called for granting Russian official status as a state language, which set him apart from Kravchuk. Furthermore, he called for a decisive suppression of crime and mafia organizations.

The incumbent's association with continued economic decline and a hostile stand-off between Ukraine and Russia hobbled him in his bid for a second term. But his challenger's relative inexperience in government and his inability to speak Ukrainian did not give him an ideal profile either. Until he became prime minister in 1992, Kuchma had built a career almost entirely in the missile industry, becoming director of the world's largest missile production facility,

---

1   Dominique Arel and Andrew Wilson, "Ukraine under Kuchma: Back to Eurasia?" *Radio Free Europe/Radio Liberty Research Report 3*, No. 32, 19 August 1994.

in Dnipropetrovsk. Kuchma won, however, because he correctly read the electorate's rapidly changing perceptions of the way out of the country's problems. If, in December 1991, electors took Ukrainian independence to be the condition for economic recovery and prosperity, by July 1994 they understood economic recovery to be the condition of continued independence. Kuchma acknowledged that the economic crisis was related directly to the breakdown of trade ties with Russia. In the pro-Western orientation of Kravchuk and the national democrats he saw no tangible benefits, let alone a substitute for Ukraine's traditional patterns of trade with the east. Kuchma's Eurasian orientation did not mean the abandonment of Ukrainian independence: rather, Kuchma argued that Ukraine's very survival depended upon economic recovery, which could only be achieved through Ukraine's fuller participation in its traditional economic area and through normalization of relations with Russia, the major regional power.

Kuchma's victory mirrored the results of the parliamentary election in March and April 1994, when the left-wing parties (Communist, Socialist, and Peasant) emerged as the largest single bloc.[2] Kuchma did not share this bloc's views on economic recovery, but there was in this election campaign a certain coincidence between the left-wing parties' regional identity (eastern and southern Ukraine) and Kuchma's own—as a defender of Russian minority interests and, of course, an advocate of renewed economic ties with Russia. The outcome of the second round showed a regional division of the electorate between Kravchuk, who gained most support in the western oblasts, and Kuchma, who gained it in the east.

Yet, this east-west division has had a paradoxical effect upon Ukraine's politicians. Their understanding of it may help them take power, but, once they assume national responsibilities they strive to overcome it. Kuchma was transformed in this way, too, after becoming president. He quickly learned to speak Ukrainian, the official language, and dropped the issue of official status for Russian. Kuchma's team in the president's administration was drawn from

---

2   See Marko Bojcun, "The Ukrainian Parliamentary Elections in March–April 1994," *Europe-Asia Studies*, Vol. 47, No. 2, 1995, 229–49.

his long-standing supporters and collaborators in Dnipropetrovsk, where he had studied and worked for many years, from the Nova Ukraina (New Ukraine) bloc of 1993 and the Interregional Bloc for Reforms of 1994, and from the Galician Nova Khvylia (New Wave) group of economic reformers. It was a broad coalition whose members were relatively young in comparison with the Kravchuk team and it included easterners, westerners, and Kyivans.

International realities also proved more complicated than Kuchma's election campaign prescriptions for them. Good relations with Russia proved more difficult to restore than many had thought, while relations with Western institutions and countries featured prominently in Kuchma's first foreign policy initiatives, contradicting initial expectations that he would turn toward Eurasia. Within months of his election, Kuchma's standing in opinion polls was higher in Western than Eastern Ukraine (though it remained relatively high everywhere), and it remained well above that of the Verkhovna Rada and its chairman, Oleksandr Moroz, throughout his first year.[3]

The Rada had elected Moroz, the head of the Socialist party, as its chairman in May 1994. His election was the left-wing bloc of deputies' first victory in parliament. Moroz did not agree with Kuchma about macro-economic reform, privatisation or foreign investment. He opposed rapid privatisation of the state economy, the privatisation of land, an open-door policy for foreign investment or any sharp reduction in the state social-security budget as a condition for Ukraine's gaining credits and technical assistance from the International Monetary Fund. He also defended the Rada's established legislative, executive, and constitutional functions against the advances of the new president. Rather, he wanted to see the president's role reduced, especially in domestic affairs. Moroz figured as a political leader whose disagreements with Kuchma were both substantial in ideological terms and indicative of the broader

---

3   *Post-Postup*, 19–25 May 1995.

struggle between the president and parliament for dominance within the state.[4]

Voting patterns in the Rada throughout the latter part of 1994 showed that, by a slim majority, it was restorationist with respect to the state power structure—that is, it wanted to return to a Soviet type of state with fused legislative, executive, and constitutional powers. But, by an equally slim majority it was reformist with regard to economic change—that is, in favour of a capitalist market tempered by strong welfare-state provisions. Such apparently inconsistent orientations within the Rada could be explained by two important facts: first, the Rada had a large body of independent, that is, non-party, deputies who swayed between the left and the national-democratic parties, often for quite pragmatic reasons, in their voting behaviour. Second, the ideological profiles of the parliamentary groupings or factions entered into by the parties were not at all firm. The deputies' regional loyalties often took the upper hand, with apparently left-wing deputies from the east and south voting for pro-capitalist measures because they were seen as beneficial for their regional economies.[5]

Nevertheless, Kuchma came into direct conflict with the Rada, as well as with vested interests in the ministries and agencies of government, as he attempted to turn his election platform into state policies. The Communists, Socialists and, to a lesser extent, the Peasant party opposed Kuchma's pro-market, pro-Western policies and his policies favouring privatisation. By 1994 much of Ukrainian society had come to hold a negative view of capitalism and the market, identifying it with the looming "grey economy" that the state could not tax for its budget, and with inflation, unemployment, the steady collapse of state industry and the appropriation of its choicest parts by the new business class. The Western capitalist countries, seen as models of development at the time of independence,

---

4   Oleksandr Moroz's interviews and speeches provide a good overview of his political orientation. See *Holos Ukrainy*, 2 April 1992, 18 September 1993, 16 July 1994, 26 August 1994, 17 and 21 September 1994, and 31 December 1994.

5   Mykola Tomenko, "The Verkhovna Rada of Today," *Ukrains'ka perspektyva*, No. 1, 1995.

came to be regarded widely as tight-fisted and bent upon penetrating Ukraine's economy and market for their own advantage.

Kuchma's anti-crime offensive encountered silent but determined resistance from state officials and elected deputies suborned by the mafia. There was an attempt on the life of the newly appointed minister of foreign economic relations in September 1994.[6] This ministry issued licences to trade abroad, which allowed some state and private firms to re-export Russian fuels and dump Ukrainian minerals, metals, chemicals, railway rolling stock, ships and other goods on world markets for considerable profit, most of it banked abroad. Kuchma's attempts to impose fiscal discipline upon the national budget, to collect taxes on company profits, to unify the exchange rate of the *karbovanets'* (in order to eliminate arbitraging between the state and market exchanges by officials with access to state hard-currency reserves), and to halt the flight of capital abroad — estimated in 1994 to be in excess of US $25 billion — ran up against powerful financial oligarchies straddling the state and private sectors.

To be sure, Kuchma was a pro-market, pro-capitalist reformer. On this general principle he had support within the country's new ruling circles. But there are many kinds of national capitalist economies in the world. Ukraine could be driven into the periphery of the world market, supplying raw materials and semi-finished goods, and developing a strong class of traders in these goods, while allowing its manufacturing sector to decline and thereby making the country more dependent on imports from the metropolitan states. On the other hand, Ukraine could preserve those industrial and technological sectors in which it has a distinct advantage in world trade and develop a more self-sufficient domestic market. It could sink into the Third World, or it could balance more evenly between the Second World (the former USSR) and the West. The social consequences of these divergent paths into capitalism and the world economy would differ markedly from each other. Kuchma openly chose the latter path, seeking to foster a private economy that could be taxed, an industrial policy to save Ukraine's

---

6   *Uriadovyi kur'ier*, 24 September 1994.

most promising extraction, processing and manufacturing sectors, and a strategic trade policy to accumulate hard-currency earnings for further economic development. The capitalist class that would emerge from this process to co-exist in a regulated relationship with the state economic sector would be different from the "robber barons" who were already engaged in the primitive accumulation of capital. Perhaps Kuchma believed that a deal had to be struck between these two tendencies. However, either a deal or a forceful confrontation with the more ruinous transition to the capitalist market would require that the state's institutions, particularly its executive arm, wield greater authority. This would be difficult to achieve because the Ukrainian state was weak and internally divided by ideology and conflicting material interests.

Kuchma's primary aim in the field of state reform, therefore, was to seek a new division of powers between the president, government, parliament and judiciary. He tried to overcome the ongoing conflict between the executive and legislature, to remove executive responsibilities from the purview of the legislature, and to establish a strong presidential arm of state that could enforce its decisions from Kyiv down to the local level throughout the country.

Why is there a conflict between the executive and legislature? In the beginning there was only the Verkhovna Rada, an instrument of the Communist Party of Ukraine, itself an instrument of the all-Union Party leadership. As the popular movement for independence gained ground in 1989 and 1990 a growing wing of Ukraine's Communists moved to accommodate and take advantage of it. The Rada, in which they held a two-thirds majority after the March 1990 elections, claimed increasing powers from the Moscow centre, expressing this claim constitutionally for the first time in the July 1990 Declaration of State Sovereignty. Throughout this period the Rada combined legislative and executive functions and operated as a kind of constituent assembly in continuous session.[7]

---

7   I have relied for this summary of the historic conflict between the legislature and the executive upon Ihor Markov's excellent analysis, "The Role of the President in the Ukrainian Political System," *RL/RFE Research Report 2*, No. 48, December 1993.

The Rada then delegated some of its higher representative and executive functions to its chairman—Leonid Kravchuk from July 1990—and a year later wrote these responsibilities into the Law on the President. The president was to be the shield of the Rada against Moscow, with the responsibility of preventing application of all-Union laws if they contradicted republican legislation. As a popularly elected statesman, he would be a legitimator of Ukrainian statehood.

In 1992, after his election, President Kravchuk became not only the head of state—a role directed essentially outward, internationally—but also the chief executive, a role directing him to domestic concerns. He assumed the right to appoint the prime minister and key members of the Cabinet, though not without the Rada's approval. The president also had the right to legislative initiative from within the executive branch. The system of president's representatives, created in March 1992, provided the chief executive with a vertical line of command from the national through the oblast, district, city and rural governments.

The Verkhovna Rada, however, took measures to limit the power of the head of state and chief executive and weaken his influence. It could veto his decrees, it could override the president's veto of its own draft legislation and, most important, it confirmed and dismissed the prime minister and Cabinet. The president, on the other hand, could not dismiss the Rada if the government resigned.

The prime minister and Cabinet emerged as an independent entity in the executive branch only with the appointment in November 1992 of Leonid Kuchma, to succeed Vitold Fokin as prime minister. The Verkhovna Rada gave Kuchma legislative initiative to rule by decree on economic matters and prevented Kravchuk from overriding him through presidential decrees. After six months, when these special powers were not extended for Kuchma and Kravchuk's were restored, the Rada nevertheless turned down Kravchuk's proposal that he should reconsolidate his executive authority by heading the new Cabinet. It sought to reimpose its authority over the government, and Kravchuk had to concede.

The erosion of recently gained presidential power that began here was illustrated in the difference between the first draft of the new constitution debated in 1992, where the president was both the head of state and chief executive, and the revised draft issued in 1993, in which the president was only the head of state. The president was forced to give up the network of his lower government representatives when parliament legislated in February 1994 that their heads be popularly elected. So began a new struggle in which the Verkhovna Rada and the president each sought to subordinate the regional and local councils.

After the Rada's acceptance of Kuchma's resignation as prime minister in September 1993 and subsequent disastrous nine months, during which Yukhym Zviahilsky held that office (currently Zviahilsky is facing prosecution for serious economic crimes), a new prime minister, Vitalii Masol, was chosen in June 1994, on the eve of the presidential elections. Ex-Prime Minister Kuchma then defeated Kravchuk in the elections on July 10.

The election of Leonid Kuchma marked a turning point in the evolution of relations between key central state institutions. As president, Kravchuk had increasingly stood aloof from domestic politics, preferring to act as a mediator and consensus maker between competing interest groups while concentrating his efforts in foreign affairs: securing Ukraine's independence and defending territorial integrity. That became his definitive role, and it was one cause of his almost complete ineffectiveness in combating the economic crisis. Kuchma, on the other hand, was handed economic recovery and reform as his principal task, and he believed that Ukraine's continued independence depended upon success in this matter. Kuchma had no alternative but to seek greater influence over domestic policy making than did Kravchuk, and this requirement drove him to redefine and expand his prerogatives as chief executive, to direct the Cabinet and prime minister, and to restore presidential control over lower levels of government. All these developments challenged the power, influence, and prerogatives of the Verkhovna Rada.

The Cabinet was overhauled in August and September 1994. Prime Minister Masol survived then, but was forced by Kuchma to resign on 1 March 1995.[8] He was widely regarded as an opponent of Kuchma's policies who had been sneaked into the prime minister's post on the eve of the second round of presidential elections as insurance against Kuchma's victory. Well before Masol's resignation, however, Kuchma had not only filled the Cabinet with his own people but had effectively shifted the locus of policy decision making to his administration. After Masol resigned Yevhen Marchuk, the minister of state security as well as the president's emissary to Crimea and Moscow in difficult negotiations, was made the acting prime minister. He was confirmed in this post and asked to form a new Cabinet in May 1995 after Kuchma reached agreement on the division of powers with the Verkhovna Rada.

Kuchma subordinated the Cabinet of Ministers directly to his office by a decree on 6 August 1994.[9] The decree was motivated by the need for effective leadership of state institutions in carrying out economic reform and consolidating market relations. It requires the president's direct participation in all cabinet meetings that address matters of economic transformation and reform, his approval of all daily Cabinet agendas and the Cabinet's participation in drawing up presidential decrees on economic reform, and establishes his right to decide appointments to all state organisations subordinated to the Cabinet.

Kuchma resubordinated all regional and local governments to the president's office by another decree issued on 6 August 1994.[10] He justified it by the need for an effective vertical command network that would ensure uniform and comprehensive implementation of policy. Accordingly, the heads of all oblast governments, of the Kyiv and Sevastopol city governments, and of all lower-tier (local) governments were made answerable to the president. The heads of these governments, elected for the first time on 26 June 1994, thus saw their democratic local authority limited by central executive authority. The capacity of the Verkhovna Rada to influence them was also diminished.

---

8   *Financial Times*, 2 March 1995.
9   *Holos Ukrainy*, 11 August 1994.
10   *Ibid.*

Kuchma sweetened the subordination of regional and local councils by promoting greater contact between them and the president through a new consultative body. To that end, a Council of the Regions was created by decree on 20 September. It was attached to the presidency and was to advise in matters of economic and social policy and central-regional-local government relations.[11] The council included the government heads of all the oblasts and the cities of Kyiv and Sevastopol, as well as the deputy Prime Minister of Crimea. The president was the council's head and the prime minister was its deputy head. Kuchma's administration worked assiduously to win explicit support from these governments for his plan to consolidate the presidency as the chief domestic executive organ and to make the prime minister and the Cabinet answerable to it, thereby diminishing the ability of the Verkhovna Rada, with its 40 percent plus left-wing bloc, to make the Cabinet answerable to it.

Quite early in his presidency, Kuchma signalled his desire to reach a constitutional accord with the Verkhovna Rada that would clearly define the separation and interdependence of their functions and powers.[12] The prime issue for both sides was who would control the government. Kuchma conceived this accord as a "little constitution" prefiguring a comprehensive constitution to be adopted later. It was needed urgently, he argued, so that the executive and legislative arms of state might work effectively towards a major economic, systemic transformation. Kuchma also warned that, unless the Rada co-operated with him, he would take the issue to the country in a referendum.

The Constitution of Ukraine had been adopted last in April 1978. It was substantially amended and expanded in the period from 1990. Naturally, the evolution of the Constitution in this latest period led to a highly complex and contradictory set of legal documents because its original Soviet terms of reference did not accord with the new historical context and the new values that accompanied it. In an effort to set Ukraine's constitutional process on a more appropriate, contemporary platform, a comprehensive new draft

---

11   *Uriadovyi kur'ier*, 22 September 1994.
12   *Holos Ukrainy*, 22 and 28 July 1994.

was considered by the Verkhovna Rada in 1992 and was released for public discussion. Parliamentary commissions incorporated many proposals drawn from public contributions and from their own deliberations in the amended draft of early 1993. As mentioned above, the document was redrafted to reduce the powers of the president as chief executive. However, it proved impossible for the Rada to muster two thirds of its deputies to agree on a new constitution, and so it was never tabled for discussion or adoption.

In November 1994 the president and the Verkhovna Rada relaunched the constitutional process by agreeing upon the composition of a Constitutional Commission of the Verkhovna Rada.[13] Kuchma and Moroz were made its co-heads. The Verkhovna Rada and the president each delegated 15 members; the Supreme Court, the Arbitration Court, and the Procuracy General delegated two each; and the Crimean Verkhovna Rada and the Constitutional Court, one each. Such proportions reflected the real balance of power between the central institutions.

There appeared to be at least three orientations within the commission: the Communist and Socialist deputies, who wished to build a new constitution on the basis of the 1978 document; the reformist centre from the national democratic and liberal democratic camps who wanted to use the 1993 draft constitution as a basis; and President Kuchma's supporters, for whom their own "little constitution" was the kernel of the future basic law they wished to see adopted.[14]

In December 1994 the president submitted his draft Constitutional Law on State Power and Local Self-government[15] to the Rada, which the latter passed on first reading. The draft contains the following essential provisions with respect to the central state institutions:

1.   There is a division of powers between the legislature, executive, and judiciary.

---

13   *Holos Ukrainy*, 30 November and 1 December 1994; and *Uriadovyi kur'ier*, 12 November 1994.

14   *Holos Ukrainy*, 1 and 15 September 1994.

15   Published in *Uriadovyi kur'ier*, 6 December 1994.

2. Judicial supremacy is exercised by the Constitutional Court, which is responsible for arbitrating between the branches of state power. Its head is to be nominated jointly by the president and the Verkhovna Rada, and appointed by the latter.

3. The president is the head of state. Executive power is vested in the president and exercised by him and through the government he establishes. He conducts Ukraine's foreign policy subject to ratification by the Verkhovna Rada. The president is the head of the National Security Council and the commander-in-chief of the Armed Forces. He appoints and dismisses the higher command and declares war and a state of war, subject to ratification by the Verkhovna Rada.

4. The president independently establishes the government. He may likewise dismiss it. The Cabinet of Ministers and the prime minister are subordinate to the president.

5. Decrees of the president in matters of economic reform not yet regulated by law have the force of law until relevant legislation is adopted.

6. The president can veto Verkhovna Rada legislation and send it back for revision. The Rada must gain support for its amended version by a two thirds majority in order to require the president to sign the legislation and make it public.

7. The president may dissolve the Verkhovna Rada, after consultation with its chairman and the Constitutional Court, if the Rada rejects his government's programme on two successive occasions or does not approve its state budget within a period of three months.

8. The president has the prerogative of nominating persons to the following key posts: the members of the Supreme Court and Higher Arbitration Court, the Procurator-General and the head of the National Bank.

9. The Verkhovna Rada is the supreme legislative authority.

10. The Verkhovna Rada can have a vote of non-confidence only on the government's programme, not its composition. Such a vote leads to the resignation of the government, but not of the president.

11. The Verkhovna Rada can veto the decrees of the president on the basis of their unconstitutionality, which must be established by the judiciary.

12. The Verkhovna Rada can initiate impeachment proceedings against the president for a serious crime and can proceed to their completion on condition of a favourable ruling by the Constitutional Court.

How a new constitution might be adopted had already been the subject of debate. Moroz proposed that a draft be adopted by the Verkhovna Rada, that a referendum be held to resolve matters on which the Rada could not agree, and that the final version be debated and adopted by an All-Ukrainian Congress of Councils composed of deputies from every level of government.[16] President Kuchma proposed that a constitution be adopted by the Verkhovna Rada, through a referendum in matters of disagreement and finally by agreement of the three central state branches in joint session.[17]

The draft Law on State Power was subjected to commission hearings from January to mid-April 1995 in an attempt to reach a compromise formulation that could be put to the Rada. Early on it became apparent that the Rada would give up its prerogative to appoint the government—the Cabinet of Ministers—but not its right to monitor and approve its programme. The main point of disagreement, however, was the perceived imbalance between the powers of the president and the legislature, in particular the president's right to dismiss the legislature if it would not accept the government's programme or its budget. Furthermore, the president would have control of appointments to the judiciary, which was meant to be the arbiter between the executive and legislative branches of state. He would also control regional and local govern-

---

16   *Holos Ukrainy*, 15 September 1994.
17   *Uriadovyi kur'ier*, 13 December 1994.

ment executives through the system of state administration, undermining their authority as elected governments and eliminating the channels of communication and influence between them and the Verkhovna Rada. In short, a majority of the Rada would not agree to a decisive shift in the direction of a presidential republic. On April 12, the Rada moved to the second reading of the draft law and began considering it article by article, raising fears that it would drag out the process even more and dilute the powers of the executive along the way.[18]

Deliberations had been proceeding for a month when President Kuchma lost patience and decided to intervene. Behind-the-scenes negotiations must have played a part in narrowing the differences between the parties. On 16 May Fedir Burchak, a presidential spokesman, proposed to the Verkhovna Rada that all articles referring to its dissolution and the president's impeachment be dropped altogether in order that the law be passed quickly. Two days later it was adopted by a simple majority of 212 deputies. The Rada's national-democratic and liberal-democratic factions (Centre, Statehood, Interregional Bloc for Reforms, Unity, and Rukh) and the Peasant party's deputies voted in favour. The Independent faction, the Communists, and the Socialists were opposed.[19] The Peasant party, representing the interests of the agricultural and agro-industrial sectors, had been aligned all year with the Communists and Socialists, so its defection to the centre right assured the latter a majority. How was this achieved? News began to leak out that Oleksandr Tkachenko, deputy head of the Rada and leader of the Peasant party, was being investigated for alleged profiteering from agro-business contracts with an American supplier of hybrid seed corn.[20] Then, on 3 June, the Rada's newspaper, *Holos Ukrainy*, carried a short item announcing that the Cabinet had instructed the National Bank to issue credits to the agricultural sector in the form of a 50 percent advance on 1995 state contracts to purchase grain

18   *Holos Ukrainy*, 20, 21, and 26 April 1995; *Uriadovyi kur'ier*, 20 April 1995; and *Post-Postup*, 3–9 February and 14–20 April 1995.
19   *Holos Ukrainy*, 18 and 20 May 1995.
20   *Holos Ukrainy*, 12 May 1995.

and seed. The Rada suspended Tkachenko's authority as its deputy head on 6 June, pending an outcome of the investigation.[21] These developments suggested that a split had occurred among the Peasant party deputies.

The fight was not over yet, because the left in the Verkhovna Rada now retreated and regrouped around the still-functioning 1978 constitution. In order to implement the Law on State Power, explicit provision had to be made to override all contradictory articles of that constitution. This would require a two thirds majority. On this matter the parties of the left managed to hold their ground and to avoid the crucial constitutional amendments that would have made the Law on State Power operative. Apparently the parties of the left were able to claw back support from deputies who were moving in Kuchma's direction. According to a statement issued later by Rukh, "a group of centrist deputies who had voted for the law ... failed to take the decisive steps to implement it."[22]

At this point the debate over the division of state power intensified again, revealing its underlying policy dimensions. Communist and Socialist spokesmen directed their fire towards the president's economic reform measures of the previous year, claiming they were responsible for the continuing economic ruin and the impoverishment of society at large, while fortunes were being made by the new class of traders and private appropriators of state property. They attacked Kuchma's pro-Western orientation, arguing that the International Monetary Fund's prescriptions for the state budget were appropriate for a Third World country, but not for Ukraine. Adherence to the IMF's demands would lead to a situation where transnational financial-industrial giants would control the country's economy. The chaos and corruption in central government ministries made it unlikely that greater executive power could lead to recovery and adequate social security provisions, they argued. Rather, the president's drive for more power in these conditions only raised the spectre of authoritarian rule. The Verkhovna

---

21   *Holos Ukrainy*, 7 June 1995.
22   *Uriadovyi kur'ier*, 6 June 1995.

Rada was the country's guarantee of political pluralism and the medium by which social grievances could be aired and addressed.[23]

On 31 May Kuchma raised the stakes and issued a decree announcing a national plebiscite for 28 June. The question to be posed — "Do you have confidence in the president or the Verkhovna Rada?" — and the fact that only two answers would be possible would force the electorate to choose between the two institutions. There would be no provision to indicate confidence or nonconfidence in both of them. Public opinion surveys suggested that the president would win hands down. In an appeal to the nation, Kuchma spoke of the inadmissibility of "political war" in conditions of economic ruin, of the unacceptable length of time it had taken to adopt the Law on State Power, and of its sabotage after adoption. He threatened to bring order to the country, either through agreement with the Rada "or through more complicated and drawn-out events." He emphasized, however, that "the president will not use force. The greatest political victory is not worth spilling blood over. God and the people will damn anyone who breaks the peace on Ukrainian soil."[24]

Two small articles accompanied the appeal in the government newspaper, *Uriadovyi kur'ier*: an instruction by the Cabinet to law enforcement agencies to strengthen the safekeeping of firearms and street control devices such as tear gas guns; and an announcement that the Council of the Regions unanimously supported the plebiscite, would assure its conduct and was ready "to share responsibility with the president for the organization of the state's socioeconomic and political tasks."

The Verkhovna Rada responded on 1 June: it vetoed the plebiscite on grounds of unconstitutionality. It forbade governments at all levels to issue funds to conduct it or any other plebiscite in 1995. It further proposed a meeting with the president to discuss reaching a compromise and asked him to submit the names of the mem-

---

23   Oleksandr Holovchenko summarizes this view in a major article *in Holos Ukrainy*, 20 and 26 April 1995. See also *Holos Ukrainy*, 12, 16, 23, and 26 May and 3 June 1995.

24   *Uriadovyi kur'ier*, 3 June 1995.

bers of his new government to the Rada for approval. The government had resigned in March after the Rada voted non-confidence in it. Yevhen Marchuk had been appointed the acting prime minister, but Kuchma was waiting for a solution to the constitutional impasse before proposing a new government. The resolution further proposed that Kuchma and Moroz jointly submit to the Rada a new list of candidates for election to the Constitutional Court. The resolution showed that the ongoing struggle for the constitutional division of powers was simultaneously a struggle over the actual composition of the next government and of the Constitutional Court, framed by the broader struggle over the direction of Ukraine's post-Communist transition.[25]

Having brought the Verkhovna Rada to the brink of dissolution, Kuchma now manoeuvred to drive his advantage home. The president had been meeting with the representatives of six factions in the Rada that supported him against the left bloc. As the conflict deepened, his support grew to eight factions by June. They proposed to sign an alternative agreement with Kuchma if the Law on State Power failed to be implemented. This agreement contained the same provisions on the division of power as the amended law, but it was framed as a temporary agreement between the president and the Rada to remain in force until a new constitution could be adopted. That is, it was not seen as the kernel of the new constitution and it was not expected to muster a two-thirds majority.

Kuchma met with the Rada's factions again on 4 and 5 June. On 6 June he met the Rada's Presidium, who agreed to put the agreement to a vote by the deputies. On 7 June the Rada considered the "Constitutional Agreement between the Verkhovna Rada and President of Ukraine on the Basic Principles of Organization and Functioning of State Power and Local Self-Government in Ukraine until the Adoption of a New Constitution." The deputies voted by name: 240 were in favour of the agreement, 81 were opposed, and eight abstained. Moroz and Kuchma signed the agreement at a ceremony in the Mariinskyi Palace the next day. The plebiscite was

---

25   *Holos Ukrainy*, 3 June 1995.

cancelled and preparations for a new constitution were announced. Kuchma named Yevhen Marchuk as prime minister and asked him to form a new Cabinet.[26]

The constitutional agreement broadly follows the provisions of the draft Law on State Power, with several important changes and elaborations:

1. The division of powers between the executive, legislature, and judiciary is affirmed.
2. The head of the Constitutional Court, exercising judicial supremacy, is nominated jointly by the president and the Verkhovna Rada, and appointed by the latter. However, these two institutions each nominate half of the court's judges. The president nominates the heads and all the judges of the Supreme Court and the Higher Arbitration Court.
3. The president is the head of state, the chief executive and the head of the Cabinet of Ministers. The Cabinet reports directly to him. The president is also the head of the National Security Council and the commander-in-chief of the Armed Forces. He appoints and dismisses the high command and declares war and a state of war, subject to ratification by the Verkhovna Rada.
4. The president must establish his government within a month of taking office or of the previous government's resignation. Within two months the government must present to the Rada its programme, which must be within the budgetary limits set by the Rada. If this condition is not met, the government can face a non-confidence motion. The Rada can vote non-confidence in the programme, but it cannot challenge the composition of the government until one year after it has been established.
5. The president's decrees on matters of economic reform not yet regulated by law have the force of law until relevant legislation is adopted.

---

26 *Holos Ukrainy*, 16 May and 6, 7, 8, and 10 June 1995; and *Uriadovyi kur'ier*, 6 and 8 June 1995.

6. The president can veto Verkhovna Rada legislation and send it back for revision. The Rada must gain support for its amended version by a two thirds majority in order to require the president to sign the legislation and make it public.
7. The president has the prerogative of nominating persons to the following key posts: members of the Supreme Court and the Higher Arbitration Court, the procurator-general, and the head of the National Bank.
8. There is no provision for the president to dissolve the Verkhovna Rada. The Rada is responsible for its own dissolution and setting new elections, both of the Rada and the president.
9. The Verkhovna Rada exercises legislative, constitutional, and control functions, as foreseen in the existing constitution and the new agreement. It will adopt the new constitution. A broad range of subjects, including the state budget, rights and freedoms of citizens, education, currency value, and state taxes are the exclusive prerogative of the legislature. All subjects not already defined as the prerogative of other branches of the state lie within the Rada's prerogative.
10. The Verkhovna Rada can veto the president's decrees on the basis of their unconstitutionality, which must be established by the judiciary.
11. There are no provisions for the impeachment of the president.
12. Elected heads of the oblast, district, and Kyiv and Sevastopol city governments are appointed as heads of their respective levels of state administration by the president. Their dismissal as state administration heads carries with it the automatic termination of their positions as elected heads of government. Higher levels of the state administration, from the president down, can overturn the decisions of lower levels. The state administration can delegate responsibilities to lower levels of government (village, town, city) and can overturn their decisions, subject to judicial review.

Conclusion

President Kuchma's first year in office was a very busy one on the domestic and international fronts. This article has investigated only one of the important developments — the effort to create a stronger presidential arm of state at the expense of the legislature, which inherited substantial executive and juridical powers from the Soviet period. By June 1995 the results were clear: Kuchma succeeded in establishing presidential control of the central government, thereby taking it out of the hands of the Verkhovna Rada. He subordinated the lower levels of government to the state administration system, undermining the elective authority and accountability of their heads. Combined with his successful courtship of elected oblast leaders by their inclusion into a Council of the Regions, Kuchma dispelled practically all hope that a Soviet system of government — with lower governments accountable to the higher ones all the way to the pinnacle of the Verkhovna Rada — could be created. The Rada thereby became — at least by definition — a more purely legislative arm of state.

Kuchma's hopes were not realized completely. He was denied the power to subordinate the Rada to his office by the right to dissolve it. He conceded to the joint nomination of the chief justice and member judges of the Constitutional Court. And, not least importantly, the Rada agreed only to what Oleksandr Moroz called "a temporary juridical and political agreement," not a constitutional agreement, between the Rada and the president. The Rada will adopt the new constitution when it is ready.

The struggle over the division of state powers is by no means a struggle for the sake of power alone. The functional division between the arms of state masks a division of another kind: the complex ideological division between the Rada's left-wing bloc and the president's team and his supporters in the Rada. It is no longer a division between capitalism and socialism/communism as the long-term goal of the transition period. It is more a choice between different paths for Ukraine to a capitalist society and the world market, with still widespread disagreement about the relative benefits of ties to the east as opposed to the west, the welfare state versus neo-liberal austerity in welfare, and so on.

Behind ideology — and in some ways beyond it as well — there are real material interests that divide Ukraine's political elite. It would be too simple to say that Kuchma is the pro-capitalist reformer and the Verkhovna Rada contains an anti-capitalist bloc, and that here the conflict rests. Indeed, de facto privatisation of productive assets has gone so far in Ukraine today that one can already speak about distinct concentrations of capital employed by their owners, who necessarily have distinct interests. Today these owners are all represented in politics in some way — within the Rada, the presidency, and other central and regional state institutions. On the one hand, they all have an interest in holding the state and the country together, building up the national market and creating a national economic leadership — this is one of President Kuchma's priorities as Ukraine's foremost elected leader. However, the struggle over the division of state powers is also the struggle between these separate and sometimes contradictory interests of privately or corporately accumulating wealth. Thus, new questions must arise: who among Ukraine's new business elites will benefit materially from a strengthened presidency in the person of Leonid Kuchma and who will suffer? And what impact, if any, will a strengthened presidency have upon the living standards of the Ukrainian population as a whole? Such questions concerning the relationship between state-political and socio-economic processes are the subject of another article.

The Ukrainian Economy since Independence*

In its first seven years as an independent state Ukraine has experienced a deepening economic crisis. What is the nature of this crisis and what are its causes? In what measure can one attribute it to the inheritance of the Soviet past, to the costs of separation from the rest of the Soviet economy, and to the transition since independence to a market economy?

A severe contraction of output in most sectors of the economy, the degradation of their fixed assets and the diminution of the labour force, both in the absolute numbers employed and their level of productivity, are the outstanding features of economic change during the 1990s. The Ministry of Statistics estimated that the value of Ukraine's gross domestic product fell between 1990 and 1996 by around two thirds, from 167 bn to 52 bn *karbovantsi* (in constant 1990 domestic prices). Measured in world prices, gross domestic product in 1996 was at 43 percent of its 1990 level.[1]

Ukrainian political leaders, business people and trade unionists, not to mention the analysts of the World Bank and the International Labour Office, all agree that the economy by the late 1990s was in a crisis deeper than the Depression of 1929–33 in the USA and was suffering its worst experience since the Second World War, when gross domestic product was reduced to a quarter of its pre-war size.

The decline in gross output over these years was not quite as severe as the official statistics suggested. Ukraine's System of National Accounts did not register all economic activity because a growing number of businesses and individuals concealed their activity in order to avoid taxation. The official statistics, therefore, need to be augmented by estimations of the shadow economy and

---

* First published in: *Working Papers in Ukrainian Studies*, No. 1 (London: University of North London Ukraine Centre, 1998).

1 *Ukrainian Economic Trends*, June 1997, pp. 8–14; V Riaboshlyk, "Realnyi podatkovyi tiahar prykhovano statystykoiu VVP" (The real tax burden is concealed by GDP statistics), *Ekonomist*, Vol. 1, No. 1, January–March 1997; pp. 28–32; *Country Profile Ukraine 1997–98*, Economist Intelligence Unit, 18.

an analysis of the flow of resources between the open and concealed spheres of economic activity. Being elusive in its very nature, the shadow economy is hard to quantify and analyse.

Features of the economic decline

According to official statistics, output of Ukraine's main agricultural goods has fallen since independence at a precipitous rate. The annual grain harvest fell by half between 1990 and 1996, from 52 mt to 26 mt. In 1997 it recovered to 36 mt. The sugar beet harvest similarly fell over the same period from 5.4 mt to 3.5 mt, or by a third. Cattle herds have been halved over this period, while meat and milk production has fallen to less than half the levels of the late 1980s.[2]

The official statistics, however, record only part of overall food production. In the case of grains and sugar beet, crops that are grown overwhelmingly on state and collective farms, the figures are accurate. However, one needs also to take account of the considerable increase of private production that is not recorded by government statistics, either at the point of harvest or in distribution. The decline of output by state and collective farms since 1990 and the subsequent drop in real wages and living conditions drove the rural workforce to give far greater time and resources to growing food on their private plots.

An even more dramatic change was the radical increase in the number of private plots taken up and worked by urban residents and a marked shift in the proportion of labour time they withdrew from the industrial and service sectors to food production. Guy Standing of the International Labour Office presents statistics showing that between 1985 and 1993 the number of households in rural areas producing food on their private plots grew by 20.6 percent to 2.9 m, while the corresponding increase of urban households was 100 percent to 6.8 m. 'In urban areas almost every second fam-

---

2   *Uriadovyj kur'ier*, 13 February 1997, p.7; Chas, 10 January 1997; *Halyts'ki kontrakty*, March 1997. 30; Country Profile Ukraine 1997–98, 31.

ily was growing fruit, vegetables and potatoes for their own consumption, for barter or for sale in open markets or on the street ... and in many cases (were) also supplying relatives'.[3]

In 1996, a worker in Dnipropetrovsk wrote: "The overwhelming majority of workers have out of town kitchen gardens, little patches of land given them by the factory management under an agreement with the agricultural authorities ... people work five days in the factories and two days on their plots."[4]

The Ministry of Statistics estimates that by the end of 1996 approximately 95 percent of potatoes, 80 percent of fruit and vegetables and around a quarter of all livestock came from the private sector. While pork output overall is estimated to have dropped by a third to 1mt in 1996, only 200,000 t of it issued from the state sector and the bulk — 800,000 t — now came from the private sector. Overall the share of food production assumed by the private sector is estimated to have grown from around one sixth in 1990 to a half in 1996.[5]

The European Union sponsored monitoring team in Kyiv, which bases its analysis upon official statistics and its own surveys, considers private agricultural production as the most important sector of Ukraine's shadow economy. The designation is accurate insofar as private agricultural production remains largely outside government monitoring, as does much of its distribution between households, through the widespread domestic network of kiosk and market trade, and into neighbouring states via the shuttle trade. Such exports on the shuttle trade to Russia were estimated in 1996 at a value of $3 bn annually.[6]

The real level of agricultural production in the years since independence would therefore seem to be greater than estimated by the official statistics. Private production has indeed grown enormously, but there is much circumstantial evidence to suggest that

3   International Labour Office, *The Ukrainian Challenge: reforming labour market and social policy* (Budapest: Central European University Press, 1995), 15.
4   Oleg Dubrovskii with Simon Pirani, *Fighting back in Ukraine: a worker who took on the bureaucrats and bosses* (London: Index Books, 1997), 5–6.
5   *Uriadovyj kur'ier*, 13 February 1997, 7; Chas, 11 October 1996, 6; *Country Profile Ukraine 1997–98*, 14.
6   *Ukrainian Economic Trends*, April 1996, 8.

it is has not compensated for the decline in gross output of the state sector. There was already a significant and unrecorded private sector of food production in rural areas before independence, where its growth since 1991 is far less dramatic than near urban centres. Secondly, the private sector has increasingly drawn labour and material resources from the state sector, including already recorded output of various food products. Thirdly, surveys of per capita food consumption show a consistent fall since independence. And finally, there has been a massive influx of foreign food products onto the domestic market, even though the purchasing power of the population has also been falling.[7]

The official statistics provide the following record for the fuel and energy sector since independence. Coal production, which peaked in 1975 at 216 mt and fell thereafter to 165 mt in 1990, continued to fall to 70 mt in 1996. Similarly, domestic output of oil was at its peak in 1975, then fell to 5 mt in 1990 and on to 4 mt in 1996. Natural gas output stood highest also in 1975 at 69 bcm, fell to 28 bcm in 1990 and continued downward to 18 bcm in 1996. The domestic shortfall in these fuels since 1975 was, of course, made up with imports from Russia and Turkmenistan, which by 1990 were supplying 50 mt of oil and 120 bcm of natural gas. Thereafter, oil and natural gas imports also began to shrink as a result both of Ukraine's inability to pay world prices for them and of the manipulation of energy trade by Russia to exert political leverage in its other disputes with Ukraine.[8]

Half of the available fuel in 1990, domestic and imported, was going into electricity or thermal energy production. In that year the republic produced 290 bn kilowatt hours. By 1996 output had fallen to 181 bn kwh. Simultaneously there was a sharp change in the structure of electricity generation. Already by 1994 over 40 percent of installed generating capacity was idle, due to the lack of fossil

---

7   *Profspilkova hazeta*, 29 January 1997; Chas, 27 December 1996 and 31 January 1997.

8   *Ekonomichni reformy s'ohodni*, No. 1, 1997, 38; *Country Profile Ukraine 1997–98*, 41–42; Ihor Yukhnovsky, *Ukraina – nezalezhna derzhava* (Lviv: Zakhidnyi naukovyi tsentr AN Ukrainy, 1994), 82.

fuels, and nuclear power stations were forced to raise their share of output from 25 percent in 1990 to 37 percent in 1995.[9] Lacking funds for repairs and replacement and pressed into continuous production to make up for the shortfalls in the thermal electricity sector, the nuclear stations were also dangerously close to breakdown.[10] By this time, it was also claimed that Ukraine had lost all its hard currency paying European customers, except Bulgaria, because of the instability of its supply. Overall, Ukraine's electricity exports had plummeted to 4–4.5 bn kwh, in 1996, about a tenth their level before independence.[11]

The Ministry of Statistics estimates the drop in industrial production by the end of 1996 to have been to around 43 percent of its 1990 level. The EU's Centre for Macroeconomic Analysis of Ukraine estimates an even steeper decline, to around 28 percent of the 1990 level.[12] Whichever figure is closer to the truth, it is clear that industry has suffered a catastrophic decline in a relatively short period of time.

The biggest declines were suffered by defense related industries, machine building and consumer goods manufacturing, while primary goods, which declined in absolute terms at a relatively slower rate, increased their share of industrial production overall. Ukraine's metallurgical plants were by 1996 working at around 40 percent capacity and producing 40 percent of their 1991 level of output. They could still sell rolled steel and pipes abroad, especially in Russia, but domestic demand had all but collapsed. The declining output of combine harvesters, bulldozers, cranes, forklifts, electrical presses, generators for steam and gas turbines and other heavy equipment actually accelerated towards the end of this period as the inventories of unsold engineering goods grew to around the equivalent of two years' output. However, declining production was also registered in sectors where domestic demand remained

9   Yukhnovsky, *op. cit.*, 85; *Country Profile Ukraine 1997–98*, 41–42; *Holos Ukrainy*, 24 February 1994.
10   *Profspilkova hazeta*, 6 March 1996.
11   *Holos Ukrainy*, 24 February 1994; *Country Profile Ukraine*, Economist Intelligence Unit, 3rd Quarter 1997, 31.
12   *Ukrainian Economic Trends*, January 1997, Table 1.3, 14.

strong. For example, the Avtozaz automobile plant, the only one in Ukraine, saw its output of Tavrias fall from 156,000 in 1991 to a mere 7,000 in 1996.[13]

By the end of 1996 the proportional contribution of different sectors to industry had markedly changed. Measured in international prices, the share of machine building had fallen from 30 percent in 1990 to 10 percent. Fuel and energy rose from 24 to 37 percent. Steel production rose 14 to 22 percent, as did food products — in the same proportions. Other categories of production — mainly consumer durables saw their share of industrial output fall from 18 to 14 percent.[14]

The critical situation faced by the machine building industry was also related to the collapse in demand for military equipment and the inability of the defense industry to convert quickly to civilian production. According to Viktor Antonov, Minister for Conversion and the Military Industrial Complex in 1992, there were 1,840 plants with a workforce of 2.7 million people producing military hardware on the eve of the Soviet collapse, including aircraft carriers, combat ships, tanks, rockets and nuclear missiles. The military industrial complex was responsible for at least one quarter of industrial output. Part of this output included civilian consumer goods, estimated at 9 to 15 percent of total consumer goods. In the year after the Soviet collapse, when Ukraine seized its portion of Soviet armed forces and military hardware and was embroiled in a dispute with Russia about their future defense and security relations, these plants received no new orders. Then, the disruption of the world market in Soviet military hardware, the disruption of ties between component manufacturers spread across the former USSR, the burden of maintaining Ukraine's sizeable inheritance in armed forces and the big budget deficits of its government all contributed to bring the military industrial complex to its knees.[15]

---

13   *Country Profile Ukraine, 1997–98*, p. 29; *Uriadovyj kur'ier*, 18 January 1997 and 13 February 1997, p. 7; *Profspilkova hazeta*, 16 April 1997.

14   *Ukrainian Economic Trends*, January 1997, Table 1.4.

15   *Central European*, July–August 1992; *Chas*, 18 October 1996, 7; *Ukrainian Economic Trends*, January 1997, Table 1.4.

Foreign trade

One of the paradoxes of the post-Soviet period is that while gross domestic production fell sharply, foreign trade remained steady. If one added to the official figures an estimation of the levels of unrecorded trade it could even be said that foreign trade boomed in the first five years of independence. In order to understand the nature of this trend a number of factors need to highlighted. First, at least a third — by some estimates over half — of domestic production relies on inputs provided by foreign trade. Secondly, by virtue of its geographic location Ukraine serves as an important transit point and re-exporter of other countries' goods. Thirdly, given its previously acquired specialization as a Soviet republic Ukraine from the moment of its independence was able to offer certain products on world markets at quite competitive prices. Fourthly, the undervaluation of the *karbovanets'* and its successor, the *hryvnia* against the Russian rouble and the American dollar provided an important additional stimulus for exports. And finally, the liberalization of imports by the government in conditions of contracting domestic production opened up the domestic market to a surge of imported consumer goods.[16]

In the period 1991–96 Ukraine rapidly diversified its trade beyond the countries of the former Soviet bloc. Although the Russian Federation remained its most important partner, trade with all the former Soviet Union republics progressively fell to 48 percent of total trade by the first quarter of 1997. The Asian component became stronger, with China emerging as its second most important trading partner, as did the European Union, headed by Germany as Ukraine's third trading partner. Turkmenistan, Belarus, Turkey, USA, UK, Greece and Italy made up the other leading partners out of more than 150 countries that traded with Ukraine.[17] Official figures suggest that foreign trade in goods remained steady over the

---

16   T. Stepankova, P. Dutkevych and M. Hkhosh (eds), *Ukraina na Perekhidnomu Etapi* (Kyiv: Academia, 1997), 145; *Ukrainian Economic Trends*, May 1996, 6; *Ekonomist*, Vol. 1, No 1, January–March 1997, 42.

17   *Holos Ukrainy*, 28 August 1995; Stepankova *et al., op. cit.*, 151.

period at around $20–23 bn annual turnover. Foreign trade in services, such as trunk line transit of Russian oil and international communications, grew steadily, reaching an annual turnover of £3.7 bn in 1995. While the volumes of trade with former Soviet republics declined their prices rose to meet world levels. With these countries, Ukraine faced serious deficits, largely as a result of its dependence upon Russian and Turkmenistan oil and natural gas. With new partner countries in Europe, Asia, North and South America (Africa and Australasia remaining insignificant) Ukraine enjoyed an overall positive balance of trade that reduced but did not cover its deficit with its former Soviet partners.[18]

Except for conventional arms and other military hardware, the structure of Ukraine's exports was dominated by goods of low-capital content such as steel plate and pipes, bulk chemicals and minerals, refined sugar and other food concentrates. It proved difficult from the outset to widen its foreign markets in machinery and instruments, given their relative backwardness compared to those of Western states and the inability of less developed and transitional countries in Ukraine's vicinity to pay for such goods. And this tendency to export mainly low-capital goods grew stronger over time as the domestic economy's capacity to re-equip, modernize and maintain production of high-capital content goods was eroded by the general economic crisis.[19]

Imports to Ukraine were dominated by fossil fuels, accounting for around 55 percent of annual totals. Other significant imports were textiles, clothing and footwear, timber and wood products, machinery and equipment, polymer feedstock and finished plastic goods. A wide range of food products and consumer durables, imported from economically developed and developing countries alike, began to flood the Ukrainian market. By 1997 more than 60 percent of consumer goods sold in Ukraine were of foreign origin.[20] The newspaper *Chas* commented on 25 October 1996: "We have lost not only the foreign market; we've almost lost our own ... One of

---

18   Stepankova *et al.*, *op. cit.*, 149.
19   *Chas*, 31 January 1997; *Profspilkova hazeta*, 26 March 1997.
20   *Chas*, 13 October 1996 and 24 January 1997.

Kyiv's supermarkets is now selling potato *varennyky* (dumplings, a traditional Ukrainian dish), and they're made in Brooklyn, New York!"

Thus foreign trade did not serve a useful purpose in the first years of independence in strengthening the country's economic performance. Rather exports markets served to strengthen the negative trends of de-industrialisation evident in the evolving structure of domestic production, while imports of fuels imposed deficits and foreign consumer goods seized a large part of the domestic market from home producers.

The Soviet inheritance

Ukraine's economic history under the USSR was marked by several key stages: recovery in the 1920s from the destruction caused between 1914 and 1921 by war and revolution; collectivization of agriculture and the forced industrialisation drive of the 1930s; destruction in the Second World War; another period of recovery that took until 1950 for industry and 1960 for agriculture; a long wave of economic growth thereafter that peaked in the 1970s, stagnated and then went into reverse in the 1980s. The economic decline which began before the breakup of the USSR deepened after independence was declared, and despite repeated predictions by Ukraine's leaders of an upturn, showed no signs of abating.

Ukraine's role in the all-Union division of labour evolved over the six decades of planned economy. First, as one of the original six regions of industrial development under the Russian Empire, south-central and eastern Ukraine served as a powerhouse of Stalin's industrialisation drive. It saw renewed and rapid growth during the 1930s with an overall three to fourfold expansion of industrial output by the War. Similarly, Ukraine's role in the Tsarist era as the breadbasket of Europe turned in the 1930ss into that of the provider of food to the new Soviet towns and cities and of surpluses for investment into industrialisation. The rate of growth in agriculture was far less dramatic than for industry, despite the mechanization of farming and the extension of land in agricultural use. Although agriculture had revived by around 1925 to its pre-World

War One levels of output, the destruction wreaked upon the countryside by forced collectivization and the Famine of 1932–33 threw the sector back again. By the outbreak of the Second World War, grain and sugar beet harvests had surpassed their 1913 levels again, but the republic's cattle herds, which the peasants slaughtered *en masse* during collectivization, had not.

Agriculture

In contrast to the pattern seen during the 1920s, the agricultural sector revived later than the industrial sector after the Second World War. Investments into fieldwork mechanization, transport, storage and processing rose and total acreage in agricultural use was expanded again to compensate for the outmigration of labour from the countryside. A decreasing rate of return on unit investment into this sector was observed in the post-war years, yet gross annual harvests of traditional proven crops of wheat, rye, barley and sugar beets seemed to grow, albeit unevenly, right up to the end of the Soviet period.

The post-war period also saw considerable experimentation and diversification, with so-called industrial crops like cotton, edible oil bearing plants, fibre flax and sugar beets accorded a far greater proportion of land, at the expense of cereals. Some of these crops, like cotton, proved to be failures. Others like corn exhibited limited adaptability to soils and climate, while certain crops grown for oils and fibres, like hemp, were supplanted by other species like sunflower or by synthetic feedstock. The record of diversification of industrial crops in the post-war period, especially from the time of Khrushchev when experimentation was ill prepared, thus shows very mixed and erratic returns.

Agriculture in the post-war period also diversified in the direction of a rapidly increasing meat producing sector to keep pace with the changing dietary patterns of the Soviet population. This new priority introduced another level of demand upon available arable land, labour and investment resources. The production statistics show that the republic's livestock in cattle, hogs and poultry, but not sheep and goats, grew quite rapidly from the 1950s on, but then declined in the 1980s, falling even more precipitously in the 1990s.

Agriculture faced a growing number of challenges to its further development in the post-war period. Ever since the forced collectivization and the Famine of 1932–33 the peasants had mistrusted the urban based Communist Party and its rural representatives. They understood that collectivization enabled the state to finance industrialisation and the growth of cities at the expense of their living standards. Peasants suffered a second-class status, lower than urbanized workers with respect to their wages, living and working conditions. They did not have even the limited rights gained by urban dwellers after Khrushchev came to power in the mid-1950s to move and take new jobs without the permission of their employers and local government authorities. Nevertheless, young people and especially men after they completed compulsory military service, found ways to migrate to better jobs and living conditions in the towns and cities. They left behind a rural population in which women and the elderly became increasingly overrepresented. Thus a legacy of mistrust, injustice, an inadequate labour force and a resistance to labour on the state and collective farms had built up.

The strategy pursued by Khrushchev and continued by Brezhnev to increase food output by extending total acreage and raising the level of technique was indeed successful in making significant improvements in the diets of the Soviet population as a whole. But it was not enough, especially for the rural population, whose standard of living remained below that of their urban counterparts. Furthermore, the state and collective farms also suffered in the same way as other sectors of the Soviet economy from the lack of labour motivation and the inefficient use of material resources, which placed an upper limit on the long term rates of return on investments. By the Brezhnev era the country had to start importing foodstuffs. Soviet leaders turned to supplementing the state agricultural sector's output by granting its farm workers the right to private plots on which to grow food and supplement their wages. They improved their own consumption, but the restrictions imposed upon such private economic activity — restrictions on labour time and permissible plot sizes, as well as on the right to trade—inevitably limited the positive effects it might have. Nevertheless, by the end of the Soviet period an estimated one sixth of total food production came from the private sector.

The agricultural sector was plagued by another systemic weakness of the economy — the inability to translate scientific inno-vation into new technique—that kept its machinery relatively back-ward. For example, the machine building industry could not assure production and maintenance of reliable tractor ploughs and com-bine harvesters. Their overall number (in use or disrepair) re-mained low: Ukraine had by 1990 around 13 tractors theoretically available for use per 1,000 hectares of ploughed land, compared with 76 in neighbouring Poland and 139 in West Germany. These tractors were of a comparatively low technical level: they could not reverse, thus adding around 1 million kilometres of unnecessary, and indeed damaging, travel over fields each year. They required a high fuel consumption. The favoured deep ploughing practices were outdated; they damaged the soil structure, leading to wind and water erosion over huge areas of the countryside.

Other kinds of problems were accumulating within agricul-ture, at microeconomic and macroeconomic levels that stemmed from the production ethos which had informed its development in the whole period since Stalin: "the conquest of nature", economies of scale, industrialisation of farming technique and labour organi-zation. The state and collective farms, very large by European standards, invariably specialized in plant cultures, animal or bird species. The advantages of mixed farming were lost while the costs of monocultural farming were incurred, for example in the treat-ment of manure as waste, in high costs of transport and in lost op-portunities to recycle the by-products of food processing.

The reclamation of marshland and the irrigation of dry soils had been pursued to extend the area under cultivation to beyond its long term sustainable limits. This strategy, combined with the often injudicious use of fertilizers, herbicides and pesticides in-curred such costs as the declining quality of seed grain and food products, soil salinity and water pollution, land erosion, and de-clining animal and human health.

Agriculture as a whole suffered a serious imbalance between grain production and pasture for animal rearing. There was not enough land devoted to pasture (5 million hectares) which, in conditions of growing meat production, made manufactured feed stocks a more important part of the animals' diet. However, the relatively low protein content of cereals and other crops harvested for feedstock, (domestically grown and protein-rich soya bean being in short supply) necessitated a very high proportion of available land to be devoted to their cultivation. By 1990 more than half of the republic's arable land was already committed to crops and pasture specifically for livestock. And even that was not enough, so grain was imported essentially to maintain production levels of meat. Thus the grain and meat producing sectors of the republic were locked in an unfavourable relationship imposed by the all-Union division of labour onto the Ukrainian republic and strengthened from year to year by the expanding Soviet population and the growing importance of meat in its diet.[21]

On the eve of independence Ukraine — a republic holding a sixth of the USSR's arable land and a quarter of the world's black earth (*chornozem*) accounted for one quarter of the Soviet Union's food output. Half of its total land area (33 million out of 60 million hectares) was under the plough. Another 5 million hectares were devoted to pasture. The limits on further expansion of agricultural land had long been reached — indeed the total area devoted to farming was retreating steadily in the face of urban sprawl. The rural population numbered some 9.2 million, of whom 4 million were directly employed in agriculture. These rural workers were organised into 10,700 collective and state farms. Their numbers were also declining.[22]

Fuel and energy

Ukraine's fuel and energy sector has been built up over the past century by the utilization of coal, hydroelectricity, oil, natural gas and nuclear power, in that order. During the first wave of industri-

---

21   Yukhnovsky, *op. cit.*, 72–77.
22   *Ibid.*, 60–70, 96.

alisation at the end of the nineteenth century coal mining developed rapidly in the Donbas region of south-eastern Ukraine. By the First World War Ukraine was producing the lion's share of coal (85 percent) and iron and steel for the Russian Empire. It maintained its pre-eminent role in the Soviet period until after the Second World War, when Soviet planners began directing greater investments into strip mining of huge coal deposits in the Siberian Kuzbas and Kazakhstan. Soviet coal production peaked in the mid-1970s at around 700 mt annually. Ukraine's share then was 200 mt.

Hydroelectric power was harnessed in the second industrialisation drive of the 1930s. The Ukrainian republic was allocated investment under the first five year plan (1928–32) to build Dniprohes, then the biggest hydroelectric station in the world. Five more such stations were built on dams along the Dnipro in subsequent years until the river's force was taxed beyond reasonable limits and it practically ceased to flow at its mouth to the Black Sea. In the Khrushchev era hydroelectric stations were built on small and medium sized rivers in Ukraine to provide electricity to towns. However, like coal, the prospect for economies of scale in hydroelectric power were far better on the big rivers of Siberia and Central Asia, to where the central planners shifted their priorities in the 1960s and 1970s.

It was in these decades also that oil and gas production in Siberia and Soviet Central Asia began to grow rapidly. Soviet oil production peaked in 1983, when it reached just over 600 mt. Ukraine had insignificant accessible deposits of its own, so it received its supplies from the eastern Soviet republics. Oil became a preferable fuel to coal in electricity generating stations and thermal heating plants. The republic had installed a set of oil refining plants with a capacity of around 60 mt annually. Fuel oil provided the feedstock to these power stations and heating plants, with the other, more valuable by-products of diesel and benzene destined for domestic transport needs as well as for export. Polymer feed stocks for the plastics industry (ethylene, propylene, chlorovinyl) were returned to the Russian Federation, because Ukraine did not have the appropriate processing facilities.

Natural gas steadily replaced other fuels in domestic heating and cooking, and even in some forms of public transport. However, the lucrative European trade in natural gas, to which the Soviet Union became connected via long distance pipelines from Siberia through Ukraine and Central Europe placed a limit on the rate that gas replaced other fuels for domestic use.

The challenge for Soviet economic planning after the Second World War was to unite the established industrial capacity and skilled labour force that was concentrated in the Western part of the Union with the plentiful deposits of energy carriers — coal, oil and natural gas — in Western Siberia and Central Asia. The remaining coal deposits in the Donbas could not meet long term Soviet demand. They were increasingly difficult to mine from their deep, thin and declivitous seams. And coal mining was environmentally taxing upon nearby conurbations and farmland. The strategy of eastward expansion came naturally to the planners, accustomed as they were to building on a massive scale, mobilizing huge material and labour resources to harness new natural reserves thousands of kilometres from their eventual point of use. But like agriculture, this fuel and energy strategy showed its systemic limits relatively soon: by the mid-1970s, coal output peaked, as did oil output by the mid-1980s. Only natural gas continued to grow in volume of output.

Then there was nuclear power, for which the Ukrainian republic was accorded a pride of place in Soviet energy strategy in the last decades of its existence. The Soviet leadership embarked upon a crash programme in the 1970s to build up its nuclear power industry. Initially, they regarded nuclear power as a supplement to coal and oil fired generating stations for the European region of the USSR. Nuclear stations could be installed and operated close to the region's dense network of industries, utilities and urban settlements. They did not depend upon faraway fuels. And as the difficulties emerged in the strategy to increase output of fossil fuels from the eastern regions, nuclear power came to be seen as the main source for future increases in electricity production. The authorities undertook to persuade the population that nuclear power was cheap, safe and clean. The "peaceful atom" was promoted as the fuel of the future. The new station sites and their entire social infra-structure were accorded priority investment. The employees of the industry enjoyed great prestige.

The growing dependence of the communist states of Eastern Europe upon Soviet energy carriers was another important reason for the rapid expansion of nuclear power. The coal reserves of Po-land, Hungary, Czechoslovakia, Bulgaria and the German Demo-cratic Republic declined after the Second World War. Soviet deliv-eries of oil, natural gas, bituminous coal and electricity, at a cost to the recipients that was well below world prices, grew accordingly. By 1980, the East European states depended upon the Soviet Union for 30 percent of their energy needs. The Soviet Union expected to be meeting 50 percent of their needs by 1990. However, Soviet lead-ers preferred to sell Siberian oil and natural gas in West European and other world markets where they earned hard currency. This trade financed the import of Western machinery for the oil and gas industry, as well as grain and other food products. Instead of meet-ing the East European states' growing energy needs with such val-uable commodities, the Soviet Union foresaw nuclear generated electricity as the most economical energy substitute. Such electricity should come mainly from Ukraine, its westernmost republic bor-dering on these states.

Nuclear power produced 6 percent of the Soviet Union's en-ergy needs in 1980 and 10 percent by 1985. The Twelfth Five Year Plan, adopted in March 1986, a month before the Chernobyl disas-ter, set forth a target of 20 percent by 1990.[23] The Ukrainian repub-lic's role in the expansion was disproportionately large. The repub-lic produced 10 percent of Soviet nuclear generated electricity in 1980 and 35 percent by the end of 1985. It was expected to produce 40 percent by 1990, considerably more than it needed to meet do-mestic needs.[24] For, indeed, Ukraine was producing electricity at its four nuclear power stations also for export to the Central European states and the neighbouring republics of the Soviet Union.

---

23   *Literaturna Ukraina*, 27 February 1986.
24   David Marples, *Chernobyl and Nuclear Power in the USSR* (Edmonton: Canadian Institute of Ukrainian Studies, 1986), 75.

Upon gaining independence in 1991, Ukraine faced the challenge to devise a national energy strategy of its own, utilizing the industries, the technologies of production and consumption that it inherited from the Soviet break-up, and necessarily facing up to the problems that came along with them. There were three major and interrelated problems inherited from the past. First, the accident at the Chernobyl nuclear power station in April 1986 incurred an enormous and ongoing burden on the Ukrainian economy and the state budget (around 12–16 percent of all budget expenditures in the following ten years), and made urgent the task of either closing down these stations or undertaking wholesale repairs and replacement of safety systems. Ukrainian public opinion was overwhelmingly hostile to nuclear power after 1986. But the power stations in the republic continued to produce electricity—the Chernobyl station never interrupted production, even at the height of the 1986 disaster—under pressure from all-Union ministries under Gorbachev that wanted to expand, not halt or close them down.

Despite the growing importance of the nuclear sector, which generated 26 percent of the republic's own electricity needs in 1990, thermal power stations still provided 66 percent (hydroelectric stations 3 percent and others 5 percent).[25] Lacking sufficient oil and gas of its own, Ukraine relied on imports from the Russian Federation and Turkmenistan. Around 13 mt of fuel oil, gained from refining Russian crude went to electricity generating in thermal stations. So when the Union broke up and Russia began to move towards world prices for its exports to former Soviet republics, Ukraine became dependent upon Russia and increasingly indebted to her for oil imports. Indebtedness and dependency carried enormous implications for Ukraine's sovereignty, for throughout the 1990s Russia's leaders became less, not more, reconciled with the loss of this most important former possession. So it was as much a political as an economic decision that the Ukrainian leadership took to maintain what it had in terms of nuclear generating capacity, including the crippled Chernobyl station. And as the economic crisis set in, as Russia curtailed her oil exports, nuclear power had to play

---

25   Yukhnovsky, *op. cit.* 85–86.

an even more important role in the structure of the country's electricity production. By 1995, nuclear power stations produced 37 percent of Ukraine's annual electricity supply — and 45 percent during the winter months — while having only 25 percent of the country's generating capacity.

The third strand in the knot of inherited difficulties, aggravated since 1991 by the economic crisis and the paucity of investment resources, was the waste and inefficiency in production and consumption of energy carriers. Soviet industrial production in general was energy, materials and labour intensive in comparison with the advanced industrial states of the West, and it had failed largely to make the technological leap to energy efficiency in the 1970s because the oil crises of that decade did not touch its autarchic economy. On the contrary, Soviet fossil fuels were available in still growing volumes. Thus the Ukraine republic had increased by the end of the 1980s its imports of Russian crude oil. Its refineries, utilizing quite inefficient refining processes, extracted only half of their throughput as benzene, diesel and other clean fuels, leaving the other half as feedstock for thermal electricity stations.[26] With modern refining processes, the extraction of clean fuels could constitute 80 to 90 percent of the original volumes of crude oil, giving enormous savings in quality of fuels, efficiency of combustion technologies and environmental protection.

The combustion technologies in use were similarly outdated in facilities producing electricity from coal, gas, oil and indeed nuclear fission. Fluidized bed combustion plants using coal and combined cycle gas turbines, for example that were being developed rapidly in the West, were practically non-existent in the Soviet Union. The RBMK nuclear reactor, a graphite-moderated, water cooled system used in Chernobyl and other stations, was based on an outdated, polluting and inherently dangerous technology. But it was maintained in service well after Soviet scientists and engineers developed their own version of the pressurized water reactor (VVER) because its maintenance was technically less demanding

---

26   *Ibid.*, 84.

and it appeared superficially to be cheaper to run. The VVER system was cleaner, safer and more efficient all round, but it demanded a higher level of exactitude in building, exploitation and maintenance. The distribution and consumption of energy carriers was similarly wasteful, from leaking oil pipelines and electricity grids to neighbourhood heating plants with above-ground, unclad steam pipes to living quarters without insulation or individual thermostatic controls.

How well Ukraine coped with these inherited problems in the fuel and energy sector depended both on the quality of Ukraine's leadership after 1991 and the propitiousness of the unfolding circumstances, both domestic and international. The latter were by no means favourable for this sector because the breakdown of the entire Comecon trading bloc and its established division of labour left Ukraine with incomplete production cycles. It could supply its own coal mining machinery, but it imported most of the oil and gas it needed. It had adequate reserves of uranium ore, but its processing into suitable fuel was carried out in Russia. It depended upon surrounding states and former Soviet republics for components or whole units of refinery equipment, combustion engines, electricity transforming and transmission equipment, nuclear reactors and pumping stations.

Industry

Ukrainian industry in the Soviet period was characterized first of all by rapid growth during the 1930s, followed by massive destruction in the Second World War, and a renewed expansion thereafter, albeit at rates of growth that declined steadily to the point of stagnation and even contraction on the eve of the Soviet Union's collapse.

The first two Five Year Plans (1928–32 and 1933–37) and the interrupted Third (1938–41) assigned the republic 20, 18 and 15 percent respectively of total Soviet investment into industry. The republic's share of Soviet industrial output by 1938 stood at around 21 percent and was weighted heavily in the producer goods sector. Industry continued to grow in the pattern that was set in the capitalist phase of industrialisation during the late nineteenth and early twentieth centuries: iron, steel, coke, cement and lumber formed the base of primary industrial goods. They supplied the machine building and metalwork industries that, in turn, provided the mining and earth-moving equipment, locomotives and railway freight cars, and other inputs necessary to further expand the production of primary industrial goods. Increases in mineral fertilizer and farm machinery secured the inputs necessary for large-scale collectivized agriculture. Food processing expanded, as did the textiles, clothing and footwear industries. And as the Second World War approached, Soviet leaders stepped up production in Ukraine of tanks and other military hardware.

Despite the massive expansion of the republic's industries in these years, their declining share of total Soviet investments was mirrored in a decreasing share of overall producer goods output. This pattern was offset somewhat by the growth of a powerful machine building and metalwork sector that was serving to expand primary industrial output in the Urals and Western Siberia. However, as in the first, capitalist, wave of industrialisation, the consumer goods sector remained distinctly underdeveloped. Semi-processed goods that were issued in growing volumes were destined largely for plants in the Russian Federation, which then distributed the finished products (consumer durables and processed food) to Ukraine and other republics.[27]

In the Second World War the republic saw most of its industrial capacity destroyed and millions of its civilian workforce displaced eastward, deported westward or killed at home or in the armed forces. Industrial output was reduced to a quarter of its prewar level. The period until 1950 was devoted to reconstruction.

The period from 1950 to 1985 was characterized by a steadily declining industrial growth rate, a renewed emphasis on machine building and some diversification of the manufacturing and light industry sectors. Official statistics, which invariably inflated plan achievements, suggested that the annual growth rate fell from around 14 percent in 1950 to around 3.5 percent in 1985. Output

---

27   *Encyclopedia of Ukraine* (Toronto: University of Toronto Press, 1985), Vol. II, 314–317.

was most likely stagnant by the mid-1980s and contracting thereafter. While agricultural machinery, mining equipment and railway rolling stock remained central to the machine building sector, there was diversification into automation equipment, computers, electricity generating equipment, automobiles, passenger aircraft and shipbuilding. A considerable investment was made into Ukraine's military industries, which by some estimates accounted for one third of Soviet military production and at least one quarter of the republic's industrial output and employed a similar proportion of its industrial workforce.[28] It was the now enormous weight of the military sector that gave the republic an opportunity to develop critical new technologies in electronics, cybernetics, radar, lasers, powders and composites. However, the priorities given to investment in the military sector denied resources to other parts of the economy, while the secrecy and enforced isolation of Soviet military production from other branches held back the diffusion of their technological advances.

On the eve of the Soviet collapse, the Ukrainian republic provided one fifth of the USSR's industrial products, around the same proportion that it gave on the eve of the Second World War. In terms of the republic's total industrial output (taking together fuel and energy, steel, machine-building and food products, with output measured in international prices) the machine building sector's share stood at 30 percent in 1990. Fuel and energy accounted for 24 percent, steel another 14 percent, food 14 percent and other goods 18 percent.[29]

The Ukrainian republic undoubtedly made enormous strides in economic development during the Soviet period, notwithstanding the destruction wreaked by the purges, the collectivization of agriculture and the Famine, the Second World War and the Chernobyl disaster. Few will dispute that the human costs of this development were too high. It is also true that the centralized and bureaucratized planning system denied the Ukrainian republic, like the others, the right to determine its own growth and its place in

---

28   *Chas*, 20 December 1996; International Labour Office, *The Ukrainian Challenge*, 2.
29   *Ukrainian Economic Trends*, January 1997, Table 1.4.

the all-Union economy. Nevertheless, it was by means of national-isation and "the command-administrative system" — the central-ized mobilisation and allocation of human labour and material re-sources — that the Soviet Union dragged into the industrial age a set of nations that were on the periphery of advanced industrial states at the turn of the century, largely agrarian and dependent upon their investments and technologies, and made out of them the world's second superpower. Ukraine was a key component of the Soviet industrialisation process before the Second World War. After the war, it maintained this position, despite the planned diversion of investments into the Union's eastern regions. The republic's sci-entists developed and applied on its territory some of the leading technological achievements of the Soviet Union. By the end of the Soviet period, Ukraine was by comparative indices a modern coun-try, able to feed, house, clothe, educate and employ its citizens. In the space of a century it left the ranks of countries we know today as the Third World and found itself at the top of the so-called Sec-ond World countries that had made a forced march to moderniza-tion by the Communist road.

Yet there were serious problems for the future that were be-queathed by the Soviet period and that remained relevant in the early post-independence years. First, the Ukrainian state leadership lacked the experience necessary to take quick and effective control of the economy on its territory. In the last decade of the Soviet Un-ion the Ukrainian republic's authorities had direct control of no more than 5 percent of the gross domestic product generated on their territory. That proportion rose from 1990 to around 40 percent on the eve of independence. The republic did not have the institu-tions necessary to conduct domestic and foreign economic policy. It is therefore not credible to speak of a Ukrainian national economy until 1991, when the newly declared state took control of its bor-ders, began to make its own laws, to determine a national economic policy and regulatory framework, to form its annual budgets and issue its own currency.

While it was part of the Soviet Union, Ukraine's resources and productive capacity had been mobilized in accordance with a planned division of labour between republics that made each one highly dependent upon the others for the completion of production cycles. So when independence came, Ukraine inherited an incomplete economy with respect to satisfying its own population's needs, while also lacking the institutional framework to rapidly overcome its shortcomings.

The disproportions within sectors of the economy noted above were compounded by the overall imbalance between the output of producer goods and consumer goods. The producer goods sector, providing around 70 percent of gross domestic product, denied the consumer goods sector the investment resources needed to diversify and complete production cycles within the republic. Instead, raw materials and semi-finished goods were exported to other parts of the Soviet Union, notably the Russian Federation, and then returned to Ukraine as finished items of consumption. Moreover, the defense industries on Ukrainian territory, which as noted above commanded a quarter of the republic's labour resources and possibly an equal share of its raw materials and installed capacity, constituted a net drain on the economy. Apart from the high quality goods of civilian use these industries produced, such as motorcycles and precision instruments, the overwhelming proportion of their output constituted goods that could not be productively consumed. That is, weapons and other military hardware are means of destruction, which contributed nothing to the reproduction of labour power or the other factors of production, except their defense in situations of military hostilities or earnings from sales on world markets. The republic authorities had little control over either of these possible benefits.

The subjective and experiential inadequacies of the Ukrainian leadership, which had been required in the past to follow, not to lead, and the objective momentum of state economic production rolling on towards the old objectives, were an inheritance that could not be corrected easily or quickly. Moreover, the transition to independence in 1991, having been neither a social revolution nor a political one, did little to shake up the old habits and priorities of those who remained in charge of the state and the nationalised economy.

The costs of separation

The definitive breakup of the all-Union economy in 1991 had a major impact upon the economic process on Ukrainian territory. The production cycles linking enterprises across the Soviet Union, already disrupted by the ill-fated reforms under Gorbachev, by civil disorder, military conflicts and the assertion of economic independence by the constituent republics, were now threatened even more. Military industries were hit immediately — Ukrainian plants had no new orders at all placed for their goods in 1992, while the completion of existing orders was jeopardized by the prevailing uncertainty and disagreement about the region's future. The Ukrainian leadership feared that Russia wanted to use economic reintegration on the basis of CIS agreements as a tool for its eventual subordination to a Russian-led super state. Therefore, no agreement could be found on maintaining a common currency, a customs union or a payments union to facilitate trade, investment and other forms of economic co-operation. Trade did continue, but in the absence of interstate co-operation which enormously increased transaction costs. Russia was more powerful economically than Ukraine and had inherited far more institutional structures and experience in foreign relations, which gave it distinct advantages coping with the aftershocks of the collapse and setting down any new terms of regional economic intercourse. The Ukrainian leadership had hopes in the first years of independence that it could replace its economic links to Russia with new links to the Western economies. When such hopes proved illusory, the Ukrainian state — now under Leonid Kuchma's leadership — had to face the long-term challenge of maintaining its independence while still engaging the economic giant next door. In the interim, the divorce proceedings imposed their costs on the Ukrainian economy.

The task of establishing an integrated national economy revealed the deep structural disproportions between its branches, in the first instance the preponderance of the producer goods sector over consumer goods production. In Soviet times it had been possible to live with these disproportions because economic activity on

Ukrainian territory was embedded in a larger whole that compensated somewhat for its inadequacies and filled in the gaps. Economic activity that was loss-making was supported by the proceeds from other domestic sectors, especially agriculture and from foreign trade in oil, gas, precious metals and minerals. After independence the Ukrainian state leadership had to face these domestic disproportions without the compensating inputs from a broader economic complex or from foreign trade, for which it had not yet acquired the necessary experience and administrative structures to conduct on its own behalf.

Basically, the real costs of production of Ukrainian coal and steel were higher than the prices charged for them to other sectors of the economy (electricity generation, machine building, consumer durables and food products). The differences had been covered by centrally disbursed subsidies to the coal and steel industries to keep their prices down. After independence, the Ukrainian state took on responsibility for these subsidies, which it could provide only by drawing off wealth from the proceeds of agriculture and from the taxation of turnover. These sources were insufficient to maintain the previous level of subsidies because the state lacked the administrative machinery and experience to gather them and, of course, because the economy as a whole—especially the official economy that could be taxed—was contracting at a fairly rapid pace.

At the same time prices were liberalized while the mines and steel plants remained state owned monopolists. Their directors did not yet face the forces of competition, so they simply raised prices for their commodities. The increases in Ukraine's base industries' prices fed through the whole economy to the point of consumption, placing the burden on the broad population. In turn the working population demanded and secured wage increases. In this way the inherited structural disproportions of the now national economy constituted the essential domestic stimulus for the wave of hyperinflation that engulfed the economy in 1993.

The other, equally important stimulus for the inflationary wave was external in origin: the steady rise to world levels and beyond of the prices of Russian and Turkmenistan oil and natural gas. Even after Russia cut back its exports in the 1990s to other CIS states in the face of falling output, these fuels still accounted for 40 percent of the total value of Ukraine's imports. Moreover, by 1993 Ukraine was buying oil from Russia at between two and three times the world price, owing to the overvaluation of the US dollar and the Russian rouble against the *karbovanets'*, the interim Ukrainian coupon currency.[30] These imports stimulated the inflationary wave in two ways: by boosting the costs of production of primary goods that were then passed on up through the economic chain to the consumer; and by increasing Ukraine's external debt, which the state then had to repay either by increasing its exports to Russia or by taxing the domestic economy through printing, releasing and then gathering in again large new issues of Ukrainian currency, that is, an inflation tax upon the broad population.

The external debt continued to rise rapidly. The Russian Federation periodically cut back fuel supplies or halted their delivery altogether in attempts to pressure the Ukrainians to repay their debt and to make concessions on other issues, such as the Black Sea Fleet and Crimea. These supply shocks contributed to production falls and eventually to plant closures. The result by 1993 was a phenomenon called hyperstagflation—massive price inflation covered by currency emissions in conditions of diminishing production levels.[31] The rate of inflation, rising in 1990–91 from around 5 to 80 percent, exploded over the following two years and reached an annual rate of 10,000 percent in 1993 before subsiding again in the first half of 1994.[32] It was only after Leonid Kuchma became President in 1994 that a concerted effort was made to suppress the inflation rate and then introduce the new currency—*hryvnia*—in conditions of macroeconomic stability.

---

30   *Uriadovyi kur'ier*, 31 August 1993.
31   *Holos Ukrainy*, 21 January 1993; Tetiana Stepankova, speaking at the Conference on the Future of Ukrainian Economy; Ukrainian Institute of International Relations, Kyiv, 27 October 1994.
32   *Uriadovyj kur'ier*, 17 July 1992; International Labour Office, *The Ukrainian Challenge*, 13; Roman Frydman, Andrzej Rapaczynski, John S. Earle *et al.*, *The Privatisation Process in Russia, Ukraine and the Baltic States* (Budapest: Central European University Press, 1993), 89; *Post Postup*, 10–16 February 1995.

The costs of transition

In considering the causes of the economic crisis one is drawn slowly from those causes having an objective nature that are inherited from the past or are external to Ukraine in their origin to causes that appear on the road to the market and private property after 1991 and over which Ukraine's leaders have far greater control. A considerable body of opinion contends that the disruption of economic activity, the closure of industries and the contraction of gross domestic product are largely unavoidable during the present transition to a market economy. And in some senses, described above in the consideration of the kind of economy that Ukraine inherited and the way it broke off from the broader Soviet and Comecon economies, such an argument has merit. However, it is necessary to examine other causes of the crisis to account for its severity. Among the most important is the particular nature of capital accumulation during the transition period and the uses to which it has been put. Here we examine this process in three broad areas: the accumulation of money capital, the government's privatisation programme and the shadow economy.

The commercial banks

In the conditions of contracting output that dominated the first five years of Ukrainian independence any significant accumulation of capital into private hands could only be achieved by redistributing the already existing capital, be it productive assets or circulating money capital.

If the state's way of holding back the pace of economic dislocation and contraction was to subsidize the costs of heavy industry production and to print money in an effort to recoup these costs from the disposed income of consumers, the resulting inflationary spiral was also conducive to the diversion and private accumulation of social wealth by commercial banks.

Ukraine's biggest banks grew out of the reorganization of republic branches of the Soviet central banks in 1988–90. They lay the foundation for the National Bank of Ukraine (NBU) and several large banks serving key state industries. Small commercial banks also made an appearance in this period to serve the new private sector. In March 1991 the Verkhovna Rada adopted the Law on Banks and Banking, which called for their consolidation into a two tier system with the NBU as the central bank responsible for national currency issuance and clearing, foreign exchange and domestic interest rate policies, and a second tier of independent banks regulated by the NBU.[33]

Three of the five big banks of the second tier—Prominvestbank, Ukrsotsbank and APB Ukraina were registered as shareholding companies in 1990, making them the property of specific state economic enterprises and government organizations. But in 1993, when the Cabinet of Ministers resolved to put all the shares of state organizations under the control of the Ministry of Finance, these banks' boards of directors handed ownership rights over to new private companies and to named individuals working in the banks, the state enterprises and government organizations, that is, to themselves as physical and juridical persons. By the end of 1994 two thirds of all the capital of Prominvestbank and 95 percent of that held by APB Ukraina and Ukrsotsbank were in private hands.[34]

Between 1991 and 1993 the five largest independent banks—Ukreximbank and Oshchadbank in addition to the three cited above—took control of 90 percent of all banking services and 95 percent of all foreign currency operations in Ukraine. However, over the next three years to 1996 their share of banking services and operations decreased to 60 percent as a result of the tremendous growth of private commercial banks. They rose in number to 220 by the end of 1994, falling back to 188 banks with 2,284 branches by the beginning of 1997 (32 banks were dissolved).[35]

The banks accumulated money capital in several unorthodox ways. The directors of loss-making state enterprises lobbied the Verkhovna Rada and the Cabinet repeatedly and successfully for subsidies to keep them afloat. Part of the subsidies was channelled through their banks to finance domestic and foreign trade by their

---

33   Stepankova *et al.*, *op. cit.*, 218, 243.
34   Oleksandr Hurevych, "Velyki banky Ukrainy v umovakh spadu inflatsii", *Ekonomist*, No. 1, Jan–Mar 1997, 44.
35   *Ibid.*, and Stepankova, *op. cit.*, 243.

own and other private companies. The big banks' directors, representing substantial sectors of the economy, had privileged access to state officials that granted export and import licences. The banks also got their credit from the National Bank of Ukraine at rates of interest that were far lower than the rate of inflation. Merely by exchanging the coupon credits into hard currency and waiting a few months before buying back enough coupons to repay the loan could the holder earn quite a few dollars. The big banks sold on some of their credits to the smaller, less well connected commercial banks for their use in money and commodity trade, and made an immediate profit from the inflated transaction fees and insurance premiums on the loans.[36] From their own premises and through a network of thousands of franchised street vendors the banks additionally traded in foreign currencies with the population at large, who regularly sought refuge from inflation for their domestic currency earnings in the dollar and were then forced to sell them back as the cost of living spiralled upwards. Thus the wave of inflation which was impoverishing large numbers of people in these years provided a profitable environment for those who received state subsidies, credits and licences to trade in their capacity as state enterprise managers and who then used them for private and corporate gain in their capacity as directors and shareholders of independent banks.

The banking community finds in inflation a very stable source of income ... the elite quickly learn how to benefit from inflation and partial reforms. Cheap credits and export quotas become bargaining chips vis-a-vis enterprises. The door to various favours and privileges narrows during transformation, but those who can still pass through, exploiting special relationships, benefit more than ever before. The more widespread is corruption, the less eager are the elites to stop inflation and pursue irreversible reforms.[37]

When Leonid Kuchma became President, his government set out to stop the run on state funds from the National Bank and the

---

36　Hurevych, *op. cit.*, 44.
37　Petr Aven, Discussion paper to Oleh Havrylyshyn, Marcus Miller, William Perraudin, "Deficits, inflation and the political economy of Ukraine", *Economic Policy*, October 1994, 376.

state budget through to the commercial banks. State officials and enterprise managers with access to various funds, especially agricultural credit and conversion funds, from which they could make speculative earnings were investigated. Under the chairmanship of Viktor Yushchenko, the NBU changed the way it extended credit to the commercial banks from an "administrative division of resources" to credit auctions, and finally by offering state bonds. Almost all the bonds issued in 1995 to cover the state budget deficit were bought by 135 commercial banks in three auctions. From 1996 foreigners were permitted for the first time to purchase state bonds. The NBU reduced the emission of *karbovantsi* as it shifted the burden of the state budget deficit over to the debt market. It steadily increased the rate of interest on loans to the commercial banks towards and beyond the rate of inflation, thus eliminating one of the important conditions for the super profits previously available to lenders and currency traders. In May 1995 the NBU reduced from 1,300 to 150 the number of firms legally entitled to conduct trade in foreign currencies. And in August of that year the government banned the use of foreign currency as payment in the domestic retail and service sectors. The commercial banks were no longer permitted to hold foreign currencies on deposit and were required to lodge them with the NBU instead. These measures helped the government to hold down the rate of inflation to single digit monthly figures and to achieve a certain macroeconomic stability. But it was not until September 1996 that the government felt confident enough to replace the temporary currency *karbovanets'* with the new *hryvnia*.[38]

The commercial banks developed into new areas when subsidies to state enterprises became more difficult to get and the sharp fall in the inflation rate eliminated the lucrative field for arbitrage. Around thirty banks went to the wall, mainly because they knew no other trade. But the remaining banks—indeed a continually growing number over the period to 1997—were involved in serving

---

38   *Post Postup*, 10–16 February 1995; Stepankova *et al.*, *op. cit.*, 115,128; *Taras Kuzio, Ukraine under Kuchma: Political Reform, Economic Transformation and Security Policy in Independent Ukraine* (London: Macmillan, 1997), 144–50.

the private sector, lending money to the government and, for the few biggest banks, providing services to state sector institutions and programmes. Services to the private sector included currency transactions, deposits and trustee operations, but perhaps even more importantly in the order of their commitments, the banks served the shadow economy by providing means to conceal capital such as channels for capital flight abroad, off-record loans and foreign currency transactions. It was estimated in 1995 that around 40 percent of the total domestic monetary mass was circulating within the shadow economy, unaccounted and untaxed. And according to President Kuchma it was the banks themselves that were responsible for that state of affairs.[39]

The commercial banks had lent the government 760 m *hryvnia* by the first quarter 1997 through debt bonds. The government itself, however, had 540 m *hryvnia* invested in the banks. Therefore the banks were lending the government its own money, and at high rates of interest.[40] This field of activity was limited, and so the biggest five banks turned to the government to ask for preferential treatment in handling such financial operations as servicing the state enterprise budgets, targeted state investment programmes, the Pension Fund and other social welfare schemes. In April 1996 the government effectively gave the monopoly on handling state finances to the NBU and to four commercial banks — Ukreximbank, APB Ukraina, Ukrsotsbank and Prominvestbank.[41]

"Banks act typically as intermediaries by pulling together savings and transforming them into productive investment."[42] Not so for the Ukrainian banks that emerged since independence. Rather, they worked mainly to extract a profit from money and commodity trade. Legislation impeded their capacity to mobilize investment.[43] The public preferred to save its earnings — if it could save — by buying dollars, consumer durables and building homes rather than

---

39   *Holos Ukrainy*, 28 August 1995; *Post Postup*, 10–16 February 1995.
40   Hurevych, *op. cit.*, 42–45.
41   *Ukrainian Economic Trends*, March 1996, 4.
42   *Ukrainian Economic Trends*, June 1997, 51.
43   Stepankova *et al.*, *op. cit.*, 139–140.

putting *hryvnia* in bank accounts. "For each *hryvnia* of deposits in national currency ... there are 1.3 *hryvnia* of cash. The corresponding relationship in most countries is one monetary unit of deposits to only 0.2–0.3 cash units".[44] Where possible, business owners and managers did not use the banking system in order to evade taxation, preferring instead to facilitate their activities with cash, debt and barter. Banks had very little capital resources of their own: a statutory fund of only £3–5 million, and in some cases less than was officially required. In the critical economic circumstances of contracting production, with the money supply very tight after 1994 as easy credits and subsidies dried up and interest rates matched inflation rates, businesses in Ukraine—both state owned and private—were in no position either to bank earnings or to borrow.[45]

> "To defeat the investment crisis requires changes in the character of banks: they must change from usurers and speculators into providers of long term investment for the country's economy".[46]

Trusts and other financial intermediaries

Another medium for the private accumulation of money capital was the institution of the financial intermediary, notably trusts and insurance companies. In March 1993 the law "On Trust Companies" was adopted defining their rights, responsibilities and regulatory framework. The legislation gave Ukrainian trusts essentially the same scope to operate as the trusts in Russia had been given. It did not take into account the lessons of the Russian experience where companies like MMM, Seleng and Hermes Finans had effectively stolen the savings of a large portion of the population. The Ukrainian legislation, moreover, was published in three different versions, each falsified in separate parts, apparently to give even greater freedom to the trusts than the original legislation permitted and some basis for protection from possible subsequent prosecution.[47]

---

44   *Ukrainian Economic Trends*, June 1997, 50.
45   *Ibid.*, 40, 51; *Post Postup*, 10–16 December 1995; Hurevych, *op. cit.*, 46; Stepankova *et al.*, *op. cit.*, 129.
46   Stepankova *et al.*, *op. cit.*, 118.
47   *Holos Ukrainy*, 29 August and 6 September 1995.

The trusts and other financial intermediaries began to draw in the savings of citizens, promising handsome dividends. They accepted hard currencies and privatisation certificates, contrary to the law, as well as people's *karbovantsi* savings. In the summer of 1995, as the government tightened its control over the monetary system, trust companies began to collapse and declare bankruptcy. The press reported investors in such companies as Hermes Finans Ukraina, Debut Fidav, Korshun, Yalta-Dim, Fintrust, Alkor, Inis Invest and Kyitrust Hermes unable to retrieve their savings. According to — Hryhoriii Omelchenko, head of the Verkhovna Rada Commission on Combating Organized Crime and Corruption, one in eight citizens lost their savings in the collapse, to the tune of around 400 bn *karbovantsi* plus $40 m. The trade union journal *Profspilky Ukrainy* estimated the losses of investors at around 25 trillion *karbovantsi*.[48]

It emerged from the official investigations that took place afterwards that the capital the trusts had accumulated was used to purchase luxury goods for their directors or was spirited out of the country or was passed on as loans to firms and enterprises engaged in trade. This tier of the financial system was less regulated than the commercial banks and was therefore more open to criminal abuse. In fact, the government did not keep track of the number of trusts and their activities. The National Bank of Ukraine failed to regulate adequately the commercial banks, which in turn were able to violate existing legislation in servicing the trusts. And when investors in the trusts discovered their losses, the legislation was inadequate to compensate them or to prosecute the trusts' principal officers.[49]

So was a considerable part of Ukraine's surviving "middle class", the minority of people living above the level of subsistence, effectively dispossessed of their modest savings. They were not the only casualties, for the private financial services sector was discredited in the eyes of many more people, henceforth to be mistrusted with one's savings. The government suffered as well, for it had hoped to allow trusts to participate in the privatisation programme as legitimate gatherers and investors of citizens' privatisation certificates.

---

48   *Holos Ukrainy*, 29 August 1995; *Profspilky Ukrainy*, No 2, 1997, 42–43.
49   *Holos Ukrainy*, 5 and 7 September 1995; *Profspilky Ukrainy*, No 2, 1997, 42–43.

Capital accumulation through trade

Trade, domestic and foreign, became an important means in the 1990s for the private accumulation of capital. Thousands, if not millions, of Ukrainian citizens became traders, from the pensioner selling matches or cucumbers on a street corner to the executive of a state enterprise selling tons of steel or oil or meat in a distant country. Most people did not make profit of any significance; they were involved in petty trade in order simply to survive. Some had been made unemployed or had failed to find employment after completing their education or were pensioners who could not survive on state benefits. They traded in anything they could get that was locally scarce, usually in miserably small quantities. Others, who were paid in kind by the enterprise where they worked because of wage arrears, sold the goods they produced in the enterprise on the streets outside.

A step further up the scale of trade was represented by the shuttle traders, many of them women, who travelled as "economic tourists" on buses and trains to as far away as China to buy up goods that were in demand in Ukraine: clothing, pots and pans, processed food, appliances, spirits. These they sold in Sunday markets, often set up in the local football stadium, or through the many kiosks that sprung up along public transport routes and in the squares of towns and cities. The private kiosks, invariably leased by enterprising families from powerful domestic wholesalers who had good connections with the government authorities that issued trading licences, competed well with the state retail network. The wholesalers entered into contracts with foreign trading firms to supply them with consumer goods of low quality but in more attractive packaging than Ukrainian goods of equivalent or superior quality. Then, of course, there were the new stores in Kyiv and the oblast capitals that sold quality Western goods at Western prices to the "new Ukrainians".

And finally there were the "commercial structures", high volume traders on domestic and foreign markets who dealt in Russian oil, Korean electronics, American cigarettes, Ukrainian steel and other goods. They could make the largest profits because of a multiplicity of advantages. Commercial structures invariably involved people who could raise capital to finance an operation in an environment of scarce credit. They had foreign partners ready to effect a transaction at dumping prices. They could get state imported, state produced and state subsidized goods at low, domestically denominated prices. They had privileged access to state officials who issued licences to trade. They knew the right people on the borders. And they knew how to conceal their profits from the taxation authorities. Their foreign trade was concealed, as was much of the petty domestic trade, and so did not appear in official statistics. But they made large profits which they banked abroad, and from them the Ukrainian state treasury — and so the domestic economy — received very little in the way of taxes, excise or customs duties. Official trade statistics of Ukraine compared with that of its trading partners show that the Ukrainian customs authorities consistently under-calculated the volume of exports: for example, to the 12 EU countries in 1992, Ukrainian authorities valued them at $624 m while the EU valued them at $1.1 bn. The hidden trade meant losses of export and import duties to both sides.[50] Tobacco smuggling, a particularly lucrative business, accounted for more than 90 percent of all foreign-made cigarettes consumed in Ukraine in 1996. The state treasury lost $500,000 a day in lost excise duties. Legal importers of cigarettes could not compete with the black market trade.[51]

According to the State Security Service in 1995 there were 500 Ukrainian citizens with $18 bn banked abroad in personal accounts. Les Taniuk, parliamentary deputy, noted in 1996 that "each year the equivalent of two annual state budgets are expatriated, more precisely, stolen from our country". Indeed for many people in these years this was the face of Ukrainian capitalism: "In our country a business person or entrepreneur, as rule, is a person engaged not in production, but in the resale of foreign goods in Ukraine. That is, people who express the interests of foreign firms in Ukraine."[52]

---

50   *Holos Ukrainy*, 22 September 1993.
51   *Profspilky Ukrainy*, No. 2, 1997, 37; Yukhnovskyi, *op. cit.*, 112.
52   Mykhailo Pavlovsky, *Shliakh Ukrainy* (Kyiv: Tekhnika, 1996), 63.

Land privatisation

The Verkhovna Rada elected in March 1990 and composed of a considerable majority of Communist deputies continued to sit for over two years after December 1991 as the legislators of independent Ukraine. They adopted a whole set of laws that lay the foundations for private property in a denationalising economy: "On Entrepreneurship", that defined what economic means could be leased from the state; "On Entrepreneurship in Ukraine", which set out the forms of ownership, namely individual, private, collective, state, municipal and joint ventures, and which explicitly permitted hiring of labour; "On Ownership", which affirmed the free economic self-determination of physical and juridical persons, their right to private property, which limited state intervention and gave equal juridical rights to private, collective and state ownership; "On Companies", defining the rights and obligations of shareholders, and their limited liability; "On Foreign Economic Activity", which gave foreign individuals and firms the same rights as their domestic counterparts; "On Investment", which guaranteed state protection of investment, state compensation for losses and a ten year guarantee of stable rules of play; "On Taxation"; "On Limiting Monopoly", and "On Banks and Banking".[53] These laws were a juridical expression of economic system change at its most general level, adopted by that section of the Ukrainian elite which occupied the state institutions. Their implementation required further enabling legislation and, more importantly, the approval of other sections of the elite who occupied the managerial posts in the economy and the leading positions in regional and local governments. In a broader sense, a radical change of property relations depended also upon the capacity of the whole social structure to cope with it; that is to say, for the working classes to accept it and for socially organised economic activity to survive through the change without too serious damage.

Such preconditions were difficult to secure in the agricultural sector. Legislation, government resolutions and presidential decrees on land reform during the period that Leonid Kravchuk was

---

53   Stepankova *et al.*, *op. cit.*, 139.

President all rested on the premise that land could not become a commodity on the market. There were powerful feelings about the land as a common inheritance, as the basis of the Ukrainian nation, its culture, that posed a formidable obstacle to any change in the status quo. The opponents of land privatisation, especially in the Verkhovna Rada, never failed to make such arguments. On a less subjective note, they argued that the property form per se did not determine the productivity of agriculture, as Israel's farm sector demonstrated. Nor did the large size of Ukraine's farms necessarily affect their performance, as the United States' prairie farms would show.[54] In fact there was no convincing argument in favour of wholesale land privatisation, except that agriculture under the existing system of land tenure was in serious trouble. So the privatisation laws were hamstrung, inching towards the private ownership of land, but failing to recognise it unequivocally as a commodity.

The so-called "private plots" were made legally so by a government resolution in December 1992, but an amendment introduced by the Verkhovna Rada the following January prohibited their sale or purchase. Similarly, the collective farms were entitled by legislation adopted in 1992 to become "collective agricultural enterprises" in which individuals owned shares. But there was no practical way that their owners could take possession of their shares in kind, nor buy or sell them. A presidential decree in August 1993 did entitle members of collective and state farms, including their pensioners, teachers and doctors, to receive a physical share of land if they left the farm. But they could not sell or buy the land themselves, only set up private farms and other kinds of business on them.[55]

Leonid Kuchma's involvement in land reform stood out as a more consistent drive to achieving a private sector, with land treated as any other commodity. As Prime Minister in 1993, he sought to make certain kinds of land holdings subject to purchase

---

54   *Holos Ukrainy*, 5 September 1996.
55   *Holos Ukrainy*, 16 February 1993 and 5 September 1995; *Ukrainian Economic Trends*, August 1996, 76.

and sale — those which lay under buildings in towns and cities; under dachas in the countryside; and the land cultivated as private plots and family farms where such farms were successfully initiated. The land holdings of collective and state farms were still excluded. However, in November 1994, after he became President, Kuchma issued the more comprehensive and radical decree "On Land Reform" aimed at dividing up the state and collective farms. It called for the juridical transfer of state held land into collective ownership by farm workers, managers and ancillary employees, followed by the division of collectively owned land among individual owners. The individuals would receive certificates of ownership of specified land portions, not an abstract percentage share of total holdings, as before, and would be legally empowered to sell, swap and purchase them and to pass them on as inheritance. Each individual owner of such land could leave the collective enterprise with his or her portion of land. This decree contradicted earlier laws, resolutions and decrees that prohibited sale or purchase of land. However, in January 1997, the Cabinet of Ministers — under control of Kuchma's administration — abolished the moratorium on sale or purchase of land. The Verkhovna Rada did not overturn the resolution.[56]

The pace of land privatisation was slow over the period from 1992 to 1996. The number of farms grew from 2,000 to 35,000, with average size of 23 hectares, and accounted for less than 2 percent of the total area of agricultural land. Just over 3 percent of all agricultural land in Ukraine — this portion including the small private plots of rural and urban residents — became private property, while 60 percent remained state property and 37 percent collective (farm) property.[57]

Prior to all other considerations about the slow pace of change there was the inertia of the existing nationalised economy. People were at least secure in their place here and the knowledge of how it worked. True, the overwhelming majority of people who were

---

56   *Uriadovyi kur'ier*, 15 November 1994; *Chas*, 7 February 1997.
57   *Uriadovy kur'ier*, 17 July 1992; *Ukrainian Economic Trends*, April 1996, 81 and October 1996, 4.

wholly dependent upon it in the 1990s grew steadily poorer, but they invariably did not abandon it because there was no easy or simple alternative. As the economic crisis set in, payment in kind became an increasingly prevalent form of remuneration for farm labour. And as it deepened in the mid-1990s, farm workers suffered from wage arrears more than any other section of wage earners. But they could not abandon their employment on the collective or state farm because they were owed up to two years in back pay and, moreover, they received social and communal services by virtue of their membership in the farm labour force. Moreover, there was the safety valve of the home economy, where a peasant family could augment its declining or non-existent wage income by growing and selling or exchanging produce without overly upsetting the established relations on the farm and in the community. And membership in the collective or state farm even served to foster such private enterprise because the farm provided some of its essential inputs, be it a little stolen feedstock or fertilizer, an agreement with the foreman to pasture a cow on a farm field, or a ride to the Saturday market with one's produce on the back of a farm truck at a price agreed with the driver.

Because they were not being paid most rural people did not have money to invest in establishing a family farm. For they could take some land, but they had no right in law to the farm machinery, transport, storage facilities and the processing plants that formed essential components of the nationalised farm sector. Many did not even have enough to pay the 52 *hryvnia* fee plus bribes needed to register their title to a parcel of land. And if they still wanted to take it, people worried whether they would earn enough from the land to pay their taxes on land and trade. So one had to have considerable confidence in one's ability to survive as an independent producer and sufficient savings to finance the early years in order to take the first step towards private land ownership.

On the other hand, the farm managers, the farm workers and trades union leaders, the officers of local government and its services had vested interests in the status quo in terms of power and material privilege, even as the property relations evolved. For some of them the familiarity of the existing system in which they were the decision makers and purse holders was sufficient reason to resist any change. Others, however, were adapting to the incremental changes already underway in the rural economy. Land may not have been privatised, but its proceeds were increasingly so. They learned how to deal with the private trader of diesel fuel as well as the government official, how to sell farm produce on the market as well as to meet state orders, and how to conceal production through barter and so avoid taxes.[58] And they managed to cope with the coming of the market without disrupting the essential relations with their farm labourers. In fact, their capacity to profit as individuals without becoming outright private landowners (which made no sense anyhow, unless they took the entire production infrastructure with them) rested upon maintaining important elements of the old system of social relations between the rural elite and the labouring classes while at the same time grafting on the new market relations.

The central government estimated in 1992 that 3.7 million people wanted to start family farms[59] but it is clear from the statistics of subsequent years that only a small fraction managed to do so. In order not to lose control either of the land or the labour force, the rural elite quietly, but firmly resisted or manipulated the privatisation process. Farm chairmen resisted leasing or parcelling out land unless it was in quite small amounts. Often a kind of tenancy agreement was struck whereby the state or collective farm allowed a peasant to legally take a land parcel while continuing to provide essential inputs such as seed grain, fertilizer and machinery. The tenant took 30 percent of the harvest and the farm chairmen 70 percent.[60] Where peasants tried to establish a holding completely on their own, the village or district council held back from registering it. The local courts refused to rule on delays, grievances and disputes. Where individuals succeeded in breaking away they were threatened not only by economic blockade by the farm they had left,

---

58   *Chas*, 24 January 1997.

59   *Uriadovyi kur'ier*, 17 July 1992.

60   Author's interview with Ukrainian local government officials, 15 November 1995.

but even by physical violence from protesting farm workers who stayed with the collective and who demanded they return the land. Several farmers were killed in such protests in 1996 and 1997.[61]

Privatisation of industry, trade and services

The Verkhovna Rada began adopting legislation enabling the privatisation of industry, trade and services very soon after the country emerged from the Soviet collapse. In March 1992 it adopted four such laws: "On Privatisation of Small Enterprises", which envisaged the sale by auction of 20,000 small manufacturing, trade and service enterprises; "On Privatisation of State Property", which envisaged the sale of medium and large scale enterprises; "On Privatisation Vouchers", which were to be distributed free to all citizens and were non-transferable; and "On Foreign Investment" which, among other rights and privileges, granted foreign investors the right to participate in the privatisation process. A State Property Fund was established, answerable to the Verkhovna Rada. Its first head was Volodymyr Lanovy, the well-known economist of liberal Western, pro-market orientation.[62]

The institutions and methods of privatisation evolved over time. The State Property Fund, with its network of regional and local branches was the central institution. After Leonid Kuchma was elected in October 1994, jurisdiction over the Fund came to be shared by the President, who nominated its head, and the Rada, which approved the nomination. Control Commissions accountable to the Rada were set up in 1995 to evaluate the Fund's performance at the regional and local levels and to interpret the regulations that governed valuation of enterprises. Valuation was a particularly contentious issue given the absence of such practice in Soviet times, the ongoing decline of production, the rapid deterioration of capital stock and the frequent removal or theft of stock. An Anti-Monopoly Committee was also established to draft legislation

---

61   *Chas*, 18 October and 6 December 1996.
62   Andrew Wilson, "'Home-made privatisation", *Central European*, July–August 1992, 14.

on the protection of consumer rights and promotion of fair competition.[63]

From the outset the State Property Fund was empowered to hold enterprises scheduled for privatisation and to organize their transfer to private ownership. The Fund would normally strike a privatisation committee composed of its own representatives and those of the enterprise management, as well as the Anti-Monopoly Committee if the object in question was indeed a monopoly. The committee drew up a share allocation plan, defining how much of the enterprise would be privatised and in what manner. The latter might include a public offering of shares for direct purchase, an auction, a commercial tender based on prices or a non-commercial tender based on competing restructuring plans. In the last case, the State Property Fund set out a non-negotiable price for the enterprise and made its decision on the basis of the best restructuring plan put forward. The privatisation of small enterprises became a fairly routine process, while medium and large enterprises took longer to decide on an individual basis. The Verkhovna Rada approved all decisions of the State Property Fund; later the Cabinet of Ministers was also required to give its approval.[64]

It was difficult at first for the public to buy shares in privatising companies because the required individual privatisation accounts in which the vouchers were held took time to be made available and the use of such accounts for transactions exacted a considerable expenditure of time and effort. Moreover, the public had insufficient access to the information it required to make an intelligent judgement about which shares to buy. In January 1995 the accounts were replaced by Privatisation Property Certificates, issued on paper directly to each citizen. Additionally, people who had lost their savings in state bank accounts during the Soviet collapse or through the rampant inflation of 1993–94 were offered Compensation Certificates, which they could use to purchase shares in privatising enterprises. The take-up of these certificates was easier and by

---

63   *Ukrainian Economic Trends*, June 1997, 83.
64   *Ibid.*

mid-1997 around 44 million Ukrainians, or 85 percent of the population, had acquired the means to take part in the process.[65]

Privatisation of state enterprises made a slow start, rising from 40 objects in 1992 to 3,500 in 1993 and reaching 11,500 in 1994. However, more than three quarters of the total number of privatised objects by the end of 1994 were small scale enterprises — shops, restaurants, services and other businesses run by individuals and families.[66] Their contribution to gross national product had probably reached around 10 percent. Taken together with the contribution to GNP made by private businesses originating entirely from outside of the state sector, the proportion was somewhat higher.

However, the non-state sector that emerged in 1992–94 included much more than the private enterprises that grew from below as the initiative of individuals and families or devolved from above in the process of official privatisation. By far the most prevalent form of exit from the state sector onto the road of privatisation was not the direct one described above, but a more circuitous route via leasehold of state enterprises by their managers and employees.

Leasehold preceded the government's privatisation programme and prevailed until 1997, when the rights of leasehold were curtailed, as the most typical point of departure towards privatisation. Viktor Yushchenko, as governor of the National Bank of Ukraine, said that leasehold was a political compromise with the pro-communist Verkhovna Rada.[67] It was a way to denationalise state enterprises while allowing their workers to retain ownership of them and the managers to remain on the inside track of their eventual privatisation.

Leasehold was permitted by decrees of the Presidium of the USSR Supreme Soviet in 1989 and 1990 and confirmed in 1992 by Ukrainian legislation.

---

65   *Ibid.*

66   Stepankova *et al. op. cit.*, 236; *Holos Ukrainy*, 17 November 1993; *Chas*, 6 December 1996; Guy Standing, "Dynamika rynku pratsi promyslovosti Ukrainy 1992–1994 rr." in *Sotsial'na polityka Ukrainy v konteksti ekonomichnykh reform* (Kyiv: 1995), 9.

67   *Chas*, 8 November 1996.

> The legislation in force vests the workers of state enterprises ... with full control over the leasing process of these firms; once the majority of the workforce votes in favour of a leasing arrangement the state has no right to refuse to lease the property involved, even if the enterprise in question has already been scheduled for privatisation by other means. In fact, then, Ukrainian workers have a veto power over the privatisation process of these enterprises.
>
> The terms of these leases are also extremely favourable ... the rent amount ... is fixed [by the Council of Ministers] for the duration of the lease and cannot exceed 5 percent of the enterprise's income, defined as after-tax profits plus total wage payments, for the last full year preceding the lease agreement ...
>
> The workforce ... can also adopt a decision ... to redeem it once it has been leased. Through such redemption the workers gradually acquire co-ownership of the enterprise.[68]

By mid-1992, more than a thousand state enterprises were being leased. They accounted for around 20 percent of industrial output. These figures remained fairly constant in 1993 and 1994 and represented the passage of the most attractive state enterprises into leasing arrangements and out again as they were then turned into closed joint stock companies (the shares held by those employed in them) and finally into open shareholding companies. A survey in early 1994 by the International Labour Office of the largest enterprises showed that 47 percent of them remained state owned, 23 percent were leased from the state, and that closed joint stock companies, open shareholding (publicly traded) companies and privately owned companies each accounted for 10 percent of the surveyed enterprises. Around 70 percent of the directors of the surveyed state enterprises and 83 percent of those in charge of leased ones were planning to turn them into share-holding firms. Ukrainian state statistics suggest that 80 percent of all enterprises that were actually privatised in 1993 and 1994 were bought out by their workforce collectives. Thus the leasehold form of ownership was regarded not as a durable alternative to state ownership but as a favoured point of transition to private property.[69]

---

68   Frydman *et al. op. cit.*, 99–100.
69   Standing, *op. cit.*, 9; International Labour Office, *The Ukrainian Challenge*, 17; *Uriadovyj kur'ier*, 17 July 1992.

How, then, did people employed in leased enterprises fare as the property forms changed? The terms of the lease were attractive for the managers and workers alike, for it took only a small proportion of the annual profits, if there were any, and wage packet. Then, when a closed joint stock company was formed, the management received 5 percent of the shares and the remainder was divided among the salaried employees and wage workers. Following this division another process of internal redistribution of ownership set in. Workers who quit or were made redundant lost their shares to the management. The managers could try to shed workers/joint owners by temporarily closing down for, say, renovations. More often than not, however, production had to be cut back and pressure was thereby increased upon managers to shed labour and upon the workforce to seek another job while waiting on administrative leave for their employment to resume. An ambitious management of an enterprise with long term potential would be preparing it for privatisation as an open shareholding company. This would require a revaluation of assets, a restructuring plan and the attraction of outside investors, be they citizens with privatisation certificates or strategic investors, domestic or foreign, with cash in hand. In order to bring them into ownership of the enterprise during the final step of privatisation, the total number of shares in the company had to be increased, thereby diminishing the value of the original shares held by the workforce.[70]

The results of the 1994 elections brought a mixed blessing for the privatisation programme. On the one hand, the bloc of left parties which wanted to slow it down took the lion's share of seats in the elections to the Verkhovna Rada. On the other hand, Leonid Kuchma's victory brought to the fore a new president much more determined than his predecessor to press ahead with it. In July the Rada passed a resolution instructing the Cabinet of Ministers to review the entire process of privatisation and to remove from the list of enterprises scheduled for privatisation about 6,300 that were deemed to be of vital national interest. The Rada imposed a three

---

70   *Chas*, 25 October 1996; Author's interview with Ukrainian local government officials, 15 November 1995.

month moratorium on these enterprises. In October it refused to lift the moratorium, provoking an outcry from the President's Administration. By this time, however, Kuchma had taken effective control of the Cabinet and subordinated it to his Administration. On 10 January 1995 the President's Advisory Council on economic reform met to consider further steps, and a week later the Presidium of the Cabinet adopted its own privatisation programme for that year. It called for 22,700 enterprises to be privatised, including 8,000 medium and large ones, 13,500 small enterprises and 1,200 unfinished construction projects. Those removed from the list by the Rada remained excluded. Thereafter, as the Rada and the President battled for control of the executive functions of government and for a division of power over other important bodies such as the State Property Fund, the National Bank and the judiciary, privatisation became one of the main litmus tests for how far their respective authority carried into these central institutions, the regions and the economy.[71]

By April 1997, 38,600 small state enterprises (shops, restaurants, service industries) had been transferred to the private sector, effectively completing the government's programme in that sector. The transfer of medium and large enterprises to private ownership was less successful: from January 1995, 5,087 of them had sold more than 70 percent of their shares, while another 3,326 had sold less than 70 percent, which left the state as major shareholder in them. Enterprises changed owners in 1995–97 in three main ways: direct buyout by the workforce, often of a previously leased enterprise; public auction or share offerings to the public of medium and large enterprises. There were still several thousand enterprises excluded from privatisation, either because they were of strategic national importance or because the State Property Fund was still preparing a more complex privatisation package involving restructuring plans, foreign investment and possibly taxation relief to the new owners.[72]

---

71   *Holos Ukrainy*, 5 August 1994; *Uriadovyi kur'ier*, 17 November 1994; *Post Postup*, 18–24 January 1995.
72   *Ukrainian Economic Trends*, June 1997, 85.

The small business/enterprise sector by mid-1996 included around 86,000 businesses employing 1.1 million people (or 5 percent of total employment) who produced 9 percent of GDP. Around 49,000 (57 percent) were still in some form of para-state or non-state ownership—that is, leasehold or closed joint stock ownership; 35,000 (41 percent) of these businesses were in private hands, having either started as private or passed from the state sector; and only 1,700 (2 percent) were still in state ownership.[73]

The origins and property forms of small businesses were not so clear cut, however, in the early period of transition. Since the end of the 1980s directors of state enterprises were setting up private small businesses as channels through which they traded a portion of their produced goods or the state subsidised imports they acquired, such as fuel. The considerable profits they made were then sunk into the shadow economy, outside the government's reach. When the opportunities for super profits through trade in state-originating or subsidised goods dried up, these small businesses were drawn into chains of companies undertaking larger production cycles. The state programme to privatise small business was more transparent than these initiatives from below that nurtured the shadow economy. Private businesses were set up openly on the basis of the legally purchased state enterprises; the established skills and experience of the workforce, the supply networks and customer/client base were preserved and passed directly into the hands of the new owners. They were publicly registered, and so could be taxed and regulated by the state more easily than those which escaped into the shadows.[74]

Of all the sectors of medium and large-scale industry, paradoxically it was the agricultural processing sector that underwent the most far reaching privatisation of its fixed assets in this period. In the period 1992–96, more than 80 percent of the sugar refineries and meat factories, 70 percent of the dairies—in all more than 800 large enterprises—passed out of state ownership into joint stock ownership and other intermediate property forms. More than 70

73   Stepankova *et al.*, *op. cit.*, 227; *Ukrainian Economic Trends*, April 1996, 80.
74   *Chas*, 6 December 1996.

percent of service enterprises in rural areas (transport, machine repair, storage facilities, etc.) — more than 2,500 — went into privatisation. A "Law on the Privatisation of the Food Industry", adopted by the Verkhovna Rada in July 1996, further stimulated the transfer to the private sector. It permitted half the property of joint stock companies in food processing to be given free of charge to the workforce of enterprises, co-operatives and individuals who provided them with raw materials or to be transferred as shares at low cost to their workforce.[75]

In an attempt to explain why agricultural processing industries were passing quickly out of the state sector and land was not, the newspaper *Post Postup* commented still on 17 February 1995:

> In agricultural production, where even individual labour can rapidly yield a good return, the loss of management control is most painfully felt. That is why, they say, peasants should not be given land! But with industrial production, established on the basis of social labour where management plays the key role — give us, they say, capitalism right away!

By the end of 1996 the government programme was focussed increasingly upon medium and large-scale enterprises in heavy industry and manufacturing that were proving most difficult to privatise. The difficulties arose from various sources. A large bloc of deputies in the Verkhovna Rada remained opposed to the scope and speed of privatisation. The President and the Cabinet, as well as the Rada, were seeking to effect privatisations that actually created jobs and improved living standards, rather than facilitated asset stripping and capital flight. The economic crisis had driven down the enterprises' output and worn down their fixed assets. They needed significant injections of capital that could not easily be mobilized. The public did not have enough savings to buy up shares that were offered in such companies. Foreign investors needed time to examine the offerings and to gain confidence in the still fragile market environment before they would bid for enterprises. And most of them were held in leasehold or as closed joint-stock companies. Given their potential to make their Ukrainian

---

75   *Ukrainian Economic Trends*, August 1996.

managers very rich one day they would not pass into outright privatisation without fights for influence and advantage between competing groups of bidders.

The privatisation programme now shifted into a new phase. Only a small proportion of the shares in the remaining big enterprises was to be offered for sale to the public through certificate auctions or on the stock exchange — around 10–15 percent — in order to assess demand. It was envisaged that purchase of shares using privatisation certificates and compensation certificates would end in 1997 and be replaced entirely by cash purchases. Moreover, the bulk of shares would be offered by a less transparent bidding process to strategic investors, including foreigners, in exchange for capital investments and detailed restructuring plans.[76]

In February 1997 the Verkhovna Rada amended the "Law on Privatisation of State Enterprise Property" in order to unblock the logjam created by the institutionalised succession of property forms transitional between public and private ownership. Workforce collectives lost the automatic right to buy out whole enterprises from the state. Henceforth they had only the right to buy shares in them, but not to determine their property form. In order to buy a controlling share in the enterprise the collective had to form itself as an "economic association" and put forward a business plan as part of its tender. Leased enterprises were now required to make share packages available to the state, to collective buyers ("economic associations") and individuals. And closed joint stock companies could no longer be created except in the case of small or family businesses. The State Property Fund was given authority to privatise leased enterprises without the agreement of the leaseholders and the leaseholders retained the right to buy out a controlling share of the enterprise only if this provision had been fixed in the original leasehold contract. Shares had to be paid up within a year, not three as previously permitted. Management of closed joint stock companies being privatised were given the right to purchase an additional five percent of the shares with their own cash on top of the 5 percent

---

76   *Ekonomichni reformy s'ohodni*, No. 2 1997, 32–33; *Profspilkova hazeta*, 23 October 1996.

to which they were already entitled. And workers were given protection from dismissal for a period of six months after eventual privatisation. The social infrastructure of enterprises, consisting of children's nurseries, housing, recreational facilities and medical services, were to be handed over to local government councils if they were not privatised along with the production assets. The councils could then return these social assets to the work collectives if they were prepared to run them as the same public services. This last provision retained some rights for the trade unions to continue administering social facilities as they had done in the past in partnership with enterprise management.[77]

How much has been privatised?

As the foregoing analysis shows the transition from public to private property was usually not a direct one, but rather a process that passed property through a number of intermediary ownership forms. Roughly speaking, the consecutive stages for large and medium sized industrial enterprises were leasehold from the state, the closed joint stock company and the open shareholding company. However, most such enterprises did not pass quickly through these stages because sufficient capital could not be raised, either within the enterprise or through public share offerings. Disputes arose as to the valuation of the enterprise's assets. And it was often necessary for those in control of an enterprise to wait in the leasehold or closed joint stock company stage for some time in order to shed some of the workforce, to seek outside investors, to separate the technologically advanced and productive part of their assets from the less efficient, loss making part, including the social facilities that state enterprises were once obliged to maintain for their employed and retired workers. Here also the struggles between factions in management and the intense lobbying of officials in the State Property Fund, the central and local governments and the courts that were required to line up the privatisation process towards its preferred outcome inevitably lengthened the time it took to complete.

---

77 *Profspilkova hazeta*, 9 February 1997.

For small service enterprises that could be run by an individual or as a family business, ownership could pass relatively easily by auction from state to private hands. This part of the official privatisation programme was almost completed by 1997.

In agriculture, the process was blocked by the strong resistance to the privatisation of land. However, the proceeds from agriculture were increasingly appropriated into private hands. State control of land was loosened with the appearance of new legal rights to occupation, exploitation and inheritance of land and by the establishment of family farms on land taken out of the control of state and collective farms. And the food processing industries passed into the private sector quite rapidly, in fact representing the advance guard of industrial privatisation in this period.

Only broad estimates can be made of the extent of privatisation achieved by the end of 1996 given the transitory nature of property forms and the fact that the State Property Fund did not maintain aggregate data about enterprises passing through these forms.[78] Official estimates of privatised enterprises are misleading because they often included all non-state property and they did not account for the fact that in the course of privatisation some enterprises were split up into several, thus inflating the figures[79]. Nevertheless, it is clear that over the period from the break-up of the Soviet Union to the end of 1996 the non-state sector had grown to account for over half of agricultural and industrial production, an even greater proportion of the service industries and around 90 percent of banking services. The state retained a share of ownership in some 5,000 enterprises, the largest in the country. Yet its overall share of total industrial equity had decreased from close to 100 percent in 1991 to less than 60 percent by the end of 1996.[80]

The impact of privatisation on economic performance

The pro-market forces in political parties and central state institutions originally hoped that privatisation would help the economy recover by disciplining the new owners to allocate their resources

---

78   *Ukrainian Economic Trends*, April 1996, 80.
79   *Ukrainian Economic Trends*, January 1996, 78.
80   *Ukrainian Economic Trends*, January and June 1996.

efficiently, to seek new markets for their products and to introduce new technology to compete more effectively, at home and abroad. Such results were not evident, however, in the first five years because managers of many of the largest enterprises were caught in the halfway house of transitional ownership forms where they both called upon central and regional state budgets to subsidise their costly inputs, such as fuel and electricity, and simultaneously hived off the more lucrative parts of their production and trade to private companies and took the proceeds into the shadow economy. Once capital was accumulated in this way, the managers were in a position to take a more active part in the official privatisation of their own and other enterprises.[81] It seems that a large part of the proceeds were unproductively accumulated or were invested abroad, and less so back into the national economy.[82]

A survey of industry in 1993–94 by the International Labour Organisation concluded that new technology was introduced, greater product assortment released and labour shed at a faster rate by companies close to privatisation or privatised than those just departing from state ownership.[83] However, it was noted three years later in *Ukrainian Economic Trends* that most enterprises privatised by insiders "have neither changed their economic behaviour nor undertaken any restructuring, and furthermore their corporate governance remains highly inefficient".[84] The reasons for this economic paralysis lay, of course, in the leased enterprises as well as in the general economic contraction, the disruption of links between enterprises within and beyond Ukraine, the looming social crisis and the investment famine.

The state, anticipating that privatisation of its holdings would stimulate an investment market and allow it thereby to cut the costs of subsidies from the state budget, progressively relinquished control of the economy. However, it was forced to continue subsidising important sectors of the economy while having less control over the

---

81   *Halyts'ki kntrakty*, April 1997, p. 76.
82   *Holos Ukrainy*, 31 December 1994.
83   Standing, *op. cit.*, 13; International Labour Office, *The Ukrainian Challenge*, Table 1.3, 19.
84   June 1997, p. 85.

use to which its subsidies were put. The state lost a big part of its tax base to the shadow economy. And in shareholding companies where the state had shares, it did not have the resources to place its own representatives on boards of directors, to take part in their decision making or indeed to take its share of dividends. It is estimated that the state failed to collect 3 bn *hryvnia* of such dividends in 1996, which were sorely needed in the state budget.[85]

Another issue concerns the legality and equity of privatisation. In the 1930s during the great upheavals of agricultural collectivisation and mass industrialisation Leon Trotsky wrote that "law is no higher than the economic structure on which it rests". In the 1990s his axiom may be seen in the way that the appropriation of state property into private hands through a myriad of partial acquisitions that start from trade of state produced goods and end in the taking of their productive means inevitably preceded its legitimisation, its legal confirmation as private property. The Ukrainian state, issuing from an administrative-territorial division of the rapidly collapsing Soviet state, did not in its early years have the capacity to pave the way to privatisation with adequate, non-contradictory legislation and to police the passage with an effective judicial system. In the absence of laws and the inadequate enforcement of existing ones, power and influence determined who got what.

The official privatisation programme was an important part, but only one part of the process. It offered each citizen 1/250 millionths of the estimated value of the national economy in the form of a voucher in a bank account, later a certificate. Legally the privatisation certificates were neither tradeable nor transferable. They represented each person's equal starting chances in the change to the market. But as many people did not know and could not find out which shares they should buy, while at the same time they were living close to or below the poverty line, an active illegal market in certificates sprung up. They were sold for $10–12 apiece, often to registered intermediaries, such as trust companies, who by force of

---

85   *Profspilkova hazeta*, 26 March 1996 and 23 April 1997; Stepankova *et al.*, *op. cit.*, 36.

published falsified legislation were empowered to collect and invest them in blocs for citizens. Certificates disappeared when trust companies collapsed.

Then there were inequalities in the ways shares in companies could be bought with privatisation certificates. Managers had the right to acquire more shares than salaried or waged employees. Then again, these employees got shares at a preferential rate to that later offered to outsiders at certificate auctions. Pensioners, disabled people, students and unemployed people did not have even these starting conditions of the employed. On an inter-enterprise level, the workers in a competitive firm naturally got more valuable shares than those in a loss-making firm. And workers who used their certificate to buy shares in the enterprise where they worked lost them if the enterprise was removed subsequently by the Verkhovna Rada from the list of objects approved for privatisation.[86]

The economy in the shadows

Informal activity, grey economy and shadow economy — such terms have been used to describe an important dimension of the private enterprise that emerged in Ukraine after the Soviet collapse. Sometimes used loosely and indiscriminately, these terms nevertheless all pointed to economic activity that successfully evaded state taxation, monitoring or regulation, that by 1996 affected up to half of all economic activity, had control over 40 percent of the mass of domestic currency and considerably more of the circulating foreign currencies.

The shadow economy, which took from the nationalised sector to extend the realm of private ownership, was the mirror opposite of Stalin's drive in the late 1920s and 1930s when he nationalised the agricultural sector, drove the peasants into the collective farms, appropriated their annual surpluses and used them for the massive expansion of state industries.

---

86   *Chas*, 11 October 1996.

The shadow economy of the 1990s effected the net transfer of capital to private hands not only by denying the state an opportunity to tax its surpluses, but more importantly by using social wealth in production and circulation for which it did not pay or paid less than it was worth: state owned productive capacity, water supplies, raw materials, fuel and electricity, transport and communications, labour educated in the state educational system and maintained at the cost of the state systems of health and social security.[87]

A vast and complex domain, intertwined with the public economy and with the state that managed it, the shadow economy operated at many levels. At the most basic level, it grew out of the natural economy where individuals and families worked private plots and were engaged in home industries. If they produced more than they needed for subsistence, their goods and services were traded, more often bartered for other goods and services, in ways that were inaccessible to the state taxation or regulatory authorities. Even where this trade was visible as commerce, requiring public space and services and the maintenance of public order, as in the lines of individual traders on the streets, the urban kiosk markets and even the farmers' produce markets run by local authorities, much of it could not be monitored, regulated or taxed. The state did not have the administrative capacity to do so. Nor perhaps did it want to interfere too energetically into this sphere of economic activity because at least it provided a way to keep people employed at a time when the nationalised sector was contracting and the social security system was under enormous strain.

Informal activity was particularly strong in residential construction and the repair, servicing and sale of automobiles. New homes were built in rural areas and near urban centres, often as dachas on the private plots and allotments. Automobiles, both new and used, were run across borders from Central and Western Europe by well organised gangs with good connections with border

---

87   *Profspilky Ukrayiny*, No 2, 1997, p. 37.

authorities and the state road inspectorate. Or they were stolen inside the country. An estimated 95,000 vehicles, half passenger cars and half vans and trucks, were registered as missing in 1996.[88] The commercial director of SC Johnson corporation in Ukraine commented that "it is a curious situation of a country in crisis, with booming residential construction and increasing car purchases".[89]

Informal or shadow economic activity in the education system manifested itself in a variety of ways: the student who used his institution's premises and equipment to earn extra money writing computer software for a private company; a lecturer offering private tuition; the catering service management diverting part of the food supplies for private sale; the admission of students and awarding of grades for sums of cash; the misappropriation of state funding by the institutions' managers, the establishment of private companies on their premises and with the help of their facilities and labour.[90]

On the railways, the shadow economy spanned from the dimly lit waiting rooms where a protection racket charged beggars for safety through the night, to the ticket counters where an absolute scarcity of seats on the trains fostered a booming trade for touts, all the way to the state officials who controlled licences to trade, service contracting, rolling stocks, warehouses and other facilities. Kuchma wondered aloud where the earnings of some 2,000 commercial organisations who leased premises and land from the railways had gone. Three quarters of the businesses and services associated with the railways violated the tax laws. Over the three years to 1997, tariffs and the costs of services had increased by nine times, the cost of passenger tickets by forty times, while the railway service had fallen below the minimum acceptable level.[91]

---

88   *Profspilkova hazeta*, 26 February 1997.
89   Cited in Taras Kuzio, *Ukraine under Kuchma*, 52.
90   See *Ekonomist* Vol. 1, No. 1, January–March 1997, 12, where President Kuchma is cited deploring the widespread misappropriation of funds in the National Academy of Sciences, while its employees were not being paid for months.
91   *Ibid.*

The directors of large state and privatising enterprises were practised in the art of concealing the extent of their output. The journal *Ukrainian Economic Trends* noted in January 1997 that "official output reporting lacks credibility". Enterprise directors invariably spoke optimistically about future performance, but routinely reported production declines when asked about past performance because they were required to pay taxes on the latter.[92] Concealed production could then be sold and the profits concealed from the state authorities.

The shadow economy was more prevalent in trade, credit and finance than in the productive spheres because money is more mobile than productive capacity. An inspection of 32,500 retail trade and service enterprises in the first half of 1995 by the State Committee for Consumer Protection found violations in 85 percent of them that pointed to a significant shadow market in their goods and services: the sale of goods unregistered or of unknown origin, overpricing and under-weighing. Within the trading network, around one seventh of bread products disappeared, as did one fifth of meat products and a third of confectionary. There were even enterprises with contracts to feed blind and sight impaired children in state care who were accused of underfeeding them.[93]

State property found its way to the private sector by a variety of other routes. Valentyn Pylypchuk, a founding member of the patriotic Union of Officers, a veteran of Vietnam and author of the first legislation on the Ukrainian armed forces, protested against "the total sell-off of military hardware, fuel, lubricants and other materiel by 'activists' in the mould of Zviahilsky" (former acting Prime Minister accused of corruption). The general staff, he wrote, "built dachas, cottages, traded and sold" using the property of the army.[94] In the spring of 1995, Yurii Kasaryk, then Minister of Agriculture was issued 54 tr *karbovantsi* from the state budget to pay for grain and other food products ordered by the government. When these funds did not reach the producers an investigation was launched

---

92   See also *Ukrainian Economic Trends*, April 1996, 68, and June 1996, 6.
93   *Holos Ukrainy*, 29 August 1995.
94   *Chas*, 15 November 1996.

by the Verkhovna Rada Commission on Organised Crime and Corruption. It traced 6.1 tr *karbovantsi* to commercial organisations, many of them of a completely fictitious nature. Kasaryk was eventually removed from Prime Minister Marchuk's Cabinet, but he later found his way back into the corridors of power as an advisor to the President[95]. Government inspectors monitoring the use of public funds at the ministerial and regional levels found that theft and misappropriation were greatest in the Ministries of Agriculture (around 62.2 m *hryvnia* missing), Industry (45.2 m), Coal (24.1 m) and Transport (8 m). Among those subsequently disciplined and dismissed were A.I. Khorishko, Minister of Agriculture and L.I. Zhelezniak, Deputy Minister of Transport.[96]

Another investigation that focussed on crime in the banking and financial sector, where 63,000 violations were uncovered and 23,000 officials were disciplined. Around 100 criminal cases that were pursued to prosecution involved the theft of state fuel supplies by people who included members of the State Committee of Oil and Gas. The Committee's Deputy Head, Sushin, was arrested. Large scale trade at home and abroad in such goods as fuel required the collusion of officials who controlled import and export licences and had access to state subsidised fuel stocks and with commercial banks that could finance particularly large trade deals.[97]

The further one looks into such cases the clearer becomes an essential relationship at work in the substantial transfers of social wealth into the private sector via the shadow economy: the relationship between the public official and the private businessman. This being a co-operative relationship, it not only follows that the shadow economy is an exercise in the evasion of state taxes and regulation by private enterprise, and the determined and sometimes illegal appropriation of state property by the private sector, but also that the state official actually helps the private businessman to evade taxes and to appropriate state property. Not surprisingly, these two agents are sometimes one and the same person.

---

95   *Holos Ukrainy*, 29 August 1995.
96   *Ekonomist*, Vol. 1, No. 1, January–March 1997, 13.
97   *Uriadovyi kur'ier*, 17 November 1994; Yukhnovsky, *op. cit.*, 112.

In May 1995 the Verkhovna Rada suspended the authority of its deputy head, Oleksandr Tkachenko, and established an Investigating Commission to look into charges that Tkachenko had illegally acquired and was profiting from state credits to import American hybrid seed grain and farm machinery.[98] It appeared he was the president of the commercial organisation called *Zemlia i liudy* (Land and People), which he presented to a government foreign currency credit committee as a state organisation under the leadership of the Ministry of Agriculture.[99] The Committee then provided his organisation with a state guarantee on an American loan of $70 m. Tkachenko was accused of misrepresenting his firm as a state enterprise and not fulfilling the terms of the credit agreement, but instead allowing the money to be used to buy luxury items for the principals of *Zemlia i liudy*. When the affair was made public Tkachenko agreed to pay the money back and concluded an agreement with the Ministry of Finance and the Ukrainian Import Export Bank that provided for an extended period of repayment. The agreement was denounced by Verkhovna Rada deputies on all sides and in October 1995 a President's Commission declared it illegal, calling on the Arbitration Court to move for compulsory return of all $70m by 1997.[100]

Products that issue from the shadow economy are estimated to have grown to around one half of the country's total output by the mid-1990s. However, if measured gross domestic output has fallen to half or less of its 1990 level, this does not necessarily mean that Ukraine's real gross domestic product is around double that recorded by the official statistics. These do reflect accurately the gross output of certain products like grain, sugar, coal and steel, commodities that cannot easily be diverted to the shadow economy. Moreover, these primary goods constitute a growing share of the diminishing total output as manufacturing of more capital-intensive producer goods and consumer goods contracts. Furthermore, most of the products and services issued from the shadow

---

98   *Holos Ukrainy*, 12 May and 7 June 1995.
99   *Chas*, 17 January 1997.
100 *Chas*, 17 January 1996.

economy utilize materials and labour that originate in the open, measured economy. The shadow economy operates largely at stages beyond the level of initial productive activity, acquiring and redeploying its material outputs in the intermediary and end stages of reprocessing, assembly and especially in trade. The shadow and open economies are thus intertwined, not isolated cycles of production. Where they do run off in separate directions is from the point of realising income from their goods and services. For while the open economy's income is in at least some small measure reinvested into new cycles of production, the shadow economy diverts far more of its income into unproductive consumption and foreign bank accounts.

Implications for the state building process

This article serves as an introduction to the grim economic predicament faced by Ukrainian society and the state seven years after gaining independence. It attempts to identify the primary causes of the crisis stemming from the past, from the disintegration of the Soviet Union and from the transition to the market. It does not analyse state economic policy in any great detail, its response to the crisis nor, indeed, its contribution to the crisis. It does not consider the role of Western and Russian capital or multilateral institutions like the World Bank in the developments since 1991. All these matters deserve detailed examination and analysis in separate articles.

Nevertheless, some broad observations can be made with respect to the relationship between the Ukrainian state and the national economy.

The deepening economic crisis of the 1990s is the single most important domestic problem of survival for the new Ukrainian state. The social and national consensus expressed in the overwhelming vote for independence in the December 1991 referendum rested on the hope, even the belief, that independence would restore economic prosperity and give Ukrainians far greater control of their destiny. In the seven years since then the economic decline actually accelerated, bringing in its wake a host of social consequences that are beyond the scope of this article to fully describe: a declining life expectancy, growing perinatal and infant mortality, a decrease in the population to below 50 million, unemployment approaching 15 percent, poverty, social inequality and crime. The contraction in output and the expansion of the shadow economy which conceals and expatriates its income prevent the state from collecting sufficient tax revenues with which to fund the social security system and help alleviate these problems and inequities. The shadow economy, preferring to seek profit through trade, reduces the capital available for productive investment. Thus the economic crisis and its social consequences undermine the consensus on which the new state was launched in 1991.

The range of problems that need to be addressed would test the abilities of any new state. First, the Ukrainian state emerged as a territorial administrative unit of the Soviet state, without the critical institutions and experience necessary to effectively regulate domestic economic activity. Second, the state had control of an economy with deep disproportions between its branches that depended upon considerable trade with neighbouring states, particularly Russia. The restoration of ties with the principal heir of the former oppressor state was problematic, especially in view of the fact that the Western states in the 1990s did not offer a comprehensive alternative in foreign trade and other kinds of economic co-operation. Third, while the new state pursued a strategy to establish a viable national economy, it was at the same time privatising it, that is, deliberately relinquishing national state ownership of whole sections of it. The search for an optimal balance between the nationalised and privatised sectors, and between the private accumulation of capital and the redistribution of wealth by the state to alleviate the social inequalities engendered by private accumulation, has become one of the most difficult and divisive issues of the transition period.

Economic recovery, effective state institutions to regulate and stimulate the economy, and the maintenance of an adequate social security net during the transition to the market all depend upon capital accumulation and its productive investment in Ukraine. This requires dismantling the shadow economy and bringing its subjects into the open, regulated and taxed economy. Here the

Ukrainian state faces its most daunting challenge: to unify and dis-cipline the new capitalist class so that it relinquishes as a matter of course a publicly agreed portion of the wealth it is accumulating for the satisfaction of social needs. Otherwise the state will rightly be regarded as an instrument for capital accumulation into private hands, rather than the redistributive agency that holds up the social and national consensus.

Russia, Ukraine and European Integration*

What are the prospects that Russia and Ukraine will be drawn further into the processes of European integration in the coming decade? Are these states destined to remain excluded from both the European Union and NATO as these key institutions spread eastward, or in only minor forms of partnership with them? Ten years ago, right after the collapse of the USSR, the prospects of Russia and Ukraine joining the West looked bright, at least from the perspective of their own leaders. Today, however, they have all but accepted exclusion or an arms-length association with the European Union and NATO for the foreseeable future.

The process of European integration appears far more complex today than it did before the complete collapse of the communist bloc in 1991. First, the process confronts the challenge of the EU's eastwards expansion into Central and East European states which were separated from Western Europe economically, politically and militarily for almost half a century. Second, there is a consensus in the Euroatlantic states that Russia and Ukraine are not suitable candidates for EU or NATO membership, with different reasoning applying to each of these states. At the same time the Euroatlantic states acknowledge that the further economic and political evolution of Russia and Ukraine has great significance for the prosperity and stability of the entire European subcontinent. Therefore, serious engagement with Russia and Ukraine is necessary, even though their full integration with European structures is not contemplated. Such engagement means both the EU and NATO on the western side and Russia and Ukraine on the eastern side developing co-operative ties that further European unity and will hopefully create preconditions for the integration of these European regions in the long term. Finally, European integration confronts the challenge of overcoming the divisions and mistrust between Russia

* First published in: *European University Institute Working Paper*, No. 2001/4 (San Domenico: European University Institute Department of History and Civilisation, Italy, 2001).

and Ukraine themselves which, like the Franco-German relationship immediately after the Second World War, has the capacity either to retard or help regenerate their neighbourhood of states.

This paper explores the prospects of Russia's and Ukraine's integration with the EU and NATO by exploring the evidence of adaptation, co-operation, interdependence and allegiance between them along the following lines:

a.   Russia's and Ukraine's experience with democratisation and the market;
b.   Ukraine's encounters with the EU and NATO;
c.   Russia's encounters with the EU and NATO;
d.   how the interdependence of Russia and Ukraine in the natural gas trade affects the prospects of both states for closer integration with Western and Central Europe.

Russia's and Ukraine's experience with democratisation and the market

If satisfaction of the EU's Copenhagen criteria were the main precondition for EU membership, then neither Russia nor Ukraine presently stand a chance of joining. The two countries are not developing market economies nor political orders like those found in the states of the European Union. Rather, after an initial start in the direction of democratisation, Russia and Ukraine have both turned towards more authoritarian government with the consolidation of strong presidential rule and the emasculation of their legislatures, restrictions on democratic freedoms and the application of a wide variety of legal, administrative and coercive instruments to limit independent civic institutions. There is pluralism in Russian and Ukrainian politics today, but it is largely the pluralism of competing oligarchic groups fighting one another for denationalised assets, markets and influence within the state. The struggle at the apex of power is augmented somewhat by those civic organisations and mass media that retain a degree of independence from both the state institutions and the business oligarchs. However, civil society is poorly developed, and the mass media in both countries is subject to heavy pressures from state institutions and powerful business interests. The political decision making process itself, both in Russia and Ukraine, is captive to this mutually advantageous relationship between big business and state officialdom. In the post-1991 transition period the state has organised the denationalisation of state property and made possible the accumulation of capital in private hands. The new business class, upon becoming wealthy, seeks to transform its economic power into political power by purchasing mass media outlets, financing election campaigns or simply buying influence with the various arms of the state. The executive power in return bestows upon them privileged access to resources and markets; the legislature adopts laws to facilitate their business and the courts become instruments to combat and punish rivals, both in politics and business.

The retreat from democratisation has been amply documented in the monitoring reports and plenary sessions of the Parliamentary Assembly of the Council of Europe.[1] The relationship between political power and capital accumulation in Ukraine was the focus of attention given by the Internet newspaper *Ukrains'ka Pravda* from its inception in April 2000, for which its founder Heorhii Gongadze paid with his life in September of that year. Its findings were subsequently augmented with the revelations of the secret tape recordings made in President Kuchma's office by his security officer Mykola Melnychenko.

Two important features of the economic change in Russia and Ukraine stand out: the peculiar multifaceted structure of oligarchic clan capitalism which combines in each of its competing entities productive enterprises, trading outlets, mass media, political parties and even security forces; and the fact that state institutions at every level—the State Property Fund, taxation authorities, courts, local governments, fire inspectors—have continued to control access to private economic activity, which results in monopolistic production, closed markets and corruption. These features and the general retreat to authoritarian and plutocratic rule seen in recent

---

1   Marko Bojcun, *Ukraine and Europe; A Difficult Reunion.* (London: Kogan Page, 2001), Part Two.

years increasingly set these successor states of the Former Soviet Union apart from the liberal democratic tradition of the West European states and of the contemporary European market economy model which both Russia and Ukraine initially chose, but failed, to emulate.

A simple comparison of the current state of affairs at both extremes of the European subcontinent suggests that a path to their integration would be hard to implement in the medium term even if there were overriding reasons of, say, geo-strategic advantage for the EU, to do so.

Ukraine, the EU and NATO

Embarking from a position of non-bloc status and neutrality on the eve of its independence, Ukrainian foreign policy evolved over the course of the 1990s into a multi-vector strategy that sought to balance Russia in the east with the USA and the EU in the west. It found a clear expression in the January 1994 Tripartite Agreement of Russia, Ukraine and the United States which offered a guarantee of Ukraine's territorial integrity and protection from the use of external force to influence its foreign policy. However, the East-West balancing act was increasingly biased in favour of a pro-Western orientation, which became explicit from 1994 after Leonid Kuchma became President. In that year Ukraine joined the Council of Europe and signed a Partnership and Co-operation Agreement with the European Union. Relations deepened with NATO, leading to Ukraine's inclusion in the Partnership for Peace and the signing of a Special Charter with NATO that projected a relationship more complex and far reaching than the Partnership for Peace, but fell short of accession to full membership.

The motives for Ukraine's westward drive in foreign policy during the 1990s were mainly to do with its international security and economic development. An abiding concern of the state leadership was to find a suitable counterweight to the historical pull of Russia onto Ukraine. The economic motive stemmed from the initial estimation in 1990 that Ukraine's economy and social structure were sufficiently developed to permit a successful transition to an effective national market economy that could engage the West European economies in a mutually beneficial way, and in the process relieve Ukraine of its strong economic attachment to Russia. Ukraine sought membership in the Council of Europe in order to be recognised as a democratising state, to seek the Council's assistance for democratic reform and to thus legitimise its claim for eventual full membership in the European Union.

Ukraine's relationship with the European Union during the 1990s was beset by serious problems. The European Union developed its orientation towards Ukraine in the light of its more important relationship with the Russian Federation. There was never any intention of offering Ukraine full membership in the EU. Rather, the EU's leaders anticipated that Ukraine would eventually be subsumed by Russia.[2] This became increasingly evident as the Ukrainian leadership from 1998 began calling for a signal from the EU that it had a chance to join, while the EU insisted that Ukraine first implement the terms of the PCA and create the necessary conditions for a free trade area with the EU.

Ukraine's frustrations with the EU and the EU's growing irritation with Ukraine were rooted not only in divergent preconceptions about the long term objectives of their engagement, but also by the Ukrainian domestic economic crisis, its failure to pursue market reforms and the unsatisfactory progress in foreign economic relations. In the background of foreign economic relations there stood a steadily deteriorating domestic economy, with declining production levels, flight of capital and scientific-technical expertise, erosion of labour skills, unemployment and mounting social inequalities, a socio-economic degradation that was not arrested even by the end of the decade. In such domestic conditions it is difficult for any country to seek advantage in its foreign economic relations.

---

2   "Ukraine has never been regarded as a potential EU member". *Annual Report for 2000*, Centre for Peace, Conversion and Foreign Policy of Ukraine, 10. "A study produced in 1999 in the depths of the German and French foreign offices and published in 2000 ... said it would be desirable for the EU to deal with united political and economic systems of Ukraine and Russia — that is, the CIS". *Zerkalo nedeli*, 14 April 2001.

Ukraine in the 1990s reduced the proportion of its trade with Russia from around 80 to 55 percent. But its trade with Central European states that were acceding to the EU was simultaneously reduced from 20 to 10 percent, while trade with EU member states rose from around 6 to 20 percent. With both Russia and the EU member states Ukraine experienced an ongoing trade deficit that was reduced, but not compensated for by its trade surpluses with other countries. The structure of its trade ties with the EU was unsatisfactory insofar as the EU protectionist regime prevented imports from Ukraine of those products in which it had competitive advantages (steel, chemicals, foodstuffs, textiles) and from which it could have generated earnings for productive investment and modernisation of its economy. Moreover, the proportion of Ukrainian exports that fell under anti-dumping investigations grew in the 1990s from around a quarter to more than a third.[3]

The EU and Ukraine had damaging disagreements about the certification of product standards to cover imports from the EU (and other countries). During the 1990s around 60 percent of the retail trade market in Ukraine was captured by foreign suppliers of surplus and second-rate goods that could not be sold in their countries of origin. There was the dispute with the EU over Ukraine's granting preferential tax treatment to the Korean firm Daewoo, which committed itself to rebuilding the country's main automobile production plant. Both sides were critical of the implementation of the TACIS technical assistance programme, blaming each other for unspent, misdirected and misappropriated funds, the lack of consultation or transparency. The closure of the Chemobyl nuclear power station became a drawn out affair that pitted powerful economic interests on the EU and Ukrainian sides over the issue of whether its generating capacity should be replaced by thermal or additional nuclear generating capacities. Finally, despite robust declarations of intent and detailed strategic documents, the Ukrain-

---

3   Commentary of Mykhailo Pashkov in *Rozvytok ta Rozshyrennia У e. S. pid chas Holuvannia Frantsii. Perspektyvy dlia Ukrainy* (Development and Expansion of the EU during the French Presidency. Perspectives for Ukraine), (Kyiv: Atlantic Council of Ukraine, 2000), 61.

ian side did not manage to establish a legal and regulatory framework that met West European expectations and in which foreign capital could confidently enter the Ukrainian markets. By March 1998, when the legislatures of EU states had finally ratified the EU-Ukraine PCA and its full terms were meant to come into effect, it was clear that the free trade area it sought to foster was a long way off. EU leaders believed by that time that the Ukrainian leadership lacked both the political will to make it work and the authority to compel the emerging oligarchic business groups to let European and transnational companies participate in the Ukrainian market. By 1999 Ukraine's relations with the EU were in crisis, and its relations with Central European states acceding to the EU were stagnant.[4]

Ukraine's participation in the Council of Europe from mid-1994 was dominated by the growing contradiction between its willingness to sign up to practically all of the Council's Charters and Covenants and their actual violation in Ukraine itself. There was a drawn out struggle which finally compelled the Ukrainian state to impose a moratorium on the death penalty by March 1997 and then to abolish it in December 1999. The Council also pressed Ukraine on its commitments to reform the system of criminal justice, to guarantee fair elections and the rights of ethnic minorities, political parties, the press and local governments. In 1999 it embarked upon unprecedented measures to suspend its membership.[5] And at the end of 2000, the tensions between the two sides erupted with even greater force over the disappearance and murder of the journalist Heorhii Gongadze and allegations of President Kuchma's involvement in his disappearance. In early 2001 Ukraine faced the prospect of complete expulsion from the Council.

Ukraine's bid to establish a distinctive relationship with NATO through the 1997 Special Charter differed from the EU-Ukraine relationship in two respects. On the one hand the Ukrainian leadership did not ever announce an intention to seek full membership in NATO. The reasons for this are not entirely clear, but

---

4   Bojcun, *Ukraine and Europe*, Part 1, 9–23.
5   Bojcun, *Ukraine and Europe*, Part 2, 24–51.

subsequent developments (see below) suggest that the Ukrainian political and military leadership had never ruled out a security alliance with Russia. This may have to do with the following set of pressures: Ukraine is of geo-strategic importance to Russia, a vital corridor to Central and Western Europe; Ukraine experienced great difficulty maintaining its cumbersome army of 400,000; by the end of the decade Russia was spending six times as much money per serviceman maintaining its own army[6]; the Ukrainian and Russian military industrial production complexes remained closely interwoven; the loyalty of the Ukrainian general staff had not been tested nor publicly confirmed (nor indeed the loyalty of its State Security Service) and both of these were rather direct transplants from their all-Union bodies. A myriad of inherited links and perceptions of common interest in the military and security fields mitigated against any clean break between Russia and Ukraine.

On the other hand, Ukraine was also of geo-strategic value to the Western alliance as a check on Russia, which overrode the relative lack of economic interest in it on the part of the West. Thus the country's geo-strategic importance stimulated the USA to envelop it militarily, short of full membership, in NATO and make it the third largest recipient of US aid, while at the same time urging on its European allies to "do more for Ukraine" to overcome the barriers to economic integration. Yet the relationship with NATO received a nasty shock in 1999 when NATO attacked Serbia. The out of area military operation inflamed public opinion in Ukraine and cast doubt in its leaders' minds about the claim that NATO's eastward expansion was consistent with strengthening European security.

Ukraine's pro-Western orientation was eroded in a major way at the end of 2000 and in early 2001 after intensive negotiations between Russia and Ukraine led to several bilateral agreements covering the energy sector, broader economic co-operation, military and security affairs (see below). These agreements appeared to signal the imminent end of Ukraine's pro-Western orientation and the

---

6   Centre for Peace, Conversion and Foreign Policy of Ukraine, *Annual Report for 2000,* 17.

beginning of its reintegration with Russia. They also graphically revealed the contradiction which had emerged by the end of the 1990s between the official pro-Western foreign policy of the President's Administration and the powerful economic links with Russia that same Administration was promoting on behalf of Ukrainian oligarchic circles tied to the Russian economy.[7] They evoked concern on the part of both the EU and NATO. But while the EU did not regard Ukraine's eventual reintegration with Russia as a retrograde step nor necessarily harmful to the EU's relations with Ukraine, the reaction of the USA, the leading force in NATO, which treated Ukraine as a counterweight to Russian regional ambitions was one of alarm.

Public opinion surveys conducted over the period 1994 to 2000 showed practically no growth in the proportion of those who favour European integration (understood as integration into the EU and NATO): the marginal rise was from 14 to 16 percent over this period. At the same time there had been a decline in public opinion favouring integration into the Commonwealth of Independent States — from 41 in 1994 to 15 percent in 2000. When asked in 2000 about Ukraine's possible integration into the Russia-Belarus Union 23 percent were opposed and 53 percent were in favour. Those in favour were more heavily represented in Eastern Ukraine. With respect to the eastward vector of integration there is a clear tendency to favour economic integration with Russia or the Russia-Belarus Union over political-military integration with Russia or the Union or the CIS. A certain sense of isolationism is suggested in the proportion of those favouring "reliance on one's own forces" growing over the same period from 13 to 26 percent. This tendency was especially marked in Western Ukraine. Young and better educated people favour European integration in proportionally greater numbers than other age and education groups. And for them the notion of integration is less of an institutional, state-to-state, geopolitical process and more of an individual opportunity for social mobility.[8]

---

7   Centre for Peace, Conversion and Foreign Policy of Ukraine, *Annual Report for 2000*, 5.

8   Sergei Makeev, "Obshchestvennoe Mnenie v Ukraine o Perspektivakh Integratsii v NATO i Yevropeiskie Struktury" (Public Opinion in Ukraine on the

Russia, the EU and NATO

Russia's outlook on European integration and security has been conditioned by several factors. Its leadership considers Russia the successor state of the USSR. It occupies the lion's share of the former Soviet space. In the wake of the collapse of the USSR, the Russian Federation has sought to maintain its status within the group of G7/8 countries, and while acknowledging that it is not a superpower anymore, it wishes to be a great power, the regional hegemon in the eastern part of the Eurasian landmass. Thus its relationship to the European project emanating from the west is envisaged as a relationship between two great powers, two pillars of potential Eurasian co-operation. Were it not for the fact that the USA is the dominant military force in Western and Central Europe and sees Russia as its rival in the Balkans-Black Sea-Caspian Sea corridor this long term perspective of Russia-EU co-operation would seem eminently feasible. However, the Russian leadership under President Yeltsin, in the aftermath of the initial illusions about Russia's rapid integration into the advanced capitalist world, had to refocus its sights and define specific objectives with respect to the former Soviet space, the European Union and to NATO. In the course of the decade the spirit of Russian foreign policy shifted from liberal-democratic pro-Westernism to a national-patriotic defensiveness, and with the assumption of presidential power by Vladimir Putin to a pragmatic re-engagement that seeks "the restoration of Russia's economic and strategic power".[9]

The first zone of re-engagement is the post-Soviet space. Russia hoped to rebuild a Commonwealth of Independent States on the ruins of the USSR, but its hopes were thwarted by the reticence of the former non-Russian Soviet republics to enter into a close alliance so soon after the break-up. Ukraine resisted more than the others and viewed the CIS as a divorce arbitration court where she

---

Perspectives of Integration into NATO and European Structures) in *Rozvytok ta Rozshyrennia У e. S. pid chas Holuvannia Frantsii. Perspektyvy dlia Ukrainy*), 63–66.

9   James Sherr, "A New Regime? A New Russia?" in Centre for Peace, Conversion and Foreign Policy of Ukraine, *Occasional Report* No. 35, 15 July 2000, 2.

would get her fair share of the assets. She maintained observer status in the CIS and refused to take part in any projects that required pooling sovereignty and creating supranational authority. Ukraine refused to sign up to two critical treaties: the Tashkent Collective Security Treaty adopted by five CIS members in May 1992 and the Customs Union, adopted in March 1996. Belarus, at the other extreme, actively sought union with Russia after the election of Alexandr Lukashenka as President in 1994. The Baltic states were, for all intents and purposes, considered a lost cause. And in the south from the Caucasus to the Chinese border, Russia had to resort to forceful means to maintain stability on its borders and influence with its allies: keeping the Fourteenth Army in Moldova in support of the Transnistrian enclave against the Romanian Moldovans; challenging Ukrainian sovereignty over Crimea; supporting Armenia against Azerbaijan; nurturing the Abkhaz insurgency as a counterweight to Georgia's efforts to break out of dependency on Russia; stationing troops on the Afghan border with Tajikistan and countering the domestic opposition to the Tajik government.[10] And, of course, the Russian Federation went to war against the Chechen independence movement within its own borders.

So in the first half of the 1990s the Russian central state tried to reclaim the post-Soviet area, but failed to secure a voluntary re-unification of the post-Soviet states or to hold the line against the northward spreading Arc of Crisis, or indeed to prevent the projection of Western power into the Balkans-Black Sea-Caspian Sea corridor. Ukraine was clearly its biggest disappointment and for reasons of imperial past history the Russian establishment could not understand why Ukraine was so determined to carve out its independence and cleave to the West, rather than return to the East Slavic brotherhood. In the process of grappling with failed strategies the Russian establishment learned three lessons about the recovery of its former power: first, that while Russia is relatively weak in its dealings with the West, it is nevertheless strong in dealing with the

---

10   Allen C. Lynch "The Realism of Russia's Foreign Policy", *Europe-Asia Studies*, Vol. 53, No. 1, 2001, 23.

fragile Newly Independent States; second, the Russian state leadership and its big business allies realised that their truly effective
lever for regional integration is not force, but the economic dependency of the NIS on trade with Russia, and particularly on Russian
gas and oil; third, as Moldovan developments in 1992 already
showed, the Western alliance is prepared to acknowledge Russia as
the guarantor of stability in her own region, if not *de jure* then at
least *de facto*.[11]

These lessons accompanied the revival of the doctrine of Eurasianism, reclaimed from the Russian White emigre intelligentsia
of the 1920s and adopted by virtually the whole political spectrum
from Ziuganov to Zhirinovsky. Eurasianism asserted that Russia is
a unique civilisation, separate from Europe and destined to unite
the Slavic, Turkic and Central Asian peoples into a great continental
power. Yet Russia's practical efforts to unite the former Soviet republics around itself in the Commonwealth of Independent States
have failed so far. The CIS is an institution built on many sweeping
declarations of intent with a poor record of adherence or implementation by its members, who have avoided above all the creation of
a CIS supranational authority to which they should relinquish a
portion of their sovereignty.[12] Therefore, the process of integration
in the west of Europe is matched in the east during the 1990s by its
opposite: the disintegration of the USSR as a supranational state
and economic entity and the stubborn resistance thereafter of most
of the non-Russian newly independent states, except Armenia, Belarus, Kyrgyzstan and Tajikistan, which are deeply dependent on
Russia economically or militarily, to any substantive reintegration.
This resistance has rebounded on the Russian state itself, causing it
to pursue bilateral relations to achieve cooperation with former Soviet republics rather than trying to build a supranational authority
for the entire CIS. In place of the CIS, other regional initiatives have
sprung up in the post-Soviet space during the 1990s: the Russia-

---

11   Lynch "The Realism of Russia's Foreign Policy", 11–20.
12   Richard Sakwa and Mark Webber "The Commonwealth of Independent States
1991–1998: Stagnation and Survival", *Europe-Asia Studies*, Vol. 51, No. 3, 1999,
379–415; "Ukraina znovu vyiavliaie pedantychnist'", *Ukrains'ka pravda*, 21 June
2000.

Belarus Union, the Central Asian Economic Community and the GUUAM alliance, uniting Georgia, Ukraine, Uzbekistan, Azerbaijan and Moldova as a tacit anti-Russian counterweight. All these regional groupings are weak and ineffectual, yet their creation testifies to the ongoing search by these states for alternatives to economic and political integration with Russia.[13]

Russian foreign policy makers at first viewed the European Union as a benign economic institution, even as a counterweight to American influence on the continent. Russian leaders were and remain concerned that their country not be isolated from the economic powerhouse of the EU, to benefit from its approach to their borders.[14] Like Ukraine, Russia joined the Council of Europe and signed a Partnership and Co-operation Agreement with the EU in 1994. But unlike its neighbour, Russia has not done so for the purpose of joining the EU, but rather to become a strategic partner of the EU on a continental matrix. The language of the PCA shows that there are far greater ambitions at play:

Russia is an essential element in the future of the continent and constitutes a strategic partner for the European Union ... The Union is already Russia's main trading partner and Russia itself provides a significant part of the Union's energy supplies ... the strategic partnership (should) develop within the framework of a permanent policy and security dialogue designed to bring interests closer together and to respond jointly to some of the challenges to security on the European continent ... continuing consultations on a multilateral transit framework which will enhance co-operation between Russia and its neighbours over access to the Russian [sic] pipeline system ... Joint foreign policy initiatives with regard to specific third countries and regions.[15]

The PCA suggests that a strategic partnership is conceived, among other things, for the purpose of a long term exchange of European technique for Russian gas and oil. Building and protecting

---

13   Centre for Peace, Conversion and Foreign Policy of Ukraine, *Occasional Report*, No. 12, April 2001.
14   *Financial Times*, Special Report on Russia, 9 April 2001, 15.
15   "Common Strategy of the European Union on Russia, 4 June 1999". Document 499XO414, *Official Journal* L157, 24 June 1999, 7–8.

such an economic partnership would require joint approaches to third countries, such as Ukraine, and mutual responsibility for meeting security challenges along the length of the network that will join the two extremes of the European subcontinent. In this context Russia views Central Europe as a region with which it must rebuild its economic ties in order to complete the bridge to Western Europe.

Trade, investment and technical assistance flowing between Russia and the EU offer some measure of the importance Russia attaches to the partnership and of its potential to become a truly strategic one in the future. The EU is Russia's largest single trading partner, the destination in 1997 of one third of its total exports and the source of more than one third of its total imports. Almost 60 percent of foreign capital invested in Russia comes from the EU, and Russia is the recipient of two thirds of the total EU technical assistance destined for the CIS states. On the other hand, EU imports from Russia are far less important, accounting for 1.5 percent of total EU imports. Nevertheless, natural gas accounts for the lion's share of these imports and it is a strategic commodity not only for the EU member states but also for the Central European states acceding to the EU. The latter states are heavily dependent on Russian energy sources.[16]

Yet the grand vision of a Europe grouped around Eastern and Western pillars that will themselves forge ever closer ties has been rendered inoperable so far by unresolved problems on both sides of the EU-Russia partnership. First, Russia has yet to make the kind of economic recovery necessary to boost capital investment, production and trade to appreciably higher levels. It has not been able, so far, to harness other states and national economies in its neighbourhood into regional co-operation that could boost economic recovery for all concerned. The second unresolved problem from

---

16   Margot Light, Stephen White and John Lowenhardt, "A Wider Europe: The View from Moscow and Kyiv", *International Affairs*, 76, 1(2000), 81; Gerhard Mangott, "Russian Policies on Central and Eastern Europe: An Overview", *European Security*, Vol. 8, no. 3, Autumn 1999, 61–72; Dmitri Danilov "A Piece of the Partnership", *Transitions*, Vol. 5, No. 4, April 1998, 60.

Russia's point of view is that NATO remains Western Europe's primary security institution. Its leading member, the United States, still sees Russia as a rival on the continent. Russia strongly opposed NATO expansion into Central Europe, tried to persuade the states involved that a pan-European security order was more appropriately the concern of the Organisation for Security and Co-operation in Europe and held onto the belief that the United Nations was the ultimate instrument for international intervention and conflict management. Russia also tried to develop an understanding with NATO during Yevgenii Primakov's tenure as Foreign Minister in 1996–97 about the limits of NATO expansion. Russia acquiesced to NATO expansion in exchange for the formation of the NATO-Russia Council, designed to ensure permanent security dialogue and consultation. It was viewed by the Russian leadership as a means to limit the damage of NATO expansion to its own interests.[17] However, the NATO bombing of Yugoslavia in the spring of 1999 revealed that Washington did not see the NATO-Russia Council in the same way. Russia in the person of former Prime Minister Viktor Chernomyrdin was reduced to delivering NATO's messages to Slobodan Milosevicz. The bombing came at the precise moment when Poland, Hungary and the Czech Republic acceded to NATO as full members. The consequences of this episode for Russia's outlook on European security were far reaching. The Russian leadership now felt morally freed to go to war a second time against the Chechen independence movement.

Thus, while the majority view in the West European states today is that NATO and EU expansion eastwards are desirable and compatible processes, the Russian establishment holds markedly different views with respect to each: it supports European expansion and integration and wishes to find its own place within that process, but it opposes NATO expansion as a challenge to its own interests.

---

17   Mangott, *op. cit.*, 67; Light, White and Lowenhardt, *op. cit.*, 78.

The interdependence of Russia and Ukraine

Relations between Russia and Ukraine have evolved in the 1990s against a historical background of Ukraine's national subordination in the Russian Empire and the Soviet Union. During the past decade Ukraine has experienced the longest period of state independence in its history, while the Russian Federation has been coming to terms with the loss of its imperial periphery. The depth of feeling about national gains and imperial losses of each side is perhaps underestimated by West European leaders whose countries experienced decolonisation after the Second World War mainly as a loss of distant overseas possessions rather than the dismemberment of a geographically compact state. The Russian nation was long accustomed to treating its Slavic neighbours as nations closely related in language, culture and religion. And the Ukrainian ethnos was itself only recently transformed by those modernising influences of literacy, urbanisation and social mobility which equipped it with the professional classes and political awareness necessary for national self-determination and independence from Russia. There was, therefore, a fundamental divergence of outlook on the Russian-Ukrainian relationship after 1991 between the two sides: those who viewed it as one between brothers, albeit quarrelling ones, and those who viewed it as one between a man and woman in the process of divorce. The two countries' leaders naturally foresaw different possible outcomes to the dispute at hand: filial bonds made reconciliation possible or, on the other hand, a bad marriage made separation necessary and in the best interests of both parties. Russia in the 1990s sought to bring Ukraine back under its roof, while Ukraine sought a new partner in the West. In fact, Ukraine so assiduously guarded its national independence against what it perceived as Russian attempts to resubordinate it through bilateral and multilateral (CIS) means that it was prepared to see its economy incur heavy losses rather than agree to restoring or deepening economic interdependence with Russia.[18]

---

18   Paul D'Anieri, "Interdependence and Sovereignty in the Russian-Ukrainian Relationship", *European Security*, Vol. 4, No. 4, Winter 1995, 608.

However, the conflict-ridden diplomatic relations between Russia and Ukraine over Crimea, the Black Sea fleet, the status of the Russian minority in Ukraine and the assets of the defunct USSR were no longer the only kind of relations between them. With the advent of market relations and oligarchic capitalist formations working the cross-border trade, the diplomatic relations were increasingly directed to the service of the latter's needs and the settlement of their disputes. Russia is by far more powerful economically and on this count alone Ukraine inevitably faced the pull of eastwards re-integration, however strong its European inclination. Because private capital was consolidated earlier and in far greater concentrations in Russia than in Ukraine Russian capitalists have been able to make decisive inroads to buy up strategic industries in Ukraine. Second, the drive to buy up Ukrainian industries has followed on the heels of the Russian natural gas and oil trade in Ukraine and through Ukraine to Central and Western Europe. Third, Russia is able to generate significant earnings from foreign trade, especially in gas and oil, while Ukrainian producers are hard pressed to retain markets both at home and abroad. Both countries are heavily indebted to foreign creditors, but Russia has greater capacity to generate earnings from foreign trade with which to pay back its debts and to deploy to the advantage of its strategic industries. Finally, the redevelopment of capitalism in both Russia and Ukraine has taken place in the 1990s under the powerful influence of their respective state institutions, which to this day control access to the resources and markets. So by the end of the 1990s Russian-Ukrainian relations were shorn of their emotional baggage, and pragmatism became the favoured description of their mutual relations for both the Russian and Ukrainian Presidents. To paraphrase a popular saying, the business of both governments increasingly became business. And as the determining influences on relations between these two states changed, so too did their outlook on the prospects of European integration for them.

The end of Ukraine's "European choice"?

The year from mid-2000 to mid-2001 may well go down in history as the point at which Ukraine abandoned its independent orientation towards the EU and its pro-NATO strategy, while Russia embarked on a new stage of integration with the EU. In this year President Putin made a determined drive to exploit the critical state of Ukraine's domestic economic situation and international standing, and to exact Russia's dues from Ukraine's dependence on its fuel and energy resources. He succeeded in the course of the year to secure several fundamentally new agreements with Ukrainian leaders:

1. To restructure Ukraine's gas debt to Russia over an eight to ten year period that will allow Russian firms to use part of the debt to buy shares in privatising industrial assets (December 2000);
2. A 52-part military co-operation accord signed by the respective defense ministers to co-ordinate the two countries' policies in relations with the European Union and to allow Russia to take part in planning all multinational military exercises on Ukrainian soil (January 2001);
3. Co-operation Agreement between the respective heads of state security services (February 2001);
4. Co-operation Agreements in aerospace and aviation industries, shipbuilding and electronics (February 2001);
5. An agreement to integrate the two countries' electricity power grids (February 2001);
6. Protocol between the Russian Conventional Arms Agency and the Ukrainian State Committee for Industrial Policy on co-operation in the production of ammunition and conventional weapons on the basis of "a single industrial policy" (February 2001).[19]

---

19 The texts of these agreements were not made public. For press reports see Hanna Liuta, "Dosiahnuta pryntsypova domovlennist'", *Zerkalo nedeli*, No. 47, 2000; *Ukraina moloda*, 21 February 2001; Centre for Peace, Conversion and Foreign Policy of Ukraine, *Reports*, March 2000, 7 and 12 February 2001,; *ITAR-TASS* 18 January and 14 February 2001; *Financial Times* 22 February 2001.

These agreements came after intense negotiations between Kyiv and Moscow throughout the year 2000 which in September brought about the dismissal at Moscow's insistence of the pro-NATO Ukrainian Foreign Minister Borys Tarasiuk in the midst of critical negotiations over Ukraine's debt for Russian gas.[20] His replacement, the veteran diplomat who held the foreign ministry portfolio at the beginning of the 1990s is Anatolii Zlenko. Zlenko downgraded Ukraine's long-standing multi-vector policy. The authoritative Kyiv think tank, the Centre for Peace, Conversion and Foreign Policy, identified in its annual report for 2000 a cardinal change of foreign policy as well as of the military and political course of Ukraine, which is characterised by a transition from the multi-vector policy, or balancing Ukraine's interests between those of the United States and Russia, to a factual, single-vectored policy oriented at Ukraine's reintegration into the Russian Federation.[21]

If indeed the above noted agreements are duly implemented, the shift in Ukraine's geo-strategic orientation they collectively represent will surely count as President Putin's first dramatic and substantial foreign policy achievement, a major step in the reclamation by Russia of the former Soviet space and, *ipso facto*, the beginning of what might prove a deep erosion of Ukraine's independence.

How did Putin persuade Kuchma to take such unprecedented steps in their mutual relations? Here we should identify a number of important developments that converged in the year 2000 to substantially undermine Ukraine's ability to manoeuvre between Russia and the Western alliance.

Russia is the biggest supplier of natural gas to Central and Western Europe. It provides around 40 percent of their needs and will be providing around 60 percent within ten years. Ukraine is a major consumer of Russian gas, as well as Turkmenistan gas, both of which are delivered to Ukraine in a total volume of 60 bcm each year by a Russian gas transit firm. These 60 bcm account for three

---

20   "Ukraina ta Rosiia domovylysia pro ostatochnu sumu ukrains'koho borhu za haz", *Ukrains'ka pravda*, 27 May 2000; "U Rosii ne duzhe vysoko otsiniuit rezul'taty vizytu Tarasiuka do Moskvy" (In Russia there isn't a very high assessment of Tarasiuk's visit to Moscow), *Ukrains'ka pravda*, 30 May 2001.

21   *Annual Report* for 2000, 7.

quarters of Ukraine's annual demand, the remainder being produced in Ukraine itself. Natural gas fuels round 87 percent of Ukrainian households and the generation of over 40 percent of its electricity (the remainder by Russian and Kazakh oil and by nuclear power). Yet Ukraine is not just a major consumer of Russian gas, but also the largest gas transit country in the world delivering across its territory around 120 bcm or 94 percent of the Russian gas consumed in Central and Western Europe. The dense network of pipelines covering 35,000 km is the property of Ukrainian para-state firms. In exchange for delivering Russian gas to European consumers the Ukrainian state and private participants involved in the gas transit network are paid in kind in the amount of 30 bcm of gas each year.[22]

Ukraine by the end of 2000 had built up a debt to Russia for the additional gas its para-state firms were drawing out of the transit network each year to meet peak winter demand and to sell on for cash to Central European consumers. Throughput in the pipelines could not easily be monitored because the international transit lines are intertwined with the Ukrainian domestic distribution network. So the amount of Ukraine's debt was disputed, but ranged between $1.4 bn and $3 bn. There was always a debate about whose debt it was—the private side of the firms transiting and trading the gas or the state side which maintains the trunk lines and guarantees the repayment of the debt.

Nevertheless, the transit and trade in Russian gas was an especially lucrative business in the 1990s, the primary initial source of super profits on whose foundation today's five or six main oligarchic groups began building their diversified empires. These oligarchs made their money in such large amounts because they learned how to turn Russian gas passing through the pipelines into hard currency profits while dumping the costs of transit onto Ukrainian state institutions. Indeed, there was close co-operation

---

22   "Ukraine at a Crossroads as Energy Uncertainty Prevails" *Gas Matters*, December 2000, 1–10; Vasyl Rozgonyuk and Zinoviy Osinchuk, "Ukrainian gas transit system expanding, modernising to meet demand", *Oil and Gas Journal*, 19 February 2001.

between state officials and private businessmen in the pursuit of this rewarding trade.[23]

In the second phase of capital accumulation—roughly 1996–1998—the Ukrainian oligarchs began to buy up downstream and ancillary assets as they were being privatised, such as the oblast electricity generating and distribution companies and the pipe manufacturing plants. They also created their own mass media outlets and political parties and succeeded in gaining representation in the Verkhovna Rada, the Ukrainian legislature, in the 1998 elections. They penetrated the entourage of President Kuchma, whose Administration has practically sole decision making power with respect to foreign policy. From this important foothold grew their ambition to take a more direct part in deciding who would occupy the chief executive positions in the country, which was clearly revealed in the key financial and organisational roles they played in the re-election of Leonid Kuchma for his second term as President in November 1999. In return they expected to gain seats in the Cabinet of Ministers, from which they could more easily direct the final phase of privatisation of the biggest and most important enterprises in the country.

Yet both Russian and Western transnational capital were also poised to take part in the final phase of privatisation of the whole fuel and energy complex based on coal, oil, gas and nuclear power and on the cycle of extraction, refinery, transit and consumption. The prize asset was the gas transit network. Russian firms such as the giant Gazprom and Western multinationals like Shell were both keen to take a controlling interest in it. Backing the western firms was the International Monetary Fund and the EU. The Russian state stood behind its own para-state and private firms which, having a hold on one of the greatest sources of gas and oil on the continent, now wanted to take hold of its distribution system beyond Russia to former Soviet, Central European and West European states. Moving into the gas transit network stretching across Ukraine was one of the most important paths for Russian national capital to transnational status and transnational competition with the Western giants.

---

23 "Z uriadu Ukrainy idut' ostanni prykhyl'nyky zviazkiv z Rosiieiu", *Urains'ka Pravda*, 25 May 2000.

The appointment in May 2001 of former Russian Prime Minister and former head of Gazprom Viktor Chernomyrdin as Ambassador to Kyiv and Special Presidential Envoy on the development of Russian-Ukrainian trade and economic relations was widely interpreted in Ukraine and Russia as a calculated move to strengthen Russia's chances of winning this important Ukrainian asset.[24]

The Ukrainian oligarchs and the state institutions did not have sufficient resources to repay the gas debt to Russia and invest simultaneously in the maintenance and exploitation of the gas transit network for their own benefit. And throughout the past two years there was growing pressure from the EU, the Russian government and major European energy companies to resolve the long term question of security of supply across the European subcontinent.[25] The other options, therefore, were for Ukraine to grant a long term concession to a foreign firm to exploit the network or to privatise it, partially or completely. For Ukraine it boiled down to the size of the stake in the network that it could retain.[26]

---

24   "Do nas pryiikhav revizor", *Ukrains'ka pravda*, 23 May 2000; "Kredyty vid MVF mozhe dadut'", *Ukrains'ka pravda*, 24 May 2000; "Ukraine at a Crossroads as Energy Uncertainty Prevails" *Gas Matters*, December 2000, 7–9. Gazprom has worked with the Russian government to acquire equity in the fuel and energy distribution systems of the NIS states in exchange for their debts so that it can control energy transit and trade further afield to Central, Southern and Western Europe. See J an Kalicki, "High Stakes Hinge on Russia's Energy Choices", *Oil and Gas Journal* 19 March 2001. On the occasion of Chernomyrdin's appointment to Kyiv, *Ukraina moloda* commented in its 2 May 2001 edition that "he will supervise Russia's participation in big privatisation and gas debt settlement. He will do everything to make Kyiv sell Russia part of its gas transit pipelines."

25   "Ukraine at a Crossroads as Energy Uncertainty Prevails" *Gas Matters*, December 2000, 1; Darius Snieckus, "EU and Russia seek co-operation and integration of energy markets", *Oil and Gas Journal*, 17 May 2001; "EBRD calls for Gazprom Break-up", *Oil and Gas Journal*, 3 July 2000.

26   In an interview given to *Rossiiskaia gazeta* on 18 April 2001 President Kuchma acknowledged that "we will be seeking compromises … we are … ready to examine the question of whether the pipeline should not be solely Ukrainian and whether both Russian and even European partners should be allowed to participate". Ukrainian Foreign Minister Anatolii Zlenko said in Brussels on 24 April 2001 that Ukraine sought to develop closer co-operation with the EU, including "the implementation of the European Union's energy strategy as an equal partner … ([and] the creation of an international mechanism for managing Ukraine's gas transportation system and invited strategic investors to participate". Centre for Peace, Conversion and Foreign Policy of Ukraine, *Report*, 21–27 April 2001.

In the battle fought out through 2000 and into 2001 the Russian side had the advantage over the Western side in dealings with the Ukrainians because: the Ukrainian oligarchs were already dependent upon Russian supply; the Ukrainian state owed a gas debt to the Russian side for which it had no cash to repay; Russian private capital had already moved onto the Ukrainian market, buying continuously into a wide range of producing enterprises, communications and mass media; and it knew how to operate in the novel conditions of the Wild East. Both Ukrainian and Russian finance capital were determined to keep Western capital of any serious weight out of the picture until they had consolidated their own positions.

Russian companies taking large shares or controlling interest in Ukrainian enterprises include Avtozaz, buying the Zaporizhzhia Aluminium Plant; Lukoil buying the Odesa oil refinery, creating a joint venture with the Kalush refinery and planning to purchase 100 Ukraine petrol stations; the Tyumen Oil Company buying the Lysychansk oil refinery and a local television station; the metals conglomerate Russian Aluminium taking the Mykolaiv Aluminium Industrial Complex; Metalls Russia investing in the Donetsk Metallurgical Industrial Complex; the companies Alliance Group, Alfa Nafta and Tat Nafta taking part in the privatisation of the Kherson, Nadvirna and Kremenchuk refineries respectively.[27]

> The (Ukrainian) oligarchs do not need the West. They do not need it in terms of economics as the overwhelming majority of money making schemes is based on the Russian economic sphere ... [The Ukrainian oligarchs are] just mediators for Russian capital in Ukraine. Take all the recent examples of the Russian privatising Ukrainian companies — you will see traces of the lobbyists from the President's entourage everywhere.[28]

Two countervailing tendencies to Ukraine's drift into a Russian orientation should be noted here. There was an agreement between

---

27 *Ukraina moloda*, 21 February 2001; *Baltimore Sun*, 29 April 200;, *Moscow Interfax*, 12 February 2001,; Centre for Peace, Conversion and Foreign Policy of Ukraine, *Occasional Report*, No. 7, 2001, 5.

28 *Zerkalo nedeli*, 14 April 2001. "Prior to President Putin's visit to Kyiv on 15–16 April [2000] Russia published a list of 30 Ukrainian enterprises of interest to Russian entrepreneurs"; James Sherr, *op. cit.*, 12.

the two countries in 1994 quite similar to the gas debt for transit assets deal signed by Putin and Kuchma in December 2000. And it was rejected by the Verkhovna Rada as too damaging to Ukraine's strategic interests.[29] Ukrainian diplomats have said privately that agreements are initialled by the executive in the knowledge that the legislature will get them off the hook. Secondly, there was from early 2001, possibly earlier, quite sustained pressure from the EU and the United States upon Ukraine to keep its Western orientation.[30] Yet are these tendencies sufficient to keep Ukraine looking westwards, given the important changes that have occurred in the overall international environment under Putin's leadership? Russia has embarked upon a more calculated reclamation of its sphere of influence in the former Soviet area. Ukraine's room for economic manoeuvre vis a vis Russia has been eroded severely by the size of its debt for Russian gas and the imposition of trade tariffs and quotas by Russia, the EU and the USA. Ukraine's international reputation is damaged by the Gongadze affair and the Melnychenko tape scandal. Ukraine's relations with Central European countries are stagnant, with the exception of Poland which may also follow suit if a centre-left government is elected at the end of 2001. Its relations with the EU and the Council of Europe are at their lowest point ever. The controversy over the US National Missile Defense project threatens to create an additional platform on which Russia and Ukraine could be driven together.[31] EU President Romano Prodi

---

29   D'Anieri, *op. cit.*, 614–15.
30   *Interfax Moscow*, 12 February 2001.
31   "Russia's strategic priority: building allied relations with Ukraine", *Moscow Interfax* 14 May 2001, in which Russian Deputy Foreign Minister Valerii Loshchinin is quoted: "Moscow and Kyiv first of all have similar views on strategic deterrence issues and in support of the 1972 ABM Treaty". Serhii Kichinin, editor of the Kyiv publication *2000*, wrote on 11 May 2001 that US officials are seeking ways to immobilise President Kuchma in order to prevent him giving Russia access to the production facilities of Pivdennmash, the rocket building complex once managed by Kuchma, which are crucial for Russia's response to the US National Missile Defense plans. "Without Ukraine's rocket plants, Russia would lag far behind the United States".

has tried to reassure Ukraine that it matters to the West.[32] But it remains to be seen whether Ukraine will maintain a pro-European or Euroatlantic orientation as an alternative to Russia, whether it will pursue the same orientation by means that are co-ordinated with Russia or whether it will drift from its pro-Western course to align with Russian foreign policy moves.

And the beginning of a new phase in Russia-Ukraine-EU relations?

We are still too close to the edge of the developments described above to draw firm conclusions about what has actually changed in a lasting way in Russian-Ukrainian relations and their implications for both countries' relations with the European Union. The long standoff marked by Ukraine's resistance to Russia's advances, its orientation towards NATO and intention to seek integration with the EU regardless of Russia's interests in European integration seems to have ended. The meaning of the agreements that were signed between December 2000 and February 2001 are still being contested by Ukrainian, Russian and American representatives. However, the parlous state of the Ukrainian economy, its wounded President and divided political elite means that the country at this point in time is even less able to influence the terms of its engagement with eastern or western powers than it ever was in the ten years of its independence.

One can hypothesise about the likely changes to the supranational dynamic between the east and west of Europe if these Russian-Ukrainian agreements are implemented. They may signal a fundamental shift in the balance of forces in Eastern Europe in favour of Russia, which is moving more decisively westward into Ukraine both in economic and military-strategic terms. Further, Russia now has a grip on key sectors of the Ukrainian economy and a strong chance to take control of its gas transportation network

---

32   Goran Persson and Romano Prodi "Ukraine's progress should be a priority for all of Europe", *International Herald Tribune*, 22 May 2001.

from the Russian border to Central Europe. If it succeeds in consolidating its advantage, Russian national corporations in the fuel, energy, metallurgical, chemical, transportation, military and other sectors will build upon the Ukrainian industrial capacities they take over and will aspire either to compete or co-operate more boldly with Western transnational giants.

For EU-Russia relations these changes may stimulate a more rapid and profound implementation of the PCA and other agreements in the fuel and energy sector, and the upgrading of the existing gas, oil and electricity transmission networks into a transcontinental energy superhighway. Russian and Central Asian fuels will flow west while European technique will go east to ensure they flow west faster. Such a development could combine the technological capacities of Western Europe with the resource rich terrain of Russia, mediated by Ukraine's transit, storage and refining capacities. An EU-Ukraine-Russia alliance built on the gas for technology trade would naturally strengthen the bargaining power of the EU (and its most powerful member states) with the Unites States of America. It could conceivably put the USA and the EU in conflict with each other over their relations with the Russian Federation and possibly as well over the exploitation of gas and oil reserves of the Caspian Sea region. That depends on whether the United States continues to see Russia as its rival. Such possible developments in the near future would be predicated also on Ukraine coming to long term agreements with both Russia and the European Union about the development of the gas-technology corridor which preserve its sovereignty and lead to productive interdependence with both sides.

The European Union's Perspective on the Ukrainian-Russian Border*

Looking through the publicly available documents of the European Union I have not been able to locate a policy statement that explicitly addresses the Ukrainian-Russian border. However, what happens on this border is of considerable interest to the European Union, and that interest can be discerned in the EU's Common Strategy on Ukraine, its Common Strategy on Russia, its programme of Technical Assistance to the Commonwealth of Independent States, the EU's New Neighbourhood policy and the emerging EU Common Immigration and Asylum Policy. One issue above all stands out in these documents that motivates the EU's interest in the Ukrainian-Russian border: the migration of people from east to west. This issue has preoccupied EU decision makers for several years, but it has become more urgent since the EU's enlargement in May 2004, when eight new member states from East Central Europe and the Baltic littoral joined (alongside Malta and Cyprus). The European Union now shares a common border of more than 5,000 kilometres with Belarus, Moldova, Russia and Ukraine.[1] EU enlargement has concentrated the minds of its decision makers on the need to work more closely with Russia and Ukraine in order to stem the tide of migration pressing on the eastern borders of the EU. What happens to migrants and refugees at the Russian-Ukrainian border is therefore an important concern of the European Union.

Migration and settlement

The overland migration path across the northern tier states of Eurasia has become the principal contemporary route for migrants and

---

*   First published in: *Eurozine*, 12 January 2005; https://www.eurozine.com/the-european-union¹s-perspectives-on-the-ukrainian-russian-border/

1   Jacek Cichocki, "Direct Neighbourhood: Border issues and visa regulations — An Eastern Perspective"; in Iris Kempe, ed., *Beyond EU Enlargement, Vol. One: The Agenda of Direct Neighbourhood for Eastern Europe* (Gutersloh: Bertelsmann Foundation Publishers, 2001), 166.

refugees coming into Europe. The path brings together people emigrating from China, South East and South West Asia, the Middle East and even Africa who move into the Central Asian states and the Russian Federation, and then on to Belarus, Ukraine and Moldova. The great majority of migrants entering Ukraine come over the border from the Russian Federation, the remainder by air and sea directly into Ukraine from their homelands or from other, third countries. These migrants from "the far abroad" are joined on the territory of the Former Soviet Union by migrants from that territory itself — Central Asian peoples, Russians, Ukrainians and others — who are also emigrating and going westward. The biggest crossing point into Central Europe for this stream of migrants is the Ukrainian western border adjoining three states that joined the European Union in May: Hungary, Slovakia and Poland, and a fourth — Romania — which will join the EU in the next wave of enlargement around 2007.

It is, of course, difficult to make precise estimates of the numbers of people involved in this ongoing migration. However, the available evidence suggests that at the present time the numbers of unregistered migrants who are either settled or still in transit across the continent are distributed thus: approximately 2–3 million people are in the Russian Federation, one million are in Ukraine, Belarus and Moldova, and about as many again are in the Central European countries. The International Organisation on Migration estimated in 2000 that there were approximately one half million migrants trying to enter the EU each year. Of this number, the great majority would be coming into the EU over the east-west path, as opposed to the south-north path out of Africa, or the considerably smaller path from Latin America.[2]

In addition to this large, long distance westward stream of migrants and refugees, there are important migration streams over

<hr>

2   Barbara Lippert, "Border Issues and Visa Regulation: Political-Economic and Social Implications — A Western Perspective" in Kempe, *op. cit.*, 182–3; Oleksandr Pavliuk in Kempe, *op. cit.*, p. 77; EU Commission, TACIS Regional Cooperation, *Strategic Considerations 2002–2006 and National Indicative Programme 2002–2003*, 27 December 200., 20; Lily Hyde, "Endless Journey", *New Internationalist* No. 335, June 2001; *Zerkalo nedeli*, 13–19 October 2001.

shorter distances, as well as recurrent migrations for seasonal labour or trade whose numbers and directions of movement are determined by changing regional disparities in the costs of labour and commodities. In the late 1980s and early 1990s participants in the very widespread suitcase and shuttle trade across the entire region from China to Central Europe and the Middle East were the first to familiarise themselves and their home communities with the opportunities for seasonal and even permanent labour migration. Labour migration became an increasingly prevalent phenomenon during the 1990s as the economic crisis throughout the Former Soviet Union deepened. For the purposes of this discussion about the Ukrainian-Russian border, the most important of these regional migration streams to mention is the north-eastwards labour migration from Ukraine to Russia. It has been stimulated by the relatively higher wages available to Ukrainian workers in Russia and made easier by virtue of an estimated 40 percent of Ukrainians having relatives living in Russia. The number of Ukrainian migrant workers in Russia grew throughout the 1990s; the biggest centre of the migrant community being Moscow, where they work mainly in transport and construction and constitute about one third of the capital's total foreign workforce. Overall, there are more than one million migrant workers from the "near abroad" countries working in the Russian Federation, and half of these have come over the border from Ukraine.[3]

Inevitably a proportion of long distance migrants have settled down before reaching their intended destination. In doing so, often against their will, they have increased the migrant stock in the populations of the key transit countries. Similarly, the East Central European states that have joined the European Union have also become net recipient countries in their own right, with significant immigration from Ukraine, Russia, Belarus and Moldova. A majority of these migrants in Central Europe do not have legal status there.

---

3   N A Shul'ha, *Velikoe Pereselenie Narodov: repatriati, bezhentsi, trudovi migranti* (Kyiv: Natsional'na Akademiia Nayk Ukrainy Instytut Sotsiolohii, 2002), 280–295, 344.

As for the older member states of the European Union, the contribution of migrants from the east to their total populations over the past 15 years has not been as proportionately large as it has been for the Central and East European states. Two factors account for this: the much larger settled population of the pre-2004 European Union (295 m) than that of the accession states of East Central Europe and the Baltic littoral (100 m) and the increasingly effective controls employed by the European Union to keep out migrants.

The marked growth in migration across Eurasia since the late 1980s — long and short distance, seasonal and permanent, westward and eastward — has been attributed to several causes: the economic crises of the post-Soviet states since 1991 and violent conflicts in some of them; the civil and military conflicts in Sri Lanka, Kashmir, Afghanistan, Kurdistan, Iraq and in North Africa; and the regional financial crises that gripped East Asia in 1997 and spread into Russia and Ukraine in 1998, disrupting national economies and entire peoples' livelihood. However, it should also be noted that the unprecedented opening of borders after 1991, starting with the partial demilitarisation of the Russo-Chinese border in the east and ending with the opening of the borders between the former Soviet Union's territory and its former East Central European satellites in the west, allowed for an unprecedented freedom of movement of people. This was an undoubtedly positive development because it gave many people a better chance to escape poverty, repression and war, not to mention the new opportunities it provided for the economic regeneration of communities living in border regions.

Immigration policy, strategy and instruments of the European Union

The reaction of the publics and governments in Western Europe to the growth of immigration during the 1990s was increasingly negative. Far right movements, particularly in Austria, Holland, France and Britain heightened this anti-immigrant sentiment and exploited it politically. National governments accommodated to the rightward shift and the European Union followed in their wake. The Amsterdam Treaty signed in 1997 by the EU member states stipulated that the Union should have in place a Common Immigration and Asylum Policy by May 2004. EU leading bodies have responded by creating tougher immigration controls at the borders of the EU and promoting closer co-operation between EU member states in matters of intelligence gathering, detention and deportation of unregistered migrants and the sharing of costs of dealing with refugees and asylum seekers. EU northern states like Britain, Germany, Holland and France have employed additional immigration controls of their own. On the other hand, southern member states like Greece, Italy, Spain and Portugal have periodically relaxed their immigration laws through amnesties and given legal status to unregistered migrant workers, while still relying upon EU policies and resources to prevent further, unwanted immigration. The general policy of the European Union with respect to immigration has become a policy of exclusion at its borders and the repatriation of unregistered migrants who are apprehended by the authorities inside the member states.

In addition to consolidating this anti-immigrant regime at its borders and on the territory of the member states, the European Union has since 1999 taken important steps to externalise its immigration policy and so to create new lines of defense well beyond its existing borders against the east-west and south-north migration streams. European Council meetings of heads of state and the Justice and Home Affairs Council meetings of ministerial representatives have addressed the need to take action in third countries beyond the expanded European Union in order to meet the EU's own immigration policy objectives. In the period from the 1999 to 2002, these bodies have developed a strategy to combat "illegal" or "irregular" immigration at its sources:

- by attempting to address in a comprehensive way through a variety of aid programmes the root causes of migration, which are identified as poverty, state institutional fragility and political instability in the countries of origin and transit;
- by identifying the key migrating groups (national, social, gender, etc.), their informal networks and organising

agents and the geographic routes of migration into the European Union;

- by gaining the co-operation of third countries in a set of joint programmes and measures designed to prevent migration to the European Union,
- by making the provision of EU aid programmes to third countries conditional upon their full co-operation in reducing migration to the EU. Those countries that do not meet the EU's demands would see their aid and trade agreements with the Union reassessed.[4]

The EU sought the co-operation of the Ukrainian and Russian governments in three principal areas. First, in its Country Strategy Paper for Ukraine for the period 2002–2006 the EU Commission stated that Ukraine should be able to effectively control and monitor all its borders, including those with Russia, Belarus and Moldova, and that the EU was prepared to provide technical assistance to help it do so.[5] Under the TACIS Regional Co-operation Programme, released in parallel with the above strategy document, the EU set out the overall task of creating "a comprehensive migration, asylum and border management system" for the whole region on the basis of national programmes and through enhanced co-operation between the relevant ministries, law enforcement agencies and border guards of Russia, Ukraine, other states of the region and EU bodies. Assistance from the EU was to include "technical capabilities for executing border controls ... surveillance ... as well as apprehending illegal migrants and migrant smugglers".

---

4   The strategy and the measures to implement it are recorded in: Presidency Conclusions of the Cologne European Council, 4 June 1999; Presidency Conclusions of the Tampere European Council, 15–16 October 1999; Presidency Conclusions of the Helsinki European Council, 10–11 December 1999; "Proposal for a Comprehensive Plan to Combat Illegal Immigration and Trafficking in Human Beings in the European Union", Official Journal of the European Communities, 14 June 2002; Presidency Conclusions of the Seville European Council, 21–22 June 2002.

5   EU Commission, Country Strategy Paper 2002–2006; National Indicative Programme 2002–2003: Ukraine, 27 December 2001.

The EU also disclosed plans to station its own liaison officers at border crossings and embarkation points in third countries to check documents and work with local authorities to detect illegal immigrants. Such liaison officers already work at some embarkation points for large numbers of travellers to the EU. They are to be introduced soon into the Western Balkans and "the experience gained in the Balkans could be extended to include other regions of strategic interest to the European Union".[6]

Furthermore, the TACIS programme aimed to improve the capacities of Ukraine, Belarus and Moldova, but not Russia, to accept greater numbers of asylum seekers by improving the legislation governing asylum claims, by training the relevant officials in asylum related matters and helping to establish asylum reception centres. The authors of the TACIS Regional Co-operation Programme concluded that, just as "financial assistance is given to the accession candidates and to the relevant partner countries in order to strengthen the future EU external border" so too was "the complementary creation of further 'filters' in the East ... in the interest both of the EU and the partner states since these are increasingly confronted with the phenomenon and the problems of illegal migration". Such filters, they noted in passing, were also to be created in the Caucasus and in Central Asia.[7]

Second, co-operation between Europol and the police and intelligence forces of third countries was to be stepped up in an effort to create an "early warning system ... to provide immediate information on first indications of illegal migration and facilitator networks, particularly in the countries in which migration operates".[8] The Common Strategy on Russia agreed by the Cologne European Council in June 1999 envisages "co-operation with Europol ... for improving the fight against illicit trafficking in human beings and

---

6   "Proposal for a Comprehensive Plan to Combat Illegal Immigration".
7   EU Commission, TACIS Regional Co-operation: Strategic Considerations 2002–2006 and National Indicative Programme 2002–2003, 27 December 2001, 20.
8   218th Council Meeting on Justice and Home Affairs, Brussels, 27–28 May 1999.

drugs as well as immigrant smuggling".[9] Similarly the EU's Common Strategy on Ukraine, adopted six months later at Helsinki, calls for co-operation between EU member states' law enforcement agencies, Europol and Ukrainian law enforcement agencies.[10] Such co-operation presumably includes contribution to and some degree of sharing of the Eurodac database of fingerprints taken from asylum seekers and illegal immigrants moving across borders towards the EU.[11]

Finally, the EU has been pressing for the conclusion of readmission agreements with Russia and Ukraine that will require the latter states to accept without delay all of their nationals as well as stateless persons and nationals of other countries who have resided on or passed through their territories and who are expelled from the territory of the European Union for reasons of unlawful entry or rejection of claim for asylum. The EU's 1999 Common Strategies on both Russia and Ukraine spelled out the need to improve co-operation regarding readmission of all categories of expelled people mentioned above. This was re-iterated in the Final Joint Statement of the EU-Russia summit of 3 October 2001.[12] The EU made repeated diplomatic contact with Russian officials to conclude a readmission agreement, but apparently got no formal response. EU officials sent Ukrainian representatives the text of such an agreement in April 2002 and formal negotiations started in November of that year.[13]

However, the EU-Ukraine summits at Yalta in October 2003 and The Hague in July 2004 revealed no substantial progress on this issue. The situation with Ukraine appeared more hopeful for the

---

9   "Common Strategy on Russia", Presidency Conclusions of the Cologne European Council, 4 June 1999.
10   "Common Strategy on Ukraine", Presidency Conclusions of the Helsinki European Council, 10–11 December 1999.
11   The extension of the Eurodac system to hold fingerprints of apprehended immigrants was approved by the 218th Meeting of the Council on Justice and Home Affairs, Brussels, 27–28 May 1999.
12   Press Release of the Belgian EU Presidency, Brussels, 3 October 2001.
13   Statewatch Report and Analysis; http://www.sdtatewatch.org/news/2002/nov/14safe.htm. Accessed 3 October 2001.

EU than with Russia insofar as Ukraine already has readmission agreements with Hungary, Moldova, Poland and the Slovak Republic. It has signed agreements waiting to be ratified with Bulgaria and Latvia, and has draft agreements under negotiation with the Czech Republic and Romania.[14] This affords the EU some recourse to the bilateral agreements of its member states to protect its eastern flank, but it does not cover all the EU member states to which immigrants manage to arrive from the east. Yet both Russia and Ukraine, it would seem, have been reluctant to conclude this type of agreement directly with the EU.

Meanwhile, the EU has moved ahead in its long-term planning: it is prepared to finance the establishment of reception centres for people sent back to third countries such as Ukraine and Russia, as well as asylum reception centres in Ukraine. The European Council has already approved the forcible as well as voluntary return of expelled people, and it can rely on specialist agencies such as the International Organisation on Migration to organise and supervise their repatriation on a large scale. The June 2002 Seville European Council expressed the EU's desire to return illegal migrants and rejected asylum seekers to their countries of origin more quickly and called for the "speeding up of the conclusion of readmission agreements currently being negotiated … [and the] adoption of a repatriation programme … by the end of the year".[15]

The proposal to establish reception centres for migrants and asylum seekers in countries across the border from EU member states, first advanced in 2002 by British representatives at Seville, proved to be highly controversial. It was opposed by other EU member states as well as a wide array of non-governmental organisations. As a result the idea was temporarily shelved, only to be revived in 2004 on the argument that such centres could prevent the deaths of many migrants and asylum seekers from Africa who were drowning in the Mediterranean Sea while trying to cross into southern Europe. Tunisia was mentioned as the location for the first

14 US Committee on Refugees, Country Report: Ukraine, 2002; http://www.refug ees.org/world/countryrpt/europe/ukraine.htm. Accessed 15 July 2002.
15 Presidency Conclusions of the Seville European Council, 21–22 June 2002.

such reception centre. Yet the proposal continued to attract widespread hostility and accusations that the EU was really trying to save itself a lot of money and at the same time absolve itself of its international responsibilities of protection and asylum.

The IOM and the EU on the Ukrainian-Russian border

The IOM was founded in 1951 on the initiative of the USA and Belgium under the name of the Provisional Intergovernmental Committee for the Movement of Migrants from Europe. In 1989 it was renamed the IOM. With 79 member states, 43 observer states and several multilateral organisations like the United Nations, the International Labour Organisation and the European Bank for Reconstruction and Development in its ranks, the IOM has become a special service advising and supporting Western governments in the control of international migration, notably by the establishment and maintenance of effective border regimes. To that end the IOM assisted the Central and East European countries acceding to the EU in 2004 to adopt the EU's framework legislation (the *acquis communautaire*) through an EU-funded PHARE project entitled "Migration, Visa and External Border Control Management". In Kosovo the IOM has fulfilled the role of an EU protectorate authority by providing support to border police and immigration authorities. In year 2000 the IOM organised for the EU member states 87,628 "voluntary returns" of apprehended migrants and rejected asylum seekers. At the 223rd Council Meeting on Justice and Home Affairs in Luxembourg, the EU's strategic planning body, the High Level Working Group on Asylum and Migration, noted the "excellent cooperation" it received from the IOM.[16]

In May 1999, following extensive consultations with the IOM, the Ukrainian Cabinet of Ministers agreed to the establishment of a

---

16   Final Report of the High level Group on Asylum and Migration, 223rd Council Meeting on Justice and Home Affairs, Luxembourg, 4 October 1999; *Statewatch Report and Analysis*, Anti-Racism Office, Bremen, "Papers for Everyone"; www.is-bremen.de/asab/Documents percent20fur percent20all.doc. Accessed 1 July 2002.

Capacity Building in Migration Management Programme (CBMMP), whose two principal aims were to harmonise and integrate Ukraine's migration policy and management system with those of its direct neighbours and of the EU, and to reduce illegal migration into and through Ukraine to Western Europe. Under the CBMMP in 1999 the IOM helped the Ukrainian government set up a demonstration project on its eastern border with Russia in the Kharkiv-Belgorod vicinity. This project involved the introduction of new border detection, control and information devices, including long range infrared monitors, motion and carbon dioxide detectors and equipment to detect document fraud. In addition, the IOM planned to help the Ukrainian government establish the capacity for detention and deportation of illegal migrants.[17]

Commenting on their early successes, IOM Kyiv Mission Chief Steve Cook noted: "that sector of the border, previously the most heavily travelled by illegal migrants, has been basically shut down ... that's what we wanted to demonstrate, and as a result we've got sufficient donor funds to develop another project on the Ukrainian-Belarusian border".[18]

The IOM did organise a second demonstration project on the Ukrainian-Belarusian border. Then it set out "to initiate work with Russian authorities, to introduce cross border elements, including shared command posts and communications infrastructure, and co-ordinated deployment of patrols. This will require the establishment of parallel inter-ministerial structures on the Russian side".[19]

This initiative also met with success and in November 2000 representatives of the Ukrainian and Russian governments toured the facilities on both sides of their common border and agreed on a set of objectives for its further improvement: a shared database about violators of the border; co-operation between central executive organs; and co-operation at the operational level in law enforcement. Reporting on these developments, the IOM foresaw the

---

17   http://www.iom.int/austria/tcc/htmlfiles/Ukraine.htm. Accessed 1 July 2002.
18   http://www.noborder.org/iom/display.php?id-155. Accessed 15 June 2002.
19   http://www.iom.int/austria/tcc/htmlfiles/Ukraine.htm. Accessed 1 July 2002.

next step being a memorandum of understanding between the two governments so that the actual work could go ahead.[20]

In February 2001 the IOM Kyiv Mission launched an EU-funded project "that will take counter-trafficking measures in Ukraine to a new and more comprehensive level by reinforcing prevention activities, promoting further criminalisation of trafficking and strengthening the national capacity to provide protection ... to victims". In addition to the IOM, the Organisation for Security and Co-operation in Europe, La Strada and the Office of the Ombudsman of Ukraine were actively involved. The IOM reported in 2002 that it had financing for its counter-trafficking work from another source as well: the Swedish International Development Co-operation Agency.[21]

Indeed, as the 2004 accession loomed ever closer, the European Union stepped up its efforts to establish a critical mass of programmes, agencies and resources to assist the Ukrainian government, among others, to relieve the new EU border of excessive migration pressure. The control of migration became a centrepiece of the newly declared EU New Neighbourhood programme, which codified EU policy priorities towards states excluded from EU accession in the foreseeable future. A "Soderkoping Process" was launched, an inter-agency initiative of the United Nations Human Rights Commission, the European Commission and the Swedish Migration Board to foster cross border co-operation on migration and asylum between EU member states on the one side and Ukraine, Belarus and Moldova on the other. This Process finances regular meetings of senior officials of all participating states. Furthermore, the EU agreed an Action Plan on Justice and Home Affairs with the Ukrainian government, that drew up priority targets to be monitored by way of a scoreboard and that included the elu-

---

20   "IOM in Ukraine: Border Management", *IOM in Eastern Europe and Central Asia*, No. 2, January–March 2001.

21   *IOM in Eastern Europe and Central Asia*, No. 2, January–March 2001 and No. 6, January–March 2002.

sive readmission agreement and effective migration border management.[22] In February 2004 the IOM announced further funding had been secured to combat human trafficking in Ukraine within the framework of the EU's Action Plan.[23]

Do Ukraine and Russia agree with the EU's objectives?

The most striking feature of these developments is the boldness and determination of the EU to reorganise and reinforce borders that it does not share in the pursuit of its own immigration objectives. The EU can behave in this way because it has considerable economic power, which it asserts over neighbouring countries through the conditions it attaches to aid, trade and other interactions with them. That it feels legitimate and comfortable in designing and supporting such interventions as the IOM's on the Ukrainian Russian border testifies to the profound transformation of development aid in the hands of the core western states. They are far more prescriptive and comprehensive about the changes they expect in exchange for the aid they provide than they were during the Cold War.

However greater the persuasive powers of the European Union may be today upon the successor states of the USSR, the effectiveness of its drive to refashion the Ukrainian-Russian border must certainly depend upon whether its objectives coincide with the objectives either of the Ukrainian or of the Russian government or of both of them.

Strengthening the EU's new external border and its Central-East European interior against the unlawful entry of migrants has automatically reverberated eastwards onto the states across whose territories these migrants tread on their way to the EU. Those who manage to cross Ukraine's western borders without visas into countries with whom Ukraine has readmission agreements are sent back

---

22   EU Commission, Commission Staff Working Paper SEC (2004) 566: *European neighbourhood Policy Country Report on Ukraine*; Brussels, 12 May 2004.
23   IOM press release 11 May 2004.

to Ukraine if they are apprehended. Should Ukraine sign readmission agreements with the EU, then the numbers of such apprehended people who are sent back to Ukraine will grow even more.

This situation evokes different reactions among Ukrainian leaders and senior officials. One kind of reaction is anger at the European Union for effectively making Ukraine (and Belarus, one should add) the EU's dumping ground of expelled migrants and rejected asylum seekers.[24] Another reaction, of course, is to fall in line with the EU's strategy and to erect stronger barriers on Ukraine's eastern borders in order to prevent migrants and refugees from entering the country.[25] Still another reaction is to accept the need for a tighter Ukrainian-Russian border, but at the same time to criticise the European Union for not doing enough to assist the Ukrainian government to create it or to meet the costs of holding and repatriating failed migrants and asylum seekers who are not Ukrainian nationals but have been sent back into Ukraine by EU states.

Ukrainian state officials continue to insist that they do not have sufficient funds to hold apprehended migrants and refugees for any length of time or to deport them to their home countries. This is the reason why the Ukrainian government is unwilling to conclude a readmission agreement with the European Union and why the latter is offering to help defray the Ukrainian government's costs. According to Hennadii Moskal, head of the State Committee for Nationalities and Migration, the Ukrainian government had not received any EU funds as of May 2004 to defray such costs, and that the funds provided by the EU to strengthen Ukraine's border with Russia are inadequate. Moskal goes on to argue that the EU should be deporting such people directly to Russia because "one hundred percent of all illegal migrants come to us from Russia".[26]

---

24   "Hennadii Udovenko made a statement last week saying that Ukraine should close its eastern borders and open its western borders so that illegal immigrants flowing from Afghanistan did not accumulate in Ukraine but go further West 'Let self-satisfied Europe feel what illegal immigration is like for itself'". *Zerkalo nedeli*, 13–19 October 2001.

25   *Den'*, 16 February 2001; *Zerkalo nedeli*, 13–19 October 2001.

26   BBC Monitoring Service 15 April 2004, citing an interview with Moskal by Iryna Nykypelova on the website *Glavred*, 13 April 2004.

Although this is a slight exaggeration, Moskal is trying to emphasise the fact that Ukraine's strategy on the readmission issue is dependent upon Russia's. Were the Russian government to fall in line with the EU's strategy of reinforced filters across the East and readmission agreements between states, then it would considerably ease the worries of the Ukrainian authorities. But like the Ukrainian government itself, the Russian government is in no hurry to sign a readmission agreement either with the European Union or with Ukraine.[27] The reason for such a stance is probably the same as the reason of the Ukrainian government — they cannot afford to honour such an agreement.

These difficulties are compounded by another: the unwillingness of the Russian government to agree to demarcation with fences and observation posts of the full length of its common border with Ukraine. There has been some progress on this issue since the collapse of the Soviet Union, when the border was an internal, inter-republican one, not an international one. Russia and Ukraine delimited their common border on maps in 1997. In April 2004 the Ukrainian and Russian parliaments ratified an agreement which acknowledges the permanency of the border and which will regulate border crossings by private individuals and commercial entities.[28] From January 2005 citizens of Russia and Moldova will require foreign passports to cross into Ukraine.[29]

However, Russia's acceptance of an international boundary with Ukraine remains partial and is countermanded by other Russian state initiatives, such as the creation of the Single Economic Space, which call for more open borders in the interests of co-operation and long term integration. The Russian authorities have also cited popular concerns about the maintenance of cultural and family ties across this border as an important reason for keeping it open

---

27 *Zerkalo nedeli*, 13–19 October 2001.
28 *Radio Liberty/Radio Free Europe Report*, 21 April 2004.
29 This requirement was agreed in September 2004 at a meeting of the Heads of Consular Services of the Commonwealth of Independent States and, according to the website of the Mission of Ukraine to the European Communities. "It is correlated with the correspondent provision of the Implementation Scoreboard of the EU Action Plan on Justice and Home Affairs of Ukraine".

for the free movement of people. This is hardly a credible argument because, like the EU external border, the Ukrainian-Russian one is freer for some to cross than for others. The great majority of local people on both sides cross this border at the few manned crossing points that exist on the major roads, where their passage is made quite difficult by long queues, bureaucratic procedures and bribe taking. On the other hand, Ukrainian, Russian and EU intergovernmental efforts are directed to easing the blockages on the flow of goods, services and capital, not of ordinary people.

As for the long distance migrants and refugees, it is still along the minor roads and tracks through the open countryside that lies between these manned border crossing points that they are being transported without detection from Russia into Ukraine. As long as there is no meeting of minds between Ukraine, Russia and the EU on east-west migration, that will probably remain the case. The Russian authorities are not interested in arresting the migration flow out of their country and the Ukrainian authorities are for all intents and purposes helpless in preventing its influx into theirs. Inaction on both sides naturally places severe limits on any attempts by the EU to strengthen the border against westbound migration.

Conclusions

Migration along the east-west path into Europe is likely to remain substantial in coming years for so long as civil and military conflicts continue to erupt east and south of the former Soviet Union's territory and the majority of people living in countries of the former Soviet Union remain substantially poorer than people in Central and Western Europe. In the face of this migration, but equally in response to the growth of racist, anti-immigrant sentiment in Europe, the EU appears determined to enforce a general policy of exclusion and to impose repatriation upon countries of origin and transit of migrants by making its aid to and trade with those countries conditional on their compliance.

The Ukrainian Russian border is a strategically important crossing point for east-west migration, and therefore it will preoccupy the EU until it is reinforced. The Russian and Ukrainian governments are in the process of resolving the status of this border in international law and for this reason their ability to contribute to the EU's objective of strengthening it is slowly improving. However, there does not appear to have been much progress in the negotiation of readmission agreements between the EU on one side and both Ukraine and Russia on the other, as well as between Russia and Ukraine.

The European Union's current policy on migration is consistent with its historical *raison d'être* to defend the common market of its member states, amongst other ways by regulating the movement of labour into its territory. The EU's policy to severely limit the numbers of incoming migrants leaves its member states free to devise their own selective recruitment and registration of foreign workers in order to fill critical labour shortages. However, a certain proportion of unregistered migrants within the EU is tolerated, in fact deemed necessary. Unregistered migrants work in the lowest status occupations for very low wages, thereby contributing directly to a higher rate of profit for employers and to a higher standard of living for the rest of the workforce. They have become all the more needed as the EU's population ages, as the proportion of its working age people diminishes and as the burden grows upon the national systems of social security. The objective impact of the threat of repatriation is to reduce the capacity of those migrants who are not apprehended and deported to win social and political rights, including the right to a minimum wage.

What can be done to resolve the knot of problems arising out of the EU's response to inward migration, and specifically the outward projection of its policy of exclusion to Ukraine, Russia and their common border? I have deliberately put the question in such a way so as to emphasise the point that migration in and of itself is not the main problem. Migration is a permanent feature of human history, a recurrent response to threats and opportunities which present themselves to individuals, communities and sometimes entire nations. Certainly, the movement of many people over large distances in search of work and refuge creates its own massive problems and challenges for both migrants and host societies. However, the way that the richer countries have responded to the flight of people out of the poorer and destabilised countries has aggravated the plight of migrants and made it even more difficult for transit countries and countries of destination to receive and help settle them, or indeed to benefit from them.

First, the criminalisation of the act of migration and the associated criminalisation of whole migrant communities in the public discourse should be vigorously opposed. It has become commonplace throughout Europe, east and west, to utter the words "illegal migration" as though they are one, as though migration is never anything but an illegal act. The principal beneficiaries of this turn of affairs are in fact the organised gangs of people smugglers, their associates in positions of state authority and the providers of informal employment to whom migrants must now turn to help them to cross borders and find employment.

Second, the states of Russia, Ukraine, Belarus and Moldova should be working together to secure a new collective agreement on migration with the European Union and to make their participation in the maintenance of their 5,000 km long common border with the EU conditional upon such an agreement. It should include the following terms:

- the legalisation of all unregistered resident migrants in the EU member states and in the states of Russia, Ukraine, Belarus and Moldova;
- an organised programme of legal migration to the EU from Russia, Ukraine, Belarus and Moldova, the annual numbers of migrants and duration of stay in the EU to be negotiated on a periodic basis;
- an equitable agreement on sharing the costs of caring for refugees, regardless of where they currently reside; the proportional burden to be determined by each country's per capita GDP.

The need for such a comprehensive collective agreement should be raised by the Ukrainian and Russian heads of state at their next respective summits with EU leaders.

Trade, Investment and Debt: Ukraine's Integration into World Markets*

The past ten years have seen the renewed development of capitalism in the countries of Central and Eastern Europe, Central Asia and Transcaucasia, and their steady integration into world markets. It still remains unclear where all the individual states that emerged in the wake of the collapse of the Soviet bloc will eventually settle in the hierarchy of the world capitalist order. And how they will become grouped into regional markets and security regimes on the continent of Europe and Asia. The countries of Central Europe are now moving rapidly towards integration with the single market of the European Union and the NATO security regime. Countries east of Central Europe face greater uncertainty. The Russian Federation attempted unsuccessfully in the 1990s to regroup the ex-Soviet area into a new supranational economic and security order on the basis of the Commonwealth of Independent States (CIS). More recently, the prospects for regional economic integration of the ex-Soviet area around the transcontinental fuel and energy trade have been heightened by the push of Western finance and the projection of American military power eastward into the Central Asian states. The Western states view their oil and gas reserves as a promising supplement to, and even a replacement of, the Middle East's supply. However, important questions remain unanswered: will long-standing Russian interests in Central Asia clash with those of the Euroatlantic states? And will the USA and the West European states co-operate or compete with one another in furthering the integration of this region with the Western centred order?

This article examines the recent entry and insertion, the "push and pull" of the second largest Eastern European state into world markets and explores the competing alternatives for its integration

---

* First published in: Neil Robinson, ed., *Reforging the Weakest Link: Global Political Economy and Post-Soviet Change in Russia, Ukraine and Belarus* (Aldershot: Ashgate, 2004), 46–60.

197

into a broader economic region in the future. One side of the renewed development of capitalism in Ukraine concerns the domestic process, which I have examined in a separate article.[1] The peculiar features of Ukrainian "oligarchic capitalism" naturally influence the way that its national market and domestic capitals have been built. The reverse side of this process is the direct impact of external markets and capitals upon the national economy and the nation state, which is the focus of this article.

The state and capitalist development in Ukraine

Until the last decade of the twentieth century, a Ukrainian state had made only two brief appearances on the world map—once in the latter half of the seventeenth century and once again in fits and starts during the years of war and revolution from 1917–1920. It hardly played much of a role in the development of capitalism in Ukraine or influenced this country's place in the international division of labour. It is significant that the year 1648 marked both the birth of the contemporary interstate system and the beginning of the first failed attempt in the modern era to establish an independent state centred in Kyiv. The Ukrainian Hetman state, created in 1648 in the midst of an anti-feudal peasant war against the Polish nobility, sought lasting protection against Poland from the Russian autocracy in 1654. Russia, however, eclipsed the Polish-Lithuanian Commonwealth and absorbed the Hetman state completely by the end of the seventeenth century, reducing it in status to a set of ordinary provinces. The erosion and loss of its national political autonomy coincided with the ending of the first major phase in Ukraine of wage labour, commodity production and long distance trade with Western Europe. These shoots of capitalist development had appeared in the early seventeenth century and had contributed to the social and national conflicts provoking the 1648 war. But they were destroyed as the greater part of Ukraine was absorbed into the

---

1   "The Ukrainian economy since independence", *Working Papers in Ukrainian Studies*, No. 1, May 1999 (London: University of North London Ukraine Centre).

Russian Empire, which had codified serfdom in 1648 and would retain it until 1861.

The second major phase of capitalist development took place in the late nineteenth and early twentieth centuries when Western finance and the Russian state jointly undertook industrialisation and the commercialisation of agriculture in the Ukrainian provinces of the Russian Empire. The absence in this period of a Ukrainian state, and indeed the relative weakness of the Russian state among the Great Powers, marked this phase of capitalism with the features of dependency: the expatriation of surpluses, underdeveloped end product and consumer goods industries, land hunger and weak domestic demand. Nevertheless, the joint effort of Western finance capital and the Russian state in these four odd decades before the First World War to invest in and build an industrial sector and commercial agricultural sector meant that Ukraine became one of the six, and arguably the most dynamic, centres of capitalist development in the Russian Empire. This placed it firmly into the semi-periphery of the evolving world capitalist economy at the beginning of the twentieth century, albeit as part of a multinational and imperial Russian state.[2]

The present, third phase of capitalist development in Ukraine is occurring in the presence of a nation state. However, the Ukrainian state, beginning as a territorial administrative division of the Soviet state, is at a fairly nascent stage of institutional development, and the economic crisis of the 1990s has retarded that development. Moreover, throughout much of the 1990s the state leadership progressively withdrew both from state ownership and from state regulation of the economy. In effect, the Ukrainian elite divided functionally into political, state-administrative and economic branches; economic activity acquired an autonomy from state regulation that was unprecedented since the 1920s.

At the same time the nascent Ukrainian state has already made a number of important contributions to the redevelopment of capi-

---

2   Marko Bojcun, "The Working Class and the National Question in Ukraine; 1880–1920", (PhD dissertation, York University, 1985), Chapter One.

talism in its territory. It has established the infrastructure of a national market (securing borders, creating the national currency, regulating imports and exports, licensing) and increasingly it has elaborated a national economic strategy of recovery and competitiveness in the global economy. The most ambitious national strategy was elaborated in the programme of the President's Administration in February 2000, entitled "Ukraine: Progress in the 21st Century".[3]

Despite all its institutional weaknesses and lack of resources in dealing with the social costs of moving to a market economy, the state played an influential role in fostering the private accumulation of capital by the five or six oligarchic formations that today dominate Ukrainian industry, trade and politics. These formations, typically built on the super profits accruing from trade in Russian and Central Asian oil and gas in the mid-1990s, which they later invested into domestic production, mass media outlets and political parties, depended upon various state institutions for their growth all along the way: to gain access to state procured energy carriers and state transit facilities, to win licences and contracts to trade aboard, to guarantee their loans and pay their debts, to privatise nationalised assets and to expatriate capital for safe-keeping abroad. Indeed, by the end of the 1990s, the erratic wavering of Ukrainian foreign policy between Russia and the Euroatlantic states could be attributed largely to the tensions between a section of the state elite that still hoped for Western/European integration and that section which was now a captive of Ukrainian businesses tied to the operations of much bigger, Russian businesses.

Finally, the new Ukrainian state appeared on the map in 1991, precisely at a time when the room for manoeuvre of all but the most powerful states in the world was being hemmed in by the might of globally mobile finance and the International Financial Institutions. In addition to the traditional function of the state to project its national interests abroad, the state is obliged to mediate between the interests of foreign capital entering its territory and its own popu-

---

3   Poslannia Prezydenta Ukrainy do Verkhovnoi Rady (Epistle of the President of Ukraine to the Verkhovna Rada), No. 276a/2000, Kyiv 23 February 2000.

lation. The obligations assumed by the state in return for loans, foreign investment, economic assistance have had a direct bearing on the domestic economy and state social policies, as well as on the development of democratic institutions and practices. For Ukraine, such external pressures have had at least two important consequences. They have required the state to shift the burden of its foreign debts, state and corporate (because corporate debts were guaranteed by the state) onto the population at large, thus driving down their living standards. And they have fuelled the bitter infighting within the state—notably between President Kuchma and various anti-Kuchma coalitions since his re-election in 1999—which is a phenomenal form of the struggle between different oligarchic formations tied to competing external economic interests. Such fighting has spilled out from the inner sanctum of the state, resulting in the legal prosecution, physical intimidation and murder of political opponents and investigative journalists, and the mutation of the political process as a whole in an anti-democratic, authoritarian direction.[4]

The former Soviet bloc enters the world market

The Soviet bloc broke up at a historical point in time when the steadily growing volume of world economic output was outstripping the capacity of the world's population to pay for and consume this output. This disparity was caused by the unequal global redistribution of accumulating wealth, which left the poorer countries' people unable to meet their consumption needs while the banks and corporations of the rich countries were increasingly unable to find new opportunities for productive investment. The objective limitations on productive investment influenced how the core capitalist states, their banks and corporations would exploit the newly

---

4   Christopher Chase Dunn suggests that peripheral and semi-peripheral states are more likely than core states to become authoritarian because they are dependent on foreign capital, which in times of tension leads to the political exclusion, and possibly repression as well, of groups that oppose the priorities of foreign capital operating inside their country. See C. Chase Dunn, *Global Formation: Structures of the World-Economy* (Oxford: Blackwell, 1989), 123–124.

opening markets of the ex-Soviet area after the break-up of 1989–91. Essentially, these territories were to be exploited as new consumer markets to absorb existing production, as additional, possibly alternative, sources of fossil fuels and raw materials and as debt markets. With one significant exception they have not been considered by Western investors as a terrain of significant productive investment. That exception is the oil and gas fields of Central Asia and the pipelines – existing and yet to be built – delivering fuel to Western markets.

The economic division of labour and trading regime of the Soviet bloc in the form of Comecon did not survive the break-up of 1989–91. Each state, new and old, now bore liabilities in terms of incomplete production cycles and skewed economies from the perspective of their national-territorial coherence that could be overcome only by forging ties anew with other national and regional economies. Each state faced entry into the world capitalist economy on its own. The whole region experienced significant economic disruption and decline in the course of transition from the largely autarchic Comecon to the open seas of the world market.

The nature and extent of international assistance to the post-Soviet bloc countries have been quite different to the American assistance offered to Western Europe under the Marshall Plan after World War Two. The Marshall Plan extended a sum of assistance equivalent in current value to $75 bn, the bulk of which was spent in the first four years of the Plan. Total committed aid to the former Soviet Union under the EU's TACIS programme amounted to $3.7 bn for the whole of the 1990s. Total EU commitments under the PHARE programme to East Central Europe for the same period were $10 bn, but as of 1997 less than half had actually been spent. The Marshall Plan was driven by long term objectives of economic recovery of Western Europe, requiring its European participant states to rebuild a regionally integrated economy that was open to international trade.[5] With respect to the Central and Eastern Europe

---

5   Umberto Triulzi, "The Partnership and Co-operation Agreement: a New Marshall Plan?" Paper delivered to the European Commission Stagiaire Conference

in the past decade, the alliance of Western states has not sought their regional re-integration, but rather their rapid insertion individually into world commodity, capital and debt markets. The European Union has embraced the goal of integrating the Central European and Baltic Sea flank of post-communist states into its single market and political institutions. However, it has no agreed perspective on the long-term integration of the bulk of the ex-Soviet area, other than to create free trade areas with its individual states.

Foreign direct investment into the former Comecon countries of East Central Europe and the Soviet Union has been small, relative to the region's investment needs. The 26 states in question have a population of 400 million people and a combined GDP of some $1,000 bn. This amounts to around 3 percent of world economic output. Foreign direct investment into the region by 1997 had grown to $18 bn per annum, amounting to less than 2 percent of the region's GDP. The Central European states which were preparing to join the European Union were at the time drawing foreign investment equivalent to 3 percent of their GDPs, whereas the states of the former Soviet Union were drawing investment equivalent to 1 percent of their GDPs.[6]

The region of the former Comecon countries accounted for 10 percent of the value of world trade in 1970, declining to 2 percent by 1994. Although their share of world trade in fact peaked in the 1970s, the fall was most precipitous after the break-up of the Soviet bloc in 1989–91 when intraregional trade was severely disrupted, each country's foreign trade objectives were redefined and the proportion of manufactured goods in exports progressively diminished.[7]

A study by the International Monetary Fund provides other evidence of this region's downward movement through the world

"A New Iron Curtain? EU-Russia Relations in Focus", Brussels, 26 June 2000. Commission of the European Communities, *PHARE Programme Annual Report 1997*, Brussels, 1999; p. 26.

6   Hans Peter Lankes and Nicholas Stern, "Capital Flows to Eastern Europe and the Former Soviet Union", *EBRD Working Papers* No. 27, 1–6.

7   Oleksandr Rohach and Oleksandr Shnyrkov, *Transnatsionalizatsiia svitovoho hospodarstva ta perekhidni ekonomiky* (Kyiv: Kyivskyi Universytet, 1999), 134.

economic hierarchy. Table 3 below shows that living standards on the territory of the USSR rose in comparison to those of the economically most powerful nations throughout the twentieth century until 1973, but then fell back dramatically by year 2000. The factors leading to this comparative fall include both the economic crisis that enveloped the Soviet nationalised economy by the 1980s and the acceleration of that crisis in the period of denationalisation and transition to the market. East Central Europe exhibits a different pattern over the twentieth century, falling back further than the USSR as a result of the Depression and World War Two, recovering, but then showing the same tendency of decline by the end of the century.

Table 3:   Regional GDP per capita as a percentage of the "leading nation" (Great Britain in 1870 and 1900; USA in 1913 and thereafter).

	1870	1900	1913	1950	1973	2000
World average	27.4	27.5	29.0	22.3	24.8	21.9
Western Europe	64.7	67.3	69.8	53.5	74.0	74.0
Areas of recent European settlement: USA, Australia, Canada, New Zealand	74.8	87.6	98.7	96.7	96.8	96.5
Eastern Europe, excluding territory of USSR	35.9	5.1	38.2	23.9	30.9	13.3
Territory of USSR	31.4	26.5	28.0	29.6	36.5	16.6

Source: International Monetary Fund, World Economic Outlook 2000; Table 5.2.

United Nations statistics show that the economic output of the Soviet bloc slowed and then stagnated in the 1980s but contracted dramatically in the first half of the 1990s. At this point the former member states of Comecon parted ways: the CIS region's output continued to contract, albeit more slowly, in the latter half of the 1990s, whereas the Central East European region's output returned to positive growth rates. By contrast, total world output and trade, and the aggregate outputs both of developed and developing countries maintained overall positive annual growth rates throughout the 1980s and 1990s.[8]

Ukraine enters the world economy

Broadly speaking, Central Europe started to recover from the shock of the break-up and the economic slump of the early nineties more quickly than the former republics of the Soviet Union. Ukraine's economy went into precipitous decline in the early 1990s and continued to fall until the end of the decade, returning to positive growth rates only in 2000. A convincing explanation for the contrast in fortunes holds that "Association Agreements with the EU [by the Central European states, leading to their accession to the EU] have brought early benefits of market access and massive technical assistance".[9] Indeed, the IMF has predicted that the divergence in economic performance between those countries accepted for EU accession and those so far denied "appears likely to widen in the period ahead".[10] Insofar as the EU represents those European states with the greatest investment capital and most advanced technologies, entry onto the world market by way of close engagement with the EU is an attractive prospect for all the post-communist states of the region.

In 1991 the research division of Deutsche Bank released a study concluding that Ukraine had the best economic potential of all republics of the Soviet Union to make a successful transition to a market economy.[11] It compared favourably to the West European states in terms of its agricultural and heavy industrial per capita production as well as the level of education and training of its workforce. It possessed transit capacity from east to west for oil,

---

8   United Nations, *World Economic and Social Survey 1999* (New York, 1999); Tables 1.1 and A.3.

9   Lankes and Stern, *op. cit.*, 6.

10   IMF, *World Economic Outlook 2000*, 26.

11   Anatolii Halchynsky, *Ukraina: Postup u Maibutnie* (Kyiv: Osnovy, 1999), 38. Ukraine got 83 marks out of 100, the Baltic states 77, Russia 73, Belarus and Kazakhstan 55.

gas, electricity and telecommunications, power generation equipment plants, aeronautical and aerospace industries, a powerful arms industry, shipbuilding, precision instrumentation and an impressive network of research institutes. The country's productive capacity well exceeded domestic demand, which accounted for the high proportion of industries geared to export.[12]

However, these assets represented merely a significant potential to enter the world market on favourable terms, not its guarantee. In addition to coping with the unfavourable international economic conditions the realisation of this potential depended also upon the pursuit of appropriate strategies by the country's leadership. On this front, Ukraine possessed some obvious deficits. Historically, it had lost its best intellectual assets to Moscow and the central Russian or Soviet governments. The brain drain continued in the 1990s, but now in all directions and especially to the West. As mentioned above, a state-building experience was largely absent and the state institutional capacity of the ex-Soviet republic was sorely lacking. So although the new Ukrainian state under President Kravchuk was able to walk away from the USSR with a good portion of its armed forces (because they were held on Ukrainian territory), it did not manage to negotiate a division with Russia and other successor states of other important joint assets. For example, all USSR property abroad and the savings of all Ukrainian citizens in Oshchadbank USSR — totalling 84.3 bn roubles, or $150 bn at the prevailing rate of exchange — were lost to the Russian Federation.[13]

The lack of cohesion or discipline within the new Ukrainian elite was evident in the way its members used the institutions under their control to accumulate personal wealth at society's expense. By 1995 around one half of the country's GDP passed through the shadow economy, where the mechanisms exist to conceal, divert and expatriate wealth. According to the World Bank in 1999 the Ukrainian unofficial or shadow economy was proportionally larger than that of Lithuania, Russia, Poland or Romania.[14]

---

12   *Ibid.*, 38–45.
13   *Ibid.*, 45.
14   International Monetary Fund, Ukraine: *Recent Economic Developments*, Country Report No. 99/42, May 1999, Figure 1.

The brain drain, the weakness of elite cohesion and discipline and the lack of state and institution building experience all contribute in some way to explaining why it took the state leadership so long to elaborate a national strategy of domestic economic recovery and competitiveness on the world market. Ukraine was the last country in the entire region to introduce its own currency, the *sine qua non* of any national economic strategy — the *hryvnia* in September 1996. After following a monetarist programme of austerity and tight money supply in order to bring down inflation and achieve a measure of macroeconomic stability, the President's Administration under Leonid Kuchma began only in the late 1990s to depart from IMF neo-liberal orthodoxy and to develop an economic recovery programme of its own.[15]

Trade

An important component of this strategy concerns trade: repositioning Ukraine's technologically advanced sectors for more effective competition on the world market and prioritising the country's involvement in key regional markets and market regimes (World Trade Organisation, EU, Russia, the Central European Free Trade Area, the Asia-Pacific region). Simultaneously, the Verkhovna Rada has adopted policies concerning discriminatory trade practices of other states vis-a-vis Ukraine, addressed issues of insurance and credit risk of exporters, adopted its own anti-dumping code and began to align the country's national product standards and norms with international ones.[16] However, the question must surely arise in the wake of ten years of economic decline and degradation of the country's productive assets as to whether the doors to a strategically advantageous export structure have already closed?

Ukraine's growing integration with the world economy in the 1990s took place principally through trade. The trading pattern of

15 Poslannia Prezydenta Ukrainy do Verkhovnoi Rady, No. 276a/2000, Kyiv 23 February 2000.

16 16. Anatolii Hrytsenko and Mikhail Pashkov, "Ukraina na mirovykh rynkakh", *Zerkalo nedeli*, 24–30 June 2000.

the decade 1988–1998 consisted of the following trends: a steady decline in the country's trade with countries of the former Soviet Union from 80 percent to 56 percent; a decline vis a vis Central Europe from 20 percent to 10 percent; a growth in trade with the EU member states from 6 percent to 20 percent, and with both China and Turkey, each with more than 5 percent of total trade turnover by 1998. Overall, Russia remained Ukraine's dominant trading partner. But while trade with the EU increased, trade with Turkey, China and other Asian countries was increasing at a faster rate.[17]

With Russia Ukraine exchanged its metals and food products for fossil fuels, timber and other primary goods. With the EU Ukraine traded its metals, chemicals, minerals and textiles for West European machinery, electrical equipment, transport vehicles, processed food and light industrial goods. It ran up significant trade deficits with both Russia and the EU which were offset, but not equalled, by its trading surpluses with other countries. In the prevailing conditions of domestic economic contraction, trade relations with both the EU and Russia served to promote "conservatism of the existing production structure and … technological backwardness".[18] In other words, an expansion of the proportion of raw materials and semi-finished goods within the country's GDP was stimulated even more by foreign trade with its major partners.

The proportion of GDP exported by Ukraine has traditionally been high, but it does not necessarily indicate a healthy economic state of affairs. For while exports may serve to stimulate an already expanding domestic economy, their maintenance at high levels in a period of domestic economic contraction means that domestic consumption has been suppressed. This was the case between 1993 and 1998 when the proportion of exported GDP doubled to over 40 percent. The proportion rose to 53 percent in 1999, when falling world

---

17   *HILFE Country Report: Ukraine*, July 1999; Igor Burakovsky and Victor Biletsky, *Ukraine's Way to the European Union* (Kyiv: Freidrich Ebert Stiftung, April 1999), 6; Anton Filipenko, "Zovnishn'oekonomichni vidnosyny Ukrainy", in T. Stepankova, P. Dudkiewicz and M. Ghosh, *Ukraina na Perekhidnomu Etapi* (Kyiv: Akademia, 1997), 151.
18   Burakovsky and Biletsky, *op. cit.*, 15.

prices of raw materials and semi-finished goods depressed demand for Ukraine's exports, principally metallurgical products, placing even greater pressure on export earnings and requiring an increase in the volume of exports at lower unit prices in an effort to maintain them.[19]

The Ukrainian state has tried to promote the exports of its technologically advanced sectors, but here it faces stiff competition from the transnational corporations of the core states in the aeronautical, aerospace and nuclear power sectors, and from the fast developing economies of Asia in the machinery and equipment sectors. In the arms trade, however, Ukraine now ranks among the top ten producers in the world and has cultivated markets in Pakistan, China and India. It seeks to expand co-operation in military hardware production with western core states, but here it faces both the direct competition of their own corporations and the rivalry of Central European countries like the Czech Republic and Poland for joint production and conversion contracts from NATO. One might assume that the export earnings of the arms industry, which formally remains under close state supervision, should provide investment capital to regenerate other, civilian sectors of the economy. But as in these other sectors, unofficial trade remains significant and the expected revenues do not always make their way back to the state treasury.[20]

There are two main obstacles to the expansion of trade with the EU. The first is the long standing protectionist EU regime which places limits on the import of metals, chemicals, textiles and foodstuffs into the member states. Such limits have effectively prevented Ukraine from mounting an export drive westward of the kind of goods it could sell in volume and at competitive prices, and from which it could generate earnings for productive reinvestment. Not only the volume of exports, but also their price is subject to controls. Unit price and volume regulation are intended to prevent

---

19 Halchynsky, *op. cit.*, 155; Hrytsenko and Pashkov, *op. cit.* By contrast, Russia's exports constitute around 15–20 percent of its GDP. Ukraine's per capita earnings from exports were $233 in 1999, compared to $500 for Russia, $690 for Poland, $2371 for Hungary and $2612 for the Czech Republic.
20 Burakovsky and Biletsky, *op. cit.*

dumping of state-subsidised products onto West European markets. (The USA had similar controls). Ukraine, together with a number of East European states, Vietnam and Mongolia, still belongs to
the list of countries defined by the EU as having a nationalised
economy, which free the EU from GATT rules to use protectionist
measures against Ukrainian exports. In April 1998 the EU Council
of Ministers adopted a regulation allowing certain Russian and Chinese exporting companies to be considered as developing under
market conditions, which permitted them to request individual
treatment in anti-dumping enquiries. This led Borys Hudyma, head
of the Ukrainian mission in Brussels, to request that his country be
recognised by the EU as having a market economy in anti-dumping
disputes.[21] By the end of the decade such recognition was still not
forthcoming.

The second obstacle to trade between Ukraine and the EU concerns the certification of imports into Ukraine and the mutual
recognition of product standards. Ukraine has since 1993 set standards for nationally produced and imported goods and raw materials. These standards were recognised as non-discriminatory by the
International Standards Organisation, of which it is a member. It
also has the right to apply such standards under GATT rules. The
European Union does not wish to recognise them for two reasons:
recognition means reciprocity, thus allowing Ukrainian producers
to export the same kinds of goods to EU member states; and the
certification of imports by such standards places barriers before
large importers of second-rate goods into the country. By the late
1990s over 60 percent of the country's retail trade turnover was controlled by wholesalers of imported goods. According to the UN
Consumer Commission in 1997 over 80 percent of consumer goods
coming into Eastern Europe were not only low grade (category B)
and technologically obsolete, but in many cases harmful to human
health. In 1997 the World Bank and International Monetary Fund

---

21   *Europe*, n.s. 7209, 27–28 April 1998; n.s. 7238, 10 June 1998. See also Mykhailo
     Pavlovsky, *Shliakh Ukrainy* (Kyiv: Tekhnika, 1996), 58; and *Ekonomist*, No. 1, Ja-
     nuary–March 1997.

placed pressure on Ukraine to revoke its National Certificate Standards with respect to imported goods under threat that it would not release $200 m credit. The standards, it argued, were used to hinder imports and competition on the Ukrainian market. Rather, the IMF wished to see in place "a non-discriminatory system of inspection of imported products on the retail market".[22]

Investment

Ukraine has had the lowest rate of foreign direct investment (FDI) on a per capita basis for all the transitional economies in the 1990s. Total FDI by April 1999 stood at $2.8 bn. Around a third was put into foreign and domestic trade, followed by food processing and light industry (15 percent), machine building and metallurgy (10 percent). On a state-by-state basis, the USA was the largest contributor of FDI (18 percent). However, three EU states — Netherlands, Germany and the UK — together contributed 25 percent of FDI, followed by Russia (7 percent), the Republic of Korea (7 percent) and Cyprus (5 percent).[23]

The statistics do not reflect the true size of Russian FDI, which was certainly larger than 7 percent in 1997 if one takes into account Russian offshore funds coming from Cyprus, the unregistered investment being made into cross-border trade and privatised state assets.[24] In fact, the pace of Russian cross border investment into Ukrainian productive assets quickened in 2000 and 2001, especially in the fuel and energy sector and metals refining. The investment drive was supported actively by President Putin as part of a wider effort to regain Russian influence over the post-Soviet space. By ex-

---

22 *Profspilkova hazeta*, 19 February 1997 and 26 February 1997; *Dilo*, 9 February 1998.

23 *Profspilkova hazeta*, 26 March 1997; *Ekonomist*, N0. 1 January–March 1997, 49; *HILFE Country Report Ukraine*, July 1999, 31; Burakovsky and Biletsky, *op. cit.*, 8.

24 Svitlana Bednazh, "Ukraine and the EU: Comparative Perspectives"; unpublished paper, March 2000, 12. Bednazh notes that Russia's investment in Ukraine is growing at the same rate as the EU's and that Ukraine's investment in Russia is larger than in any other country.

ploiting Ukraine's state debt for Russian natural gas supplies, variously estimated at between $1.4 bn and $3 bn, Putin succeeded in getting his counterpart Leonid Kuchma to initial a debt for equity deal in November 2000, yet to be ratified by the Ukrainian legislature. This deal is aimed prospectively at securing control by the Russian transnational Gazprom of Ukrainian gas transit pipelines to Central and Western Europe. Meanwhile, other Russian companies have been taking large shares or controlling interest in large Ukrainian enterprises.[25]

While the size of total Russian investments in Ukraine is hard to calculate, it does appear that Russia may in the short run recover through such investments what it has lost through the contraction of commodity trade links with Ukraine over the past decade. Moreover, Russian companies which have grown capital-rich through trade in energy carriers and raw materials will aspire to transnational status and competition with Western transnational giants in the first instance by purchasing the facilities located in Ukraine that process, refine and transport their primary materials on the way to world markets. This is certainly a logical step for Russian gas exporters which depend upon Ukraine's transit pipelines to deliver more than 90 percent of the gas they sell throughout Europe.

A number of reasons can be cited to account for the relatively low level of Western originating FDI in Ukraine and for its application mainly to trade, services and other non-productive activities. The North American and West European regions are interested mainly in securing new markets for their own products. The Central European states are more attractive than Ukraine because they are geographically more accessible and have greater domestic consumer purchasing power. Moreover, the institutional and legal conditions in Central Europe are now better developed, more stable and secure for foreign companies. As for Ukraine, not only does it lag in the harmonisation of its legal and regulatory frameworks with those of the EU and the international trading regimes, but the

---

25 *Ukraina moloda*, 21 February 2001; *Baltimore Sun*, 29 April 2001; *Moscow Interfax*, 12 February 2001; Centre for Peace, Conversion and Foreign Policy of Ukraine, *Occasional Report* No. 7, 2001, 5.

widespread corruption of government at all levels also makes foreign investment difficult and the repatriation of profits hazardous.

The same factors explain why Ukrainian business men and women themselves do not invest a great deal into their own country's economy. The bigger players in the economy use the banking system neither for savings nor for credit, but as a conduit to expatriate capital. The unofficial sum of Ukrainian capital now abroad in Western banks and companies is around $20 bn. Ironically, this is about the same amount that the Ukrainian state is seeking as credit from the International Monetary Fund.[26]

Debt and the international financial crisis of 1997–98

Debt represents the third important path of Ukraine's integration into the world economy. The foreign debt is not large in comparison with that of some Central European states, like Hungary. However, the ongoing contraction of Ukraine's GDP, the growing proportion of primary and semi-finished goods within the GDP and exports, and the chronic difficulties of raising domestic revenues through taxation together exert enormous pressure on the country's capacity to repay the debt. Looked at from this perspective Ukraine's debt burden can be compared to that of some of the poorest countries in the world. In 1995 Nicaragua was carrying a $10 bn foreign debt, equivalent in that year to 67 percent of its GDP. Ukraine's foreign debt grew to $12.4 bn by the end of 1999, equivalent to 54 percent of its GDP.[27]

The country's difficulties in repaying its foreign debt showed up clearly during the international financial crisis of 1997–98. From 1996 the government resorted to offering treasury bills on the domestic, and then foreign, markets in order to cover the state budget deficit. In the first seven months of 1997, when investor confidence in Ukraine's recovery was still firm, around 800 m *hryvnia* a month

26   Hrytsenko, Pashkov, *op. cit.*
27   United Nations Development Programme, *Human Development Report*, (New York: Oxford University Press, 1999), 108.

were being raised in this way. By the end of 1997 45 percent of treasury bills were held by foreign investors, 28 percent by Ukrainian commercial banks, (which had put 85 percent of their investment portfolios into bills, and 24 percent by the National Bank of Ukraine.[28]

The first signs of the financial crisis in East Asia undermined investor confidence in the transitional economies in Europe, in the first place Russia and Ukraine. Foreign investors began to withdraw their money from treasury bills. In August 1997 the Ukrainian government switched over to international capital markets and floated a succession of high interest yielding bonds denominated in Euros and Deutschmarks, the total value of which exceeded $2 bn by June 1998. But by the end of August when the international financial crisis enveloped Russia and decimated its currency, investor confidence in Ukraine had evaporated and capital inflow ceased altogether. In fact, the National Bank, like its Russian counterpart, had been fighting a rear guard action for some months, selling its foreign reserves in an effort to hold up the *hryvnia* exchange rate. If in September 1997 the NBU had $2.7 bn of reserves, by August 1998 they had fallen to below $1 bn.[29]

Debt accumulation is in some respects like an investor pyramid scheme, where the second round of investors is used to pay obligations to the first round, the third round to the second and so on. Facing mounting wage and pension arrears to state employees and pensioners, as well as a general crisis of social expenditure (from an inability to collect sufficient taxes) the state first resorted to borrowing more money from residents in order to cover its annual budget deficit. When that proved insufficient, foreign investors were invited to buy bills whose proceeds were meant to cover repayment of bills that were already coming due. Bonds on international markets followed. In the end the loss of investors' confidence in the government's ability to pay back these loans with the promised interest drove investors to sell before their due date, taking a loss and undermining further the value of their loans in the

---

28   International Monetary Fund, No 99, 30–40; Halchynsky, *op. cit.*, 154.
29   Halchynsky, *op. cit.*, 47.

eyes of other would-be purchasers. In the closing months of 1998 the Ukrainian government all but defaulted on its debt when it negotiated a voluntary programme with domestic and external creditors to change short term debt into longer term government bonds.

The international financial crisis impacted in several ways upon the Ukrainian economy: capital flight, devaluation of the national currency by some 80 percent, an increase in the trade deficit and the loss of important export markets for metallurgical goods and foodstuffs. One positive by-product of the crisis was the decline of imports of consumer goods which the Ukrainian public could no longer afford, leading to a certain revival of demand for domestically produced goods. On the whole, however, this crisis demonstrated how the domestic economy and the state's regulatory instruments could be damaged by international capital and price movements.

The rapid fall in world commodity prices, including oil, in 1997–1988 was largely responsible for Russia's default on its foreign debts in August 1998. Ukraine's economy is closely tied to Russia's, so Russia's crisis was bound to spread into Ukraine. Between September and December 1998 Ukrainian exports to Russia fell by one third, in January and February 1999 by 40 percent. The flow of metallurgical exports between the two countries began to change direction, now going from Russia to Ukraine. In 1998 as a whole the value of Ukrainian exports fell by $2.8 bn, or by 13 percent compared to the previous year.[30] And while Russia's financial crisis was in most respects deeper than Ukraine's (its currency devalued by 300 percent), the subsequent recovery of its foreign trade and its currency reserves has been more rapid. This had to do with the fact that Russia has oil and gas, the world prices of which recovered in 1999 and allowed the country to return to a trade surplus. The world prices of other primary commodities did not recover in 1999, leaving countries trading in such goods and dependent on imported fuel, like Ukraine, with trade deficits. Central European states, by and large, withstood the international financial crisis, saw

---

30   Halchynsky, *op. cit.*, 165–66.

their economies grow in 1998 (with the exception of the Czech Republic and Romania) and even attracted investments that were fleeing out of the CIS region.

Conclusion

It is difficult to express in concise terms where Ukraine finds itself in the hierarchy of the world economy. The difficulty arises mainly because such quantitative indices of its domestic economic growth/decline as GDP need to be compared with the indices of other countries of the world. The comparison, moreover, needs to be made several times over an extended period of time in order to have a sense of the direction of change of the global economy, its groups of countries and regions, and its individual states. There is no doubt that the region of the former Soviet Union has suffered considerable economic damage and lost ground to other regions and groups of countries. However, the recovery of individual countries of the FSU region from its break-up and the transition to the market differ considerably in the latter 1990s and these countries can hardly be treated as a group any more.

In the work of analysts dealing with global trends, the Ukrainian economy became disaggregated statistically from the economy of the Soviet Union and the CIS region only in the early 1990s. So while it has been possible on the basis of Ukrainian statistics alone to track the country's economic evolution by way of comparison with its own previous performance, including performance in the Soviet period, it is more difficult to compare its performance over an extended period with other countries. For example, the United Nations Human Development Index, which combines measures of per capita GDP, education and life expectancy, placed the country in 1999 in 9st place among the 174 countries of the world. The Central European states were considerably higher on the Index, with Slovenia in 33rd position, the Czech Republic in 36th, Poland in 44th and Hungary in 47th. Belarus was at 60th, Kyrgyzstan at 67th, Russia at 71st and Kazakhstan at 76th. Below Ukraine on the Index came Uzbekistan, Turkmenistan, Azerbaijan and Tajikistan—all of them the traditionally poor republics of the USSR and now politically unstable states.[31]

We can only assume, albeit with confidence, that Ukraine would have been in a better position on the Index in 1990 had it figured there as a separate state. And we need to wait for the next major compilation of the Index to get a sense of the direction and pace of the country's economic and social evolution in the context of regional and global change. What is clear, however, from the Index is that the collapse in GDP per capita was mainly responsible for driving Ukraine down into 91st position. The decline in life expectancy at birth to 69 years (in 1997) was less important, while the level of education, which remained comparatively high, had the least impact. Declines in life expectancy and educational levels tend to lag behind declines in per capita GDP, so one could see a further erosion of Ukraine's position on the Index even if its economy recovers in a sustained manner from year 2000.

The general impression is of a country moving rapidly downward from the upper quartile of the world's semi-peripheral states, where it stood at the end of the 1980s, to its lower quartile. Upon becoming an independent state it still had quite favourable prerequisites to cleave towards the group of core states of the world economy, most likely by way of integration with the EU. Now one has a far more contradictory scenario: a country that on the one hand still possesses advanced technological sectors and a highly educated workforce, while more than half its population lives below the official poverty line on the other; launching Zenith rockets carrying communications satellites from the Pacific Ocean, selling world-class tanks to Pakistan, offering heavy lift Antonov aircraft to West European states while at the same time fighting to retain its primary goods markets in Russia and Turkey.

Ukraine still has no secure place in one stable regional market. As in its foreign security policy of "active neutrality" and engagement with states on all sides, economically it remains partially and precariously balanced between several regional markets. Membership in the European Union remains the principal long-term goal of

---

31   *Human Development Report*, pp. 134–137.

its foreign policy. But that has been ruled out by the EU for the fore-seeable future. Ukraine's leaders see the Central European Free Trade Area as a possible back door route into the EU, but CEFTA's construction as a regional market has been overshadowed by the Central European states' accession negotiations with the EU. A long-term economic engagement with Russia is taken for granted, but it is constrained by Ukraine's fear of domination and absorption by Russia. The development of new markets across the Middle East and Asia is considered indispensable for survival, but these regions already contain powerful competitors in many of the commodities that Ukraine wishes to sell there. The problem for Ukraine's leaders is that they balance between these regions but are not able to achieve sustained capital accumulation from engagement with any one of them. Nor are they prepared to sacrifice a portion of the country's sovereignty for the sake of more advantageous economic arrangements, bilateral or multilateral, with neighbouring states. Engagement with a number of regions can be seen as an important advantage. However, it is in the nature, not the number, of Ukraine's external economic relations that the problem lies. For if such relations cannot in the long run contribute to a steady capital accumulation at home there is little hope for a domestic economic recovery. The Ukrainian economy could recover over time and become an arena of modest accumulation, but given the extent of the country's debt obligations to Western and Eastern creditors, accumulated capital will be expatriated, not reinvested to any great extent. And this pattern could become the defining feature of the country's integration with world markets for a long time to come.

The Ukrainian Economy and the International Financial Crisis[*]

This chapter examines the impact of the international crisis of 2007–09 on Ukraine's economy. The crisis manifested itself on a number of levels, impacting successively on the banking system, the volume of external trade, domestic production, consumption, indebtedness and employment. It was tackled from the end of 2008 by a state programme of recovery agreed by Prime Minister Yulia Tymoshenko with the International Monetary Fund (IMF) in exchange for a loan of $16 billion. The failure of Tymoshenko's government to deal adequately with the crisis during 2009 contributed to her defeat in the 2010 presidential elections.[1] It also diminished the capacity of the incoming administration under President Viktor Yanukovych to manoeuvre between Russia on the one side and the Euroatlantic core states on the other. The entire previous period of the Yushchenko presidency had seen a significant growth in foreign direct investment and a heightened rivalry between European and Russian investors for strategic assets and market share in Ukraine. Thus Ukraine's overall place in the world capitalist economy, its linkages with rival transnational capitals, and its capacity to manoeuvre in the world market have been deeply affected by the crisis.

The first objective of this chapter is to examine how the international crisis impacted onto the national economy and the response to the crisis by Tymoshenko's government in 2008-9. This section looks at the crisis as an external force confronting the national economy and state. The second objective is to examine how the Ukrainian state leadership under Presidents Leonid Kuchma and Viktor Yushchenko sought to integrate their country into the world market over the decade leading up to the crisis. This section, looking at the transition to capitalism from within the national

---

* First published in: Gareth Dale, ed., *First the Transition, then the Crash: Eastern Europe in the 2000s* (London: Pluto Press, 2011), 143–168.

1 Marko Bojcun "The International Economic Crisis and the 2010 Presidential Elections in Ukraine", *Journal of Communist Studies and Transition Politics*, Vol. 27, Issue 3-4, 2011, 496–519.

economy and state, seeks answers to two important questions: What did the crisis reveal about the adequacy of the development strategies pursued during the past decade by the Ukrainian state? And how has the crisis affected Ukraine's position in the world capitalist economy, in particular its relationship to rival centres of transnational capital in Western Europe and Russia that seek to incorporate it into their own growth strategies?

The course of the crisis

According to Bohdan Danylyshyn, economics minister in the second Tymoshenko government (December 2007–March 2010), the international financial crisis hit the Ukrainian economy in a succession of waves.[2] The first appeared as a promise, not a threat. In 2006 and 2007 share prices of the biggest investment banks and hedge funds in USA and Western Europe began to fall. Facing a growing mountain of irredeemable debt in the US sub-prime mortgage market, these big players stepped up their investments in the markets of the Far East, Central and Eastern Europe. One of the publicly held assumptions in financial circles at the time was that emerging markets were immune from the sub-prime mortgage crisis. Foreign direct investments in Ukraine rose sharply from a $1.7 bn net inflow in 2004 to $9.2 bn in 2007. Capital inflows climbed even higher in 2008, but from August of that year the collapse of Ukraine's foreign trade and the seizure of its banking system prompted massive capital outflows, leaving net FDI at $6.2 bn for the year as a whole.[3]

The inexorable rise of FDI flows, particularly after the 2004 Orange Revolution, was the result on the one hand of the growing volumes of investment capital available to the region of Central and Eastern Europe, and on the other hand the liberalisation of its financial markets. For the first time since independence commercial

---

2   Bohdan Danylyshyn, "Svitova finansova kryza—test dlia Ukrainy"; www.dt.ua/1000/1550/64350/ Accessed 30 October 2008.

3   According to Anatolii Federenko, Ukraine Vice President of Kinto, the asset management firm, around $17.5 bn in bonds alone were transferred for deposit outside Ukraine in 2008. www.epravda.com.ua/markets/4ac5de2747aca/. Accessed 2 October 2009.

banks in Ukraine became the most important intermediaries and allocators of investment capital. A range of foreign banks — both EU based and Russian — started operations in Ukraine, usually buying up Ukrainian banks to serve as subsidiaries. They saw good opportunities for profit both from retail banking services, which were wholly undeveloped, as well as for corporate investment in production for export, retail and wholesale trade, transport and real estate. The share of foreign capital in Ukraine's banks grew from 13 percent in 2004 to over 50 percent in 2009.[4]

The second wave of the crisis came at the beginning of 2008 when FDI started to concentrate in the sectors that account for the main share of Ukraine's exports. The shift of foreign direct investment was prompted by the huge rise in prices on international primary commodities markets. In Ukraine there was a big jump both in the earnings of firms producing steel, wheat, mineral fertilizers, coal, coke, etc., and in the debt obligations they assumed to finance new rounds of expanded production.[5]

Already in 2007 signs of economic overheating appeared as commercial banks took larger amounts of short term foreign credits to pass on as loans both to Ukrainian firms caught in the thrall of booming export demand and to individuals, in the form of mortgages, car purchase loans and other forms of consumer credit. The FDI surge financed imports to Ukraine of machinery, automobiles and luxury goods that, together with the high price of oil and gas imported from Russia, resulted in a deepening trade deficit and contributed to the deficit of the government's current account. At the end of 2007 the National Bank of Ukraine responded to overheating by limiting the short term loans commercial banks could take from abroad. Then, in spring 2008, the government abandoned the *hryvnia's* peg to the falling US dollar and allowed it to float within a defined band. This was meant to ease the pressure of the

---

4   Roman Kornyliuk, "Ukrains'ki banky u tenetakh inozemnoho kapitalu"; www.epravda.com.ua/publications/2009/05/12/192705/. Accessed 12 May 2009.

5   *Ibid.*

rising cost of Euro-denominated imports, as the Euro was growing strongly against the US dollar at that time.[6]

The third wave of the crisis came in the summer of 2008 when world prices of oil and metals fell sharply. Prices of petrochemical products and food, heavily reliant on intensive energy inputs, fell in succession. Price falls were followed by the hasty departure of hot money (around 5–7 percent of FDI in Ukraine) and the suspension of further outlays by the stable, longer term investors.[7] The big producers of primary and semi processed goods now faced a choice: either to push out even greater volumes of goods onto external markets where they might at least hold market share while earning much lower unit prices, or to sharply curtail output and cut their losses, conserving capacity and laying off workers. Invariably they took the latter course because international demand for their goods kept shrinking as the crisis deepened in the fourth quarter of 2008, and there was no domestic demand to replace it.

A fourth wave, generated by the global contraction of production and trade, pushed deep into the national economy. Stagflation set in; from September 2008 the *hryvnia* steadily devalued. Lines of credit to Ukraine's commercial banks dried up as foreign banks and corporate investors lost liquidity in their core institutions on the one hand, and on the other hand Ukraine's collapsing exports, real estate market and domestic consumer demand threw into doubt the ability of borrowers to repay what they already owed. Savers, on the other hand, who had just learned to trust the banks enough to deposit money in them, lost confidence again and began to withdraw their deposits. Their massive exchanges of withdrawn *hryvnia* into US dollars put more pressure on the exchange rate. The NBU was forced to intervene to prevent a run on the banks: savings accounts were frozen for six months, affecting millions of ordinary savers.[8]

---

6   Anders Aslund, "Floating the hryvnia arms the National Bank to fight inflation now"; www.unian.net/eng/news/news-245168.html. Accessed 7 April 2008.

7   Danylyshyn, *op. cit.*

8   For analysis of the Ukrainian currency crisis see *EBRD Transition Report 2009*. See also Yurii Skolotiany, "Novi derzhbanky — use shche valiza bez ruchky?"; www.dt.ua/2000/2040/68173/. Accessed 26 December 2009.

The government's response

The government of Yulia Tymoshenko faced a difficult situation at the end of 2008. Although public external debt was relatively small (about 20 percent of GDP), the private sector was facing a total external debt in the region of US$104 bn — around 108 percent of the GDP achieved in 2009. And $43 bn of that amount was short term debt, due for repayment in 2009.[9] The government was under great pressure to help restore confidence and liquidity to the banks and to prevent the weakest from going under. With such a large proportion of bank capital foreign owned and a large number of Ukrainian firms holding foreign loans, it seems very likely that pressure was put on Tymoshenko by the international financial institutions and the governments of significant foreign investors to take speedy action to prevent defaults in the private sector.

However, collapsing foreign trade, contracting domestic production and demand and growing unemployment had sharply reduced the government's revenues from taxation and increased its social welfare payments. Preparation of the 2009 state budget showed a shortfall of approximately $17 bn in meeting the anticipated expenditures. Without a sizeable sovereign fund (NBU foreign currency reserves totalled around $28 bn in January 2009) Tymoshenko saw no option but to seek external financing of the state budget. She turned to six states and to the IMF. One of these was Russia, which offered a $5 bn loan.[10]

In November 2008, Ukraine and the IMF concluded a memorandum setting out the conditions of a $16.4 bn loan. This amount worked out to around $360 per capita. The interest rate on it was set at 2 percent per annum, the loan to be repaid by 2014.[11] Tymoshenko sold the IMF loan to the public in such terms — a low interest rate, adequate reserves to cover the amount, and a relatively small burden on a per capita basis. President Yushchenko supported

---

9   "Ukraine — the spectre of default", *Economist Intelligence Unit — Business Eastern Europe*, 23 February 2009.

10   *Kontrakty*, No. 7 16 February 2009; See also BYUT Inform, 12 December 2009.

11   Roman Kornyliuk, "Spivpratsia Ukrainy z MVF: tsina pytannia"; www.eprav da.com.ua/publications/4b011f720268f/. Accessed 16 November 2009.

Tymoshenko on the loan, seeing that it would serve to anchor Ukraine to the Euroatlantic core states.

From the camp of the Party of Regions sharp criticism of the IMF loan came from Mykola Azarov, the party leader who would become Prime Minister under the Yanukovych presidency in 2010. Putting forward an alternative bill to the government's October 2008 legislative package in conjunction with negotiations over the IMF loan, Azarov argued that it wasn't needed. He saw no looming crisis of the banking system. His alternative proposal amounted to two essential points: the creation of a Stabilisation Fund to stimulate economic recovery and raising the amount of bank deposits guaranteed by the state. Azarov saw the main danger at the end of 2008 in an area that was not addressed by the government and the IMF at all in their joint memorandum: the collapse of Ukraine's external markets. To counteract it he proposed mobilising domestic demand for steel, mineral fertilizers and machinery, traditionally the country's main exports. He also proposed the government use the still-to-be created stabilisation fund to finance reconstruction of state railways and rolling stock, build bridges, subsidise farmers' purchases of fertilizer, and give tax breaks to the machine building industry:

> The current situation requires a considerable mobilisation of the domestic market ... Under pressure from the IMF our government is doing precisely the opposite. We have to lower taxes, but it is raising them; we have to relax fiscal policy wherever possible to increase domestic demand, but it is making this tougher ... If we implement all the demands of the IMF the situation will only get worse.[12]

Prime Minister Tymoshenko, however, retained a slim majority in the Verkhovna Rada and her coalition carried the day. The IMF loan and its terms were accepted (though later amended — see below) and became the centrepiece of the government's strategy to deal with the crisis. According to the IMF-Ukraine memorandum, its main aims were:

---

12   Mykola Azarov, "Iakshcho my zaraz pidemo na vykonannia vsikh vymoh MVF" Zerkalo tyzhnia, 25 October 1008.

- to restore the banks' liquidity; this measure to include re-capitalisation of the stronger banks, liquidation of the weaker, state purchase and sale of bank shares, all in an effort to make credit available again;
- to raise the guarantee on individual bank deposits from 50,000 to 100,000 *hryvnia*;
- to monitor corporate sector debt with a view to anticipate peak periods of debt service and avoid any massive default across the private sector;
- to create a floating exchange rate without a defined band, as a way of dealing with further external shocks to the economy;
- to target inflation at 17 percent in 2009, falling to 5–7 percent by 2011;
- to strengthen fiscal discipline and bring the current account deficit down to 1 percent of GDP by raising end-user costs for energy resources, preventing increases in salaries and wages in the public sector as well as holding social expenditures to the rate of inflation, and postponing by two years the planned alignment of the national minimum wage with the defined minimal living standard (poverty line);
- to restore Naftogaz, the state gas importer, to financial health by bringing up end user prices of imported gas to those of domestically produced gas and by simultaneous abolition of the state subsidy of gas consumed by public housing and communal facilities.[13]

The IMF released three tranches of its loan—the first $4.5 bn in November 2008 upon adoption of the agreement with Ukraine, the second of $2.8 bn in May 2009 and the third of $3.3 bn in September 2009.[14] The fourth and final tranche was held up by the presidential election campaign. However, at the very end of 2009 the IMF agreed to amend its deal with Ukraine and allow its government to use $2 bn of the NBU's own reserves (thereby limiting the NBU's

---

13   "Memorandum Kabminu ta MVF"; www.epravda.com.ua/publications/4909 aebce9644/. Accessed 30 October 2008.
14   Kornyliuk, *op. cit.*

minimum international reserves requirement) to prop up Naftogaz Ukrainy and pay the government's pressing gas bill to Russia.[15]

The Tymoshenko government implemented its rescue package from the end of 2008 broadly in line with the aims set out in its memorandum with the IMF. It used the IMF loan, as well as additional revenues of its own, to pay off $7.1 bn of the commercial banks' debts to foreign creditors and a further $5.7 bn to honour the savings accounts of Ukrainian depositors. Total savings in all banks by Ukrainian citizens was 207 bn *hryvnia*, worth about $20 bn on 1 December 2008. Some of the funds were used to increase the minimum reserves of two state banks — Ukreksimbank and Oshchadbank, and to buy out controlling shares and thereby nationalise five commercial banks to prevent them from failing. Tymoshenko said in an interview in August 2009 that one of these five — Ukrprombank — went bankrupt after its biggest shareholders stole the initial funds advanced by the NBU to recapitalise it.[16] The Kyiv weekly *Dzerkalo tyzhnia* reported that the National Bank had already issued 111 bn *hryvnia* (worth $15 bn in December 2008) in credits between September and December 2008 (that is, before the disbursement of the IMF loan) for the recapitalisation of commercial banks, but that some of these credits had disappeared into the shadow economy through immediate purchases of foreign currencies on the interbank currency market. And some of the money was lent out unsecured to private clients who then went bankrupt. Bank Nadra, for example, "lost" 380 m *hryvnia* ($51 m) in this way.[17]

Meanwhile, the Ukrainian currency had been allowed to float on international currency markets, and it devalued against the US dollar from an average rate of 5:1 in 2008 to around 9:1 in September 2009. It subsequently began to rise in value again, albeit slowly, registering an annual average rate for 2009 of 8.1 *hryvnia* to the dollar.

The IMF loan and the release of NBU funds with the IMF's agreement in January 2010 were critical to ensuring that Ukraine

---

15   *BYUT Inform*, 4 January 2010.
16   "Tymoshenko obitsiaie vesele zhyttia kolyshnim vlasnykam bankiv"; www. pravda.com.ua/news/2009/08/6/4128348/. Accessed 6 August 2009.
17   *Dzerkalo tyzhnia*, 14 January 2010.

managed to meet its monthly payments for gas imports from Russia. These payments proved a significant burden on the state budget, as the government continued to subsidise end user gas prices to public housing and communal institutions. Tymoshenko had renegotiated the gas contract with the Russian government in January 2009 but secured a purchase price only 20 percent lower than the price Russia charged EU consumers. However, the agreement removed Rosukrenergo, the private intermediary trading body, and established a direct purchasing and payments procedure between Naftogaz and Gazprom. Tymoshenko aimed to establish a transparent trading arrangement that ensured stability and predictability of prices and supply both to Ukraine and its western neighbours.

Tymoshenko's government also seized Rosukrenergo's gas reserves stored under the Carpathian Mountains. She thereby provoked a bitter fight with Dmytro Firtash, a principal partner in both Rosukrenergo and the troubled Nadra Bank, who was backing Viktor Yanukovych in his bid for the presidency. The gas trade was also one of the subjects of ongoing dispute between Yushchenko and Tymoshenko, who traded accusations of benefiting from allegedly corrupt arrangements and betraying Ukrainian national interests.[18]

Finally, the government was obliged to respond to the social consequences of the sharp economic downturn. These included growing indefinite layoffs and unemployment reaching 9.6 percent in 2009, mounting wage arrears, deepening household indebtedness and persistent price inflation of essential consumer goods.[19] Strikes against wage arrears and layoffs began in the autumn of 2009, and there were fairly widespread protest marches organized by the trade unions against poverty. The marchers denounced the IMF agreement as evidence of the government's willingness to bail out big business at the expense of working class people who now bore the costs of the crisis.[20]

The government and the IMF were at odds over the 2009 state budget, which held up the release of the second tranche of the IMF

---

18   *BYUT Inform*, 12 February 09; *Financial Times*, 15 January 2010.

19   L. Shanhina and V. Yurchyshyn, "Struktura dokhodiv I vytrat domohospodarstv 'ne vidchula' kryzy", *Makroekonomichyyi ohliad Ukrainy*, December 2009.

20   Ihor Zhdanov, "Holodni budni v Ukraini" (Hungry days in Ukraine), *Dzerkalo tyzhnia*, 28 February–7 March 2009.

loan. The IMF was insisting on a budget deficit of 1 percent of government expenditures over income, to be calculated on the basis of a projected 8 percent drop in GDP in 2009 and an inflation rate of 16 percent. Such a small deficit could have been achieved in such projected macroeconomic circumstances only by sharply lowering government expenditures on public sector salaries, pensions and other social services, as well as by reducing state subsidies on domestic energy prices. However, the Rada adopted a 2009 budget with a projected deficit of 3 percent GDP (31 bn *hryvnia*, equivalent to $3.7 bn). This was unacceptable to the IMF delegation, which left Ukraine to wait for the Cabinet to modify its position. But the Cabinet remained divided. Finance Minister Viktor Pynzennyk, supported by Yushchenko, insisted that the Cabinet follow the prescription set out in the memorandum with the IMF. Tymoshenko was clearly resisting such a course and holding out for a concession from the IMF. Pynzennyk resigned from the Cabinet and the IMF agreed to accept a state budget deficit of 4 percent of GDP, which everyone knew was unrealistic because month by month GDP contracted, squeezing government revenues accordingly.[21]

The second tranche of $2.8 billion was released to the government only in May 2009. The third was released in September, but the fourth tranche was held up because on the eve of the presidential elections the government failed to increase domestic prices on gas supplies and the Rada adopted legislation in October to increase social welfare payments by an average of 20 percent. The legislation was pushed through the Rada by a coalition of the Party of Regions and the Communists against the will of Tymoshenko's reduced parliamentary coalition. President Yushchenko signed off the legislation.[22]

The annual decrease in GDP in 2009 turned out to be 15.1 percent. The state budget deficit at the end 2009 was a matter of some

---

21   "Kraina v nebezpetsi: sekretna dopovidna ministra finansiv na im'ia Tymoshenko"; www.epravda.com.ua/publications/497ee1f14c7d6/. Accessed 27 January 2009. Viktor Chyvokunia, "'Minus 8 protsent: MVF vymahaie vid Tymoshenko vyznaty ekonomichnu iamu"; *Ukrains'ka pravda*, 13 February 2009; www.pravda.com.ua/articles/2009/02/13/3732266/. Accessed 13 Febuary 2009.

22   *The Guardian*, 15 November 2009; Kornyliuk, *op. cit.*

dispute between political leaders, but the dispute was voiced openly only after the elections were over. While the Cabinet of Ministers under Prime Minister Tymoshenko had reported a surprisingly low year end deficit of 19.9 bn *hryvnia*, the incoming government under Prime Minister Azarov calculated it at 103.8 bn *hryvnia*. Azarov added together the deficit declared by Tymoshenko, the costs of recapitalising the banks and Naftogaz, further loans taken from the IMF under Special Drawing Rights and the government's outstanding repayments of VAT to businesses. Further, in calculating the state debt, as opposed to the annual budget deficit, Azarov also added in the cost of honouring state bonds. By his calculation the state debt stood at 211.6 bn *hryvnia*, or 23 percent of GDP.[23] Interestingly, Azarov did not take into account the huge obligations of the state pension fund, which would have driven up the calculated state debt to around 40 percent of GDP. He needed to show just how badly Tymoshenko had managed the state finances during her time in office, but not to reveal the full extent of the state's indebtedness for fear of undermining the confidence of international creditors and investors.

The government's response to the crisis in 2009 may be summarized as follows: the Cabinet led by Tymoshenko, and supported by President Yushchenko, took the IMF loan and made it the centre piece of its strategy to combat the impact of the financial crisis on the economy and state finances. By using the IMF loan to recapitalise the commercial banks, nationalise the five banks facing collapse and to honour Ukrainian depositors' savings accounts the government in effect transformed part of a massive private sector debt into a public debt. Adherence to the terms of the IMF loan about limiting state budget expenditures came under pressure as the presidential elections loomed and the candidates sought to provide additional social support to those worst affected by the economic downturn. However, the government neither formulated nor implemented any significant measures to stimulate economic recovery, although there was a lot of talk about it from the end of 2008 and throughout the presidential election campaign period.

---

23   *Dzerkalo tyzhnia*, 30 April–14 May 2010.

The immediate impact of the 2007–9 crisis on the Ukrainian economy, measured in the most basic indices, can be summarized in the following terms:

1. after climbing steadily at strong annual rates of growth, real GDP fell in 2009 by 15.1 percent;
2. net foreign direct investment fell from its peak of $9.2 bn in 2007 to $4.5 bn in 2009;
3. a collapse in Ukraine's principal exports, notably steel and chemicals, and a similarly sharp contraction in imports;
4. after its revaluation during the boom years, a devaluation of the national currency *hryvnia* by around 40 percent;
5. a rise in unemployment levels to 9.6 percent in 2009;
6. a year on year decrease in real wages of 10.9 percent by October 2009;
7. a sharp reduction in the capacity of the population to meet their household debt obligations: consumer loans and mortgages denominated in foreign currencies have to be paid back in devaluated *hryvnia*;
8. an increase in the public debt to at least 23 percent of annual GDP (40 percent including the state pension fund's obligations) as a result of the government's assumption of private sector debt obligations to foreign creditors and domestic savers.

The immediate causes, the moment of impact and the quantitative dimensions of the crisis can only tell us a limited amount. Its wider significance for the Ukrainian economy can be understood better by analytically situating the crisis in the context of Ukraine's emergence as an independent state and its leaders' efforts subsequently to insert their national economy into the world capitalist economy. Such an analysis can begin by way of addressing the following two questions: What did the crisis reveal about the adequacy of the national development strategies pursued during the past decade by the Ukrainian state? And how has the crisis affected Ukraine's position in the world economy, in particular its relationship to rival centres of transnational capital in Western Europe and Russia seeking to incorporate Ukrainian economic territory into their own growth strategies?

Kuchma's strategy of development

In its first seven years as an independent state Ukraine experienced a continuing economic decline. The decline had begun in the 1980s, but it accelerated rapidly as the Soviet and Comecon networks of production and trade disintegrated. A severe contraction of output in most sectors of the economy, the degradation of their fixed assets and the diminution of the labour force, both in the absolute numbers employed and their level of productivity, were the outstanding features of the 1990s. The value of Ukraine's GDP measured in constant domestic prices fell by around two thirds between 1990 and 1997.[24] Hardest hit were the sectors with the highest levels of technique, which had also been the most closely integrated sectors within the Soviet division of labour: armaments, aeronautical and aerospace industries, heavy engineering and consumer durables. Mining and processing of fuels, minerals and chemicals, whose gross output declined in absolute terms at a relatively slower rate, increased their share of industrial production overall. These sectors enjoyed strong international demand in the 1990s and figured prominently in the structure of Ukraine's exports. They survived better because they were not affected by the collapsing domestic demand and they could find markets beyond the disintegrated Soviet bloc.

Not only did the Ukrainian economy contract, but it also splintered into several autonomously reproducing layers: a subsistence economy in the production of food, on which all the rural population and up to half the urban population depended in the mid-1990s[25]; a nationalised sector of arms, aerospace, aviation, as well as

24   *Ukrainian Economic Trends*, June 1997, 8–14; V Riaboshlyk, "Realnii podatkovyii tiahar prykhovano statystykoiu VVP" (The real economic burden is concealed by GDP statistics), *Ekonomist*, Vol. 1, No. 1, January–March 1997, 28–32.

25   International Labour Office, *The Ukrainian Challenge: reforming labour market and social policy* (Budapest: Central European University Press, 1995), 15; Oleg Dubrovskii with Simon Pirani, *Fighting back in Ukraine: a worker who took on the bureaucrats and bosses* (London: Index Books, 1997), 5–6.

the major utilities, which the new state was not eager to privatize; and a private sector emerging from petty trade and services, and from the first rounds of privatisation of state owned small and medium sized enterprises. Much of this last layer belonged to the shadow economy, beyond the reach of statistical measurement, state regulation or taxation.

It was only during Leonid Kuchma's first term as president (1994–1999) that the state leadership acquired minimal institutional capacity to put the brakes on the economic decline. In 1996 it introduced the national currency (*hryvnia*), the last to do so among the post-Soviet states. It implemented a monetary stabilisation, tightening the money supply and bringing down the raging inflation rate. And it started to build up state finances and regulatory institutions mainly on the basis of implementing the first rounds of privatisation. However, it could not undertake a pro-active strategy of economic and social development until after the decline hit rock bottom in 1999. The devaluation of the *hryvnia* in the wake of the 1998 financial crisis provided the kick start for a recovery of the food processing sector, allowing it to compete effectively with food imports that had managed by the end of the 1990s to capture more than 60 percent of the domestic retail market.

The devaluation and favourable world market prices spurred a recovery of Ukraine's exports of steel, chemicals and food products. From these altered price conditions on domestic and external markets, and with the help of recently built state institutional capacity, came strong renewed growth from 2000 onwards.

By the end of the 1990s, Kuchma's leadership team had concluded that Ukraine should not try to follow the prescriptions of the International Monetary Fund and the World Bank. No-one but themselves would help pull Ukraine out of "the widening bloc of poverty" that such prescriptions had fostered in past decades and into which most post-Soviet countries had now fallen.[26] Rather, Kuchma's strategy of development aimed to create "a social market

---

26   A.S. Halchynsky *et al.*, *Stratehiia ekonomichnoho isotsial'noho rozvytku Ukrainy 2004–2015 roky shliakhom ievropeis'kyi intehratsiyi Ukrayiny* (Kyiv: 2004), 15–16. This is a collective work by Ukrainian academics and experts working under the direction of then Prime Minister Viktor Yanukovych.

economy" integrated into the world market on terms that capitalised on its strengths and resulted in its insertion on a relatively high technological echelon. It was in the first instance an export led strategy to accumulate surpluses from foreign trade in steel, chemicals, and food products, as well as refined petroleum products and machinery. The accumulated surpluses would be used to fund the upgrading of existing high technology sectors of production and to create new ones, leading in the long run to an import substitution strategy of growth, one more reliant on domestic demand and less vulnerable to external fluctuations and shocks.[27]

An integral part of the strategy was to establish a strong national capitalist class and to restrict foreign ownership of strategic industries, the banking system and the fuel and energy complex.[28] The principal mechanism for establishing this class was privatisation of the large nationalised economic assets. After the privatisation of small and medium sized enterprises was completed, the State Property Fund began organising the distribution of the first set of big industrial enterprises. It chose to sell these assets in 2003 and 2004 at low prices to just a few powerful capitalist clans, which were vertically integrated corporations of production, trade and finance that had accumulated their initial capital in the 1990s through various legal and illegal means. The five largest corporations were Interpipe, headed by Viktor Pinchuk, Pryvat by Ihor Kolomoisky, System Capital Management by Renat Akhmetov, the Industrial Union of Donbas by Serhii Taruta and Vitalii Haiduk, and the Ukrsybbank group by Oleksandr Yaroslavsky. Of the 18 big enterprises privatised in 2003 and 2004, 13 of them went to just four corporations. Renat Akhmetov, a close ally of then Prime Minister Yanukovych, got seven.[29] Thus, the new historical phase of capitalist development in Ukraine was being shaped by a state strategy that preserved the concentration of industry on a very narrow social base.

---

27   *Ibid.*
28   *Ukrains'ka pravda*, 26 December 2003, citing Mykhailo Chechetov, head of the State Property Fund.
29   Aleksandr Paskhaver and Lidiia Verkhovodova, "Privatisation Before and After the Orange Revolution", *Problems of Economic Transition*, Vol. 50, No. 3, July 2007, 5–40.

Further privatisations would of course follow. Let us not forget that in 2004 the technologically most sophisticated sectors of the economy — aeronautics, aerospace, armaments, transport, telecommunications, as well as the public utilities providing energy, water and environmental protection — were not yet even considered for privatisation. They remained state owned, either giving added revenues to the state coffers (arms, for example) or requiring substantial state support to maintain them in the face of highly competitive and restricted foreign markets (aeronautics and aerospace)[30].

Kuchma's "multi-vector" foreign policy served his economic development strategy. Maintenance of strong ties with Russia was essential for three reasons: cheap Russian oil and gas fuelled the Ukrainian economy and its public utilities; Russia was the biggest importer of Ukrainian machinery and processed food products; and Ukrainian firms were locked into joint production with Russian ones in a number of sectors, the most important of which was the production of armaments. Nevertheless, the Ukrainian leadership under Kuchma aimed to utilise its competitive advantages vis a vis Russia, as well as other ex-Soviet states, in order to acquire the resources it needed for eventual westward integration into the single market and the governing institutions of the European Union. Building a social market economy and entering on a high echelon into the global division of labour would make Ukraine an attractive candidate for membership in the European Union.[31] European integration remained the priority of Ukraine's foreign policy throughout Kuchma's term in office, even when after 2000 he was diplomatically isolated in the West and faced mounting pressure from a resurgent Russia to yield to deeper penetration of the

---

30   *Central European*, July–August 1992; *Chas*, 18 October 1996, 7; *Ukrainian Economic Trends*, January 1997, Table 1.4.

31   Halchynsky *et al., op. cit.*, 18. The strategy of European integration was a long term one. It foresaw mastering an "innovative" model of further economic development, reducing the per capita income gap between the EU and Ukraine, incorporating Ukrainian industrial production into European production chains, building a strong middle class, democratizing political institutions, adapting the legal code to EU law, joining the World Trade Organisation and NATO by 2008.

Ukrainian economy by Russian firms.[32] Kuchma made concessions to Putin, but steadfastly refused to consider going any further into the Russia-led Single Economic Space than participation in a free trade area (which was not established anyhow).

Kuchma's determination to keep foreign capital out of the strategic heights of the national economy applied as much to the Russians as it did to the West Europeans. However, it was difficult to keep Russian investments out of the middle tiers of the Ukrainian economy once the Russian economy started to recover and its state took a more determined stance in staking out a westward, downstream trail for its primary resource producers. Ukraine's processing and refining industries and its transport infrastructure were these Russian producers' obvious targets. The pace of Russian cross border investment into Ukrainian assets quickened in 2000 and 2001, especially in the fuel and energy sector and metals refining. By using Ukraine's state debt for Russian natural gas supplies as leverage (variously estimated at between $1.4 bn and $3 bn at the time) Putin succeeded in getting Kuchma to initial a debt for equity deal in November 2000 to cede control to Gazprom of Ukrainian gas transit pipelines to Central and Western Europe. Kuchma managed somehow to wriggle out of this initialised deal. Meanwhile, other Russian companies did succeed in taking large shares or controlling interest in a number of powerful Ukrainian enterprises.[33] Undoubtedly, the inability of Western investors to buy such assets at the time explains much of the coolness of European and American diplomacy towards Kuchma after 2000.

---

32   Marko Bojcun, "Russia, Ukraine and European Integration", (San Domenico, Italy: European University Institute Working Paper HEC No. 2001/4, EUI, 2001).

33   Avtozaz bought the Zaporizhzhia Aluminium Plant; Lukoil bought the Odesa oil refinery, creating a joint venture with the Kalush refinery and purchasing a network of petrol stations; the Tuymen Oil Company bought the Lysychansk oil refinery; the metals conglomerate Russian Aluminium took the Mykolaiv Aluminium Industrial Complex; Metalls Russia invested in the Donetsk Metallurgical Industrial Complex; the companies Alliance Group, Alfa Nafta and Tat Nafta took part in the privatisation of the Kherson, Nadvirna and Kremenchuk refineries respectively. *Ukraina moloda*, 21 February 2001; *Baltimore Sun*, 29 April 2001; *Moscow Interfax*, 12 February 2001; *Occasional Report No. 7* (Kyiv: Centre for Peace, Conversion and Foreign Policy of Ukraine, 2001).

Table 4:   Ukraine 2000–2009: Selected indicators of economic growth

	2000	2001	2002	2003	2004	2005	2006	2007	2008	2009
Growth in real GDP (in percent)	5.9	9.2	5.2	9.6	12.1	2.7	7.3	7.9	2.1	−15.1
Inflation (percentage change)	28.2	12.0	0.8	5.2	9.0	13.5	9.1	12.8	25.2	11.2
Real income of the population (percentage change)	4.1	10.0	18.0	9.1	19.6	23.9	11.8	14.8	7.6	−10
Government current account balance (in percent of GDP)	4.7	3.7	7.5	5.8	10.5	2.9	−1.5	−4.1	−7.2	−1.7
Foreign direct investment (net inflows in $m)	594	769	698	1411	1711	7533	5737	9218	6181	4463
Percentage share of output of sectors of industry										
Mining	12.0	10.9	10.4	9.0	7.3	8.3	8.2	8.5		
Food and agricultural products	17.7	19.1	19.1	18.5	15.8	16.3	15.5	14.4		
Light industry goods	1.7	1.6	1.6	1.3	1.2	1.1	1.1	0.9		
Petroleum refining, coking coal	3.7	5.5	7.7	9.5	9.1	9.4	8.0	8.2		
Metallurgy and steel processing	23.0	20.6	20.5	21.8	23.3	22.1	21.9	24.7		
Engineering	13.1	11.5	12.1	13.1	13.4	12.7	12.5	14.4		
Production and distribution of electricity, gas, water	15.2	14.1	13.2	11.3	16.3	15.9	18.3	14.8		
Other sectors	13.6	16.7	15.4	15.5	13.6	14.2	14.5	14.1		

Sources: EBRD 2009; NBU 2010; State Committee of Statistics of Ukraine; Ya. A. Zhalilo, *Teoria i praktyka formuvannia ekektyvnoi ekonomichnoi stratehii* derzhavy, Kyiv, National Institute of Strategic Studies, 2009.

The economic statistics suggested that Kuchma's growth strategy was working (see Table 4). Gross domestic product grew solidly year on year, the rate of inflation was reduced to single digits and the current account balance rose into positive figures. The income of the population rose markedly in real terms for four years. Investment in fixed capital grew year on year, although from a very low base. Foreign direct investment remained distinctly modest on a per capita basis, though one has good reason to suspect that investments from the Russian side were underreported.

However, there were also shortcomings in the strategy and the political regime that was built by Kuchma to manage and direct it. First, the export led strategy relied in 2000–02 on expanding production of export commodities through increasing labour and raw materials inputs. But these inputs were maximally applied and quickly exhausted, while fixed capital itself had already been exhausted by the long decline of the 1990s. And while the real incomes of the workforce were growing, the owners of industry and their state sponsors were failing to address domestic demand. In 2003–4 exports soared again, but the earnings from exports were not sufficiently reinvested in fixed capital, nor were they targeted to diversifying production in order to meet the still expanding domestic demand.

One may well ask what happened to the earnings of the big exporting firms? Why were they not reinvested and redirected to serve domestic demand? A larger part of these earnings were expatriated to offshore havens to protect them from both devaluation and the taxation authorities. Tiny Cyprus, where numerous Ukrainian and Russian firms opened up bank accounts, became the source of the largest recorded share of foreign direct investment into Ukraine. Furthermore, in 2004 the President's Administration intensified the collection of taxes and compulsory purchases of state bonds by VAT indebted firms. Yet these obligations were avoided through corrupt agreements between firms and regional taxation authorities, and a large portion of the taxes which were collected in 2004 were diverted into the presidential election campaign to support Viktor Yanukovych, the president's chosen successor. Such practices contributed to the consolidation of regionally based political formations around the most powerful firms, whose leaders balanced off against the centre and competed against one another for influence within its central institutions.[34] In turn, their success at minimising their own taxes threw the burden onto the smaller businessmen, who invariably served the domestic market. In 2004 this burden potentially fell onto 2.5 million legally registered small business and self employed people out of a total working population of 20 million.[35] They naturally passed on the greater tax burdens to their own clients. But they were deeply resentful both of the Kuchma regime and the clans it protected.

Regionally concentrated centres of production serving export markets and enriching regionally aligned elites aggravated social and economic disparities across the country as a whole. One of the most evident disparities was a growing regional differentiation in the wage packet. By October 2004 the average monthly wage in the heavily populated and industrialised eastern oblasts of Donetsk, Dnipropetrovs'k and Zaporizhzhia was over 700 *hryvnia*, while in the predominantly agricultural and more sparsely populated western oblasts of Ternopil, Rivno and Khmelnytsky it was barely over 400 *hryvnia*. Western Ukraine, moreover, was haemorrhaging from a mass emigration due to a lack of jobs. And while wage arrears were highest in the eastern oblasts at the beginning of that year, they were paid off more quickly there than in the western oblasts, leaving the strong impression among the population of unequal treatment and unequal distribution of the rewards from the economic recovery.[36] These regional disparities in income explain why more rural workers and urban workers from the central and western oblasts tended to support Yushchenko's Orange camp, and the industrial heartland of Eastern and Southern Ukraine backed Yanukovych's Blue camp during the upheaval at the end of 2004.[37]

---

34   Ya. A. Zhalilo, *Teoriia i praktyka formuvannia efektyvnoi ekonomichnoi stratehii derzhavy* (Kyiv: National Institute of Strategic Studies, 2009), 129–31.

35   Paskhaver and Verkhovodova, *op. cit.*

36   Zhalilo, *op. cit.*, 129–31.

37   "... the Orange revolutionary coup was broadly a product of real economic grievances and 'decremental relative deprivation' suffered by the majority of the Ukrainian electorate during the transition." Vlad Mykhnenko, "Class voting and the Orange Revolution: A Cultural Political Economy Perspective on Ukraine's Electoral Geography", *Journal of Communist Studies and Transition Politics*, Vol.25, Nos.2–3, June–September 2009.

The Ukrainian state leadership was always mindful of the need to maintain a consensus between the classes as it tried to navigate through the transition. During the 1990s and into the new century Ukrainian leaders regularly expressed their fear of "an uncontrollable social explosion", not knowing what were the socially acceptable limits or the consequences of their actions. And this fear was quite understandable because a new sovereign state power was breathing life into a new class of very wealthy people by handing over to them the accumulated social wealth of past generations while the absolute living majority, the legal heirs of that wealth, was being impoverished. The mechanism of this historic redistribution of wealth was privatisation. The majority of the population were bitterly disappointed with the coupon privatisation of the early 1990s and the worker and management buyouts that followed. Their allocated shares in both failed to bring them even a glimpse of the promised prosperity. Everyone saw the first big enterprises denationalised in 2003–04 go to regime insiders. And then a wave of illegal and hidden privatisations of production facilities, research institutes, communal housing, trade outlets and natural resources mounted on the eve of the 2004 presidential election and carried on right up to the deciding round of voting. It rightly provoked popular outrage and condemnation as corrupt and "antinational".[38]

The industrial working class in Ukraine did enjoy rapidly growing real incomes after 1999. But these incomes were recovering from a terribly depressed state when close to 95 percent of household incomes was spent on food and essential services, when life expectancy and the birth rate both plummeted, and infant mortality rose. And these incomes recovered in a highly uneven manner, aggravating regional tensions within the working class. Tensions also increased between the professionals, the small and medium sized businesses and the state supported billionaires. Not only had Kuchma failed in his strategy to establish a workable cycle of domestic economic and social reproduction mediated by the world market. He also failed to contain the social tensions arising from

---

38   Paskhaver and Verkhovoda, *op. cit.*, p. 30.

this strategic failure, which then took on a complicated political life in the struggle between the Orange and Blue camps.

Thus, concludes the economist Ya. Zhalilo, "the processes of unregulated expansion of capitals concentrated in the exporting sectors became one of the reasons for the socio-political crisis in Ukraine at the end of 2004 ... [it was] the direct result of the chronic ineffectiveness of the socio-economic strategy of the state to build mechanisms for the harmonious redistribution of resources ... for the purpose of development".[39]

From the Orange revolution to the international financial crisis

The 2004 Orange revolution marked a watershed in the Ukrainian state's declared domestic and external policies. While this is not the place to analyse the course of the revolutionary events, it is never-theless important to identify the mass expectations arising from them and their influence upon regime strategy. These expectations included above all: to end corruption in privatisation, taxation and state regulation in general; to end state protection and favouritism towards the biggest corporations and to assure equal legal, regula-tory and tax treatment of self employed people in small and me-dium sized businesses; to end the various kinds of coercion used by the state authorities against their parliamentary and extra-parlia-mentary opponents, such as spying, press censorship, murders of journalists, denial of basic rights of assembly and expression; and to improve the standard of living of those parts of the population who had benefitted the least from the economic upturn since 1999 — pensioners, small town and rural workers, inhabitants of economi-cally depressed regions. These people were an important contin-gent of the multiclass alliance that made up the Orange camp. Meanwhile, the Orange leaders could not afford to alienate any more the mass base of the defeated Blue pro-Yanukovych, camp, which in electoral terms was almost as large as its own. The indus-trial workers concentrated in eastern and southern oblasts did not

---

39   Zhalilo, *op. cit.*, 125–31.

want to see the material gains they had made in previous years eroded.

Both Yushchenko and Tymoshenko felt compelled to restore a sense of national unity. However, they were not ready to restore unity within the establishment itself. Before continuing with any new privatisations the Orange leaders decided to take back the biggest assets privatised under Kuchma and to reprivatise them by an open and transparent tender. In this way they were killing three birds with one stone. First, they were responding to public outrage over the way that privatisations had been conducted in the past. Second, they were set on weakening their rivals from the Blue camp by confiscating their wealth. Viktor Pinchuk, Kuchma's son in law and Renat Akhmetov, the richest man in the country, were the first to be targeted. They lost the steel plant complex Kryvorizhstal. Pinchuk also lost the Nykopil Southern Pipe Plant and Oranta Insurance Company. Some 1700 other privatisations were hastily challenged and reclaimed by the state before the whole process was brought to a halt by protests over its selective nature. Threats were issued both at home and abroad that the loss of business confidence in private property rights would cause big business to withdraw from Ukraine altogether.

The third bird at which reprivatisation was aimed represented the biggest of the impending changes to state economic strategy: to open up to foreign investment. The new government demonstratively organised a show piece reprivatisation of Kryzorizhstal, which was won by competitive tender by the Indian steel tycoon Lakshmi Mittal in October 2005 and which brought into the state treasury more than six times the price at which Pinchuk and Akhmetov had acquired it in the first place. But then privatisation of large industries and utilities like Ukrtelecom and the Odesa Port Authority faltered and got bogged down in face of renewed public opposition. The Verkhovna Rada refused to approve further privatisations.[40] Therefore foreign capital could not take this direct route to the productive assets of the Ukrainian economy, but rather had

---

40   Paskhaver and Verkhovoda, *op. cit.*, p. 31

to approach by other routes, such as investing in foreign and domestic trade.

Like Kuchma, Yushchenko was dedicated to integrating
Ukraine into the Atlantic core of advanced capitalist states, their
economic, institutional and security structures. In contrast to
Kuchma, his pro-EU, pro-NATO foreign policy was aimed against
Russia. Yushchenko wanted to weaken the grip of Russia on
Ukraine's economy, its information space and security environment. This much is clear in the foreign policy pursued after 2004,
notwithstanding Tymoshenko's attempts while Prime Minister to
blunt Yushchenko's edge and seek an accommodation with Russia.
Yet with respect to the state's strategy of economic development,
which concerns us here, Yushchenko's enthusiastic engagement
with the EU and NATO at the political level was accompanied by a
major opening up to transnational capital flows from the Euroatlantic states into Ukraine. These two engagements were seen as mutually reinforcing by those who wanted Ukraine to rapidly become
a member of the EU and NATO. It was as if the new leadership
under Yushchenko had concluded that Kuchma's strategy of European integration would take too long, and that it might be achieved
more quickly if the doors were thrown open to let European finance
sink roots into the national economy. Surely the EU's political institutions and its security umbrella would have to follow finance in,
so as to protect it? And it definitely was the accepted wisdom in the
Ukrainian liberal-democratic, pro-western camp that foreign direct
investment invariably brings benefits: it introduces new technologies, stimulates upgrading and diversification of domestic production and links it to transnational production and distribution
chains. Western capital, it was believed, would also help create
those still missing or chronically weak economic sectors that were
needed to serve growing domestic demand.

For domestic demand did indeed continue to grow, both as a
result of growing real income (see Table 4) and government social
policy. Honouring its commitment to improve the lot of the poorer
sections of society, the government extracted a greater proportion
of GDP from businesses and boosted household incomes. Wages

and salaries in the public sector went up rapidly. Pensions and social welfare benefits went up in 2005 by the equivalent of 4 percent
of GDP to 25 percent of GDP, while overall GDP growth in that year
rose only by 2.7 percent. So it was not just the explosion of cheap
foreign credit that led to the expansion of effective demand. But
without an equivalent expansion in the domestic production of
goods and services in demand, only foreign producers and suppliers could satisfy it.

Foreign direct investment leapt forward after the Orange revolution, from $1.7 bn in 2004 to a peak of $9.2 bn in 2007 (see Table
4). As noted earlier, much of this inflow came through the banking
system. The proportion of capital held in Ukraine's banks that was
owned by foreign shareholders grew from 13 percent to over 50
percent between 200 4 and 2009. The EU and Russia were the most
important sources. Between them six EU member states held 61
percent of foreign owned banking capital, (Austria 16 percent; Italy
14 percent; France 13 percent; Hungary 7 percent; Sweden 6 percent; and Germany 5 percent). Financial institutions based in Russia
held another 21 percent. The Russian share was distinguished by
the predominance of state banks among their holders—VTB,
Vneshekonombank, Sberbank, BM Bank and Prominvestbank, and
by four other banks closely tied to the Kremlin. The European presence was headed up by Raiffeisen of Austria, Unicredit and Intesa
San Paolo of Italy, and BNP Paribas, based in France.[41] By April
2009 a majority of assets in seven out of the largest ten banks were
foreign owned. Ukrainian state owned banks, meanwhile, held less
than one eighth of the country's bank assets.[42] This state of affairs
made it increasingly difficult during the boom period for the National Bank to enforce monetary policy. And at the time of bust,
when the private sector owed over $100 bn to foreign creditors
these private banks pressed the government to save them by taking
on a loan of $16 bn from the IMF and to turn their bad debts into a
public liability.

41   Kornyliuk, *op. cit.*
42   Vlad Mykhnenko and Adam Swain "Ukraine's diverging space economy: The
      orange Revolution, post-soviet development models and regional trajectories",
      European Urban and Regional Studies, Vol. 17, No. 141, 2010, 158.

Foreign direct investment in the years 2005–09 did not go into technologically upgrading and diversifying the economy, except in a very limited way. Rather it went mainly into acquiring and expanding networks of retail bank branches which released the cheap credit to the population (cheap at the time of boom), expanding wholesale and retail trade in high tech goods, consumer durables and luxuries, many of them imported, financing mining and processing plants geared for export, and buying up real estate. In 2007, the peak year for FDI, 29 percent went into expanding financial services. Another 9 percent went into construction, which at the time was closely tied to a booming real estate market in the cities. Twenty five percent of FDI went into industry, but it was targeted at the plants exporting most of their production (steel and chemicals) into soaring world commodities markets. Engineering got just 1.7 percent of all FDI in 2007. So, machinery became an ever growing component of the country's imports, squeezing the Ukrainian machine building sector and reducing its capacity to serve both domestic and foreign demand.[43]

Conclusion

Table 4 shows that Ukraine experienced eight years of GDP growth from the beginning of 2000 to the end of 2007. That period saw two phases of strong growth which were divided by a moderate downturn right after the Orange revolution. Both of these phases saw growth driven by strong international demand for steel and chemicals. However, the structure of industrial GDP remained fairly static over this eight year period, with some clearly negative trends, notably a diminution of the share of food production and light industry in GDP. The engineering sector, whose output enjoyed demand in Russia and other ex-Soviet markets, hardly grew at all. That can only mean that neither the private owners of industry, who were making big profits from exports, nor the state, which reclaimed part of these profits through taxation, was redirecting these

---

43   Zhalilo, *op. cit.*, 143–50.

resources to the sectors of the economy most in need of development.

These eight years of export-led growth did not fundamentally improve the structure of Ukrainian industry, or its overall technological level or the nature of its insertion into the world economy. The question arises whether this failure arose for different reasons in the phases of GDP growth presided over by Kuchma and by Yushchenko. It has already been argued here that Kuchma's strategy failed because of an internal brake: his political regime could not manage the social and regional tensions arising from the unregulated expansion of capital in the exporting sectors. On the other hand, the Orange revolution opened up the political process and promised to overcome these tensions. In contrast to Kuchma, Yushchenko invited foreign capital from the Euroatlantic core, both to balance it off against Russian capital and to help satisfy the still growing domestic demand for commodities and services that the domestic economy could not provide. Yushchenko and his allies believed foreign capital would help upgrade the Ukrainian economy technologically and diversify domestic production of goods in demand. However, foreign capital did not put its money there, but rather into domestic and foreign trade, financial services and the high earning exporting sectors. Foreign owned capital expatriated its earnings, as indeed did domestic capital. Thus, Yushchenko's strategy came up against an external brake on development. And when the international financial crisis mounted in 2007–08, freezing capital flows and driving down prices and demand on world commodities markets, the Ukrainian economy and the state were left with their pants down, without reserves or alternative demand to fall back on. Yushchenko and Tymoshenko had to turn to the IMF to keep their ship of state afloat. Yanukovych and Azarov, who succeeded them in 2010, have had to go to the IMF for a second loan.

In these ways, the international crisis offered an opportunity for centres of foreign capital to strengthen their positions within the Ukrainian economy. The Euroatlantic centre has marched into the banking system and in response to the international crisis it has put up an umbrella over its investments in the form of two IMF loans totalling more than $30 bn. So it insures its risk and gives itself leverage to influence the policies of the indebted government. These developments insert Euroatlantic capital into the economy's financial heights. Russian private investors, on the other hand, had a head start on their Western counterparts in the productive sectors. By 2008 they had already occupied commanding positions in non-ferrous metallurgy, petroleum refining and petrochemicals, mobile telecommunications—and had strong positions in iron and steel and the dairy industry. The crisis allowed Russian investors to buy new assets. The Russian state bank Vneshekonombank took 75 percent ownership of the troubled Prominvestbank in late 2008. And in January 2010 Vneshekonombank supported a successful bid by Russian private investors to take majority ownership of the Donbas Industrial Union, the now deeply indebted steel producer that was once one of Kuchma's chosen national champions.[44] The Russian government stepped up its efforts to gain control of the biggest Ukrainian asset of all—the state owned network of oil and natural gas pipelines. It has for the moment failed to get this coveted prize, not least because the IMF allowed—or rather, required—the Ukrainian government to use part of its loan to pay Natfogaz Ukraina's monthly bills to Gazprom. But for how long can it go on in this way? After the election of Viktor Yanukovych, Prime Minister Putin proposed to him that the Ukrainians and Russians merge Gazprom and Naftogaz Ukrainy, as well as their military industrial complexes, the aviation and aeronautical industries, and some others for good measure. President Yanukovych is truly in a tight spot; he has managed to pay only some of his country's debts to Russia by extending the Russian lease on the Black Sea naval port at Sevastopol for another 25 years to 2042.

The resulting structure of ownership of the privatised Ukrainian economy now consists of three layers—at the top the financial layer is divided between European, Russian and Ukrainian-owned banks. It has not gone so far as, say Poland or Latvia, but the trend

---

44   *Financial Times*, 6 January 2010; "Rosiis'ki aktsionery kupyly 50+2 aktsii"; www.epravda.com.ua/news/4b471de2882e4/. Accessed 8 January 2010.

is towards outright foreign control of the banking system. The middle layer is occupied by Ukrainian owners of mining and industrial processing, with Russian investors making big inroads into the technologically higher end of the processing chains. They are working closely with the upstream suppliers of Russian energy and raw materials that feed the processing industries and the public utilities. And the bottom layer—agriculture and food production—seems secure in majority Ukrainian hands. The processing plants of the "agro-industrial complex" were already privatised in the 1990s. And land itself has been kept off the privatisation agenda altogether. The big challenge for the food processing sector is therefore not about ownership, but about finding adequate external markets to realise returns. Controllers of those external product markets and sources of finance—the EU and Russia in particular—act as gateways for Ukrainian producers into the world economy.

The international financial crisis has shown how vulnerable the Ukrainian economy is to external shocks. Its growth strategy in the past decade has relied heavily on external commodity markets that have seen massive swings in price and demand. The political leaders and private owners of industry have failed to generate a production and distribution of values through their national economy that can satisfy domestic demand and allow such demand to replace a significant portion of external demand. Furthermore, Yushchenko's team in office tried to deal with that failure, first committed by Kuchma, by admitting a bigger inflow of foreign capital, which they expected would complete a virtuous circle of harmonious and balanced growth. The revised strategy has not only failed, but introduced an even more destabilising external ingredient, which has no obligations to the Ukrainian people, not even the kind that elected representatives should honour. Capital, whether foreign or domestic, has revealed itself as fundamentally *anational* in outlook and obligation. No sooner has Ukraine acquired a sovereign state and a capitalist class than its people have begun to realise who they are working for.

Origins of the Ukrainian Crisis[*]

This article explores the origins of the Ukrainian crisis in several
historical developments that came together in 2014. The first development, and the condition necessary for activating all the others, is
the situation that has unfolded inside Ukraine itself since 1991 with
the establishment of a new nation state simultaneously with the return of capitalism. The second is the isolation of Ukraine from the
regional economic and security blocs of the Euro-Atlantic core
states to the west and of Russia to the east. The third is the revival
of Russian imperialism, and the fourth is the ensuing rivalry between Russian and European imperialisms to incorporate Ukraine
into their respective transnational strategies. The fifth development
is the overarching confrontation between a declining American
power and a reviving Russian power in Europe. Russia is observed
as the proactive power that militarised and internationalised the
Ukrainian crisis in 2014 by seizing Crimea and arming the separatist insurgency in the east. It brought the question of European
security to the centre ground, making a confrontation inevitable between Russia and the USA. However, it also has the potential to
open up cracks in the Euro-Atlantic core between the USA on the
one hand and the most powerful European states on the other.

My findings are at odds with the claim made by academic and
political figures right across the political spectrum in the West that
the USA bears primary responsibility for the Ukrainian crisis by
having encroached too far into Russia's traditional sphere of
influence.[1] Rather, I see the US-Russia rivalry as only one contributing factor. The Euro-Atlantic core states had the initiative after
the collapse of the Soviet bloc. They integrated Central European

---

[*]   First published in: *Critique*, Vol. 43, Nos. 3–4, 2015, 395–419.
[1]   They have included John Mearsheimer, "Why the Ukraine Crisis is the West's
Fault", *Foreign Affairs*, September–October 2014; Stephen Cohen, "Why is
Washington Risking War with Russia", *The Nation*, 18–25 August 2014; Jeremy
Corbyn, British Labour Party MP, "NATO Belligerence Endangers Us All",
Morning Star, 17 April 2014; Marine le Pen, leader of France's National Front,
"France's le Pen in Moscow blames EU for new 'Cold War'", *Reuters*, 12 April
2014.

and Baltic littoral states into the EU and NATO on their own terms from the end of the Cold War right up to the international financial crisis and the Russo-Georgian war in 2008. Thereafter, however, the Russian state retook the initiative in Eastern Europe and the Caucasus, the eastward drive of NATO and the EU stalled, and the role of the USA in the region's affairs became increasingly a reactive one. This was the broader context of the Ukrainian crisis, which matured and then erupted in the period from 2008 to 2014.

The fragility of the Ukrainian state

The Maidan[2] arose in 2013, as it did in 2004, because the new Ukrainian ruling class failed to share state power democratically or to invest in the development of its own society. Lacking democratic legitimacy or an adequate social consensus made the state weak and less capable of dealing with the challenges and opportunities it faced from neighbouring powers.

This past quarter-century we have seen the simultaneous construction of a new nation state and its still incomplete transition to a capitalist economy. State building and the privatisation of the nationalised assets have been not only simultaneous, but also symbiotic processes. The state was built as the instrument for the wholesale transfer of these assets into the hands of a very narrow class that we call the oligarchs. This social class then turned the state to enabling new rounds of wealth accumulation from the living labour deployed in the growing private sector.

The old Stalinist bureaucracy was not driven out of the collapsing nationalised economy. Rather, it made its own way to the individual and corporate ownership of the economy's commanding heights. So too did it ensure its own resurrection in the political sphere where it became the absolutely dominant subject of the multi-party system.

---

2   Maidan Nezalezhnosti, Independence Square in central Kyiv, lent its name to the mass revolts in 2004 and 2014 against corruption, social injustice and oligarchic rule.

The state rested on a fragile social consensus of a population holding onto an ever-fading promise that prosperity would come from leaving the Soviet Union and joining the West. The Ukrainian masses rose up in frustration and anger over this broken promise in 1994, 2001 and 2004,[3] but their increasingly massive protests failed each time to fundamentally change things. On the contrary, the Ukrainian people are as poor today as they were in the last year of the USSR, and they are riven by far more inequalities than they were then. Their influence over public policy and public institutions remains weak, even if they have managed repeatedly to recover their basic rights to free expression, assembly and self-organisation.

Thus the present crisis is in the first instance attributable to the failure of a newly independent state to meet the mass expectations on which it was founded in 1991. The Maidan in the winter of 2013–2014 was the latest revolt against this manifest failure, a mass movement that briefly undermined the new ruling class, drove its most powerful faction out of the country, but ultimately failed to dislodge it from the political and economic institutions. However, the Maidan was sufficiently threatening to compel the Russian state — gendarme of the transnational ruling class in its region — to intervene and seize Crimea, to arm a revanchist insurgency in the Donbas, and so to prevent the revolutionary process from spreading into the east and south.

The international isolation of the Ukrainian state

The second historical development that contributed to the outbreak of the current crisis was the failure of the Ukrainian state — for reasons not entirely of its own making — to integrate successfully into

---

3   In 1994 the threat of a general strike forced the Verkhovna Rada and President Leonid Kravchuk to finally call the first democratic elections to both institutions in the independent state. In 2001 the encampment on Independence Square — Maidan — in Kyiv that called itself "Ukraine without Kuchma" demanded the second president's resignation before being violently suppressed. The 2004 Orange Revolution overturned the falsified presidential election and brought Viktor Yushchenko to the presidency.

either the Euro-Atlantic alliance or the Russia-led alliance. Its resulting isolation from the integration projects on either side made Ukraine particularly vulnerable to shifts in the relations between the big powers in the region.

After succeeding Leonid Kravchuk as president in 1994, Leonid Kuchma pursued a strategy to build a national ruling class that could hold its own place in the international political economy. His strategy required keeping Western and Russian capital out of the first big privatisations of nationalised property, accumulating wealth at home and upgrading technologically so as to prepare the country for membership in the EU and its single market. Kuchma's strategy failed because the state leadership could not compel its own capitalists to keep their wealth in the country to upgrade and diversify the domestic economy. Rather, Ukraine became a low wage, energy and materials intensive exporter of primary goods and semi-finished products in agriculture, energy, chemicals and minerals, the profits from which the oligarchs sent abroad.[4] The mounting social inequalities in the midst of a rapid rate of economic recovery on the back of an export boom and an increasingly repressive regime were the triggers for the 2004 Orange Revolution.

From Kuchma's second term in office and Putin's first in Russia, Russian capitalists succeeded in placing substantial investments in the Ukrainian economy. Kuchma's successor in 2004, Viktor Yushchenko, tried to offset the Russian advance by inviting in European investment capital. By 2008 the Ukrainian economy was well penetrated by both Western and Russian investors, neither of whom contributed much to diversifying or upgrading it. Rather, each side was trying to incorporate Ukraine's natural resources, cheap labour and markets onto a low technological echelon of its own regional chains of production and consumption.

Yet the 2008 financial crisis prevented either side from making a bid for a dominant position. The Ukrainian oligarchs still held onto their hope of remaining an independent capitalist class in the

---

4   The government retained state ownership of land, the arms, aeronautical and aerospace industries, communications and energy transportation pipelines.

global political economy. They resisted incorporation into the succession of Russia-led integration projects: the Commonwealth of Independent States and the Customs Union. The European Union, on the other hand, did not want them in as members, and it made that abundantly clear in 2005–2007 by rejecting the requests for a membership path from Yushchenko, the most pro-Western of all Ukraine's leaders. Moreover, the EU's biggest states—Germany, France and Italy—remained steadfastly opposed to offering Ukraine membership in NATO.

So Ukraine ended up in the grey zone between US-led Europe and Russia, and the likely recipient of friction between them that grew as Russia revived and US influence in Europe waned.

The revival of Russian imperialism

The third historical development contributing to the current crisis has been the revival of Russian imperialist ambitions. Throughout the 1990s the Western powers set the agenda, incorporating Central European and Baltic states into the EU and NATO, and all the time holding Russia, Ukraine and Belarus at arm's length outside their integration project.

From around 2000 Putin began to restore Russia's position as a power in Eurasia. He focussed first on rebuilding Russia's economic ties in the ex-Soviet space by reclaiming state control over Russian energy and mineral resources and promoting several national corporate champions in these sectors. Later, the restored economic links with Russia's near abroad would lay a path to securing transnational competitive status for Russia's biggest energy and mineral producers.[5]

In terms of strategy, although not of scale, the Russian model of imperialism is similar to that of the USA in the twentieth century: the provision of military security to countries in exchange for their alignment with Russian foreign policy, and their access to Russian

---

5   Putin's strategy also required subordinating the oligarchs politically, destroying the insurgent Chechen state at the cost of tens of thousands of lives, substantially recentralising the loose federal system he inherited from Boris Yeltsin, and undertaking neoliberal reforms of the welfare system.

markets in exchange for the removal of barriers against Russian capital penetrating their national economies. It is different from the USA experience insofar as Russian expansion has relied on its competitive advantages in global markets of fuel, energy and mineral resources whereas American capitalism expanded globally with a far more diversified production base and with already saturated domestic demand.

The Russian economy is weakly driven by domestic demand, and it does not satisfy it. It is not diversified nor is its bourgeoisie willing to invest significantly in its diversification. Property ownership in Russia is too insecure, access to domestic resources and markets is in the gift of state authorities, and better security and investment opportunities exist for Russian capital investment abroad. Therefore, while the Russian national economy is not diversified, Russian capital has become diversified both sectorally and geographically along transnational chains of production, trade and investment.

A Deutsche Bank report in 2008 concluded that Russia had become by 2006 the largest outward investor of its capital of all the BRIC countries (Brazil, Russia, India and China). Russian overseas direct investment (ODI) was double that of its nearest rivals India and China at $160 bn, up from $20 bn in 2000. Russia was already the second largest source of ODI in emerging markets after Hong Kong. Russian private capital was invested first in the near abroad and then expanded outwards, seeking new markets, financing and new technologies principally in the fields of fuel, energy and metals.

A survey of 25 top Russian firms shows they sent 52 percent of the ODI into Western Europe, followed by 22 percent to the near-abroad countries and 11 percent to Eastern Europe. Several Russian companies made new large purchases abroad in 2008: Evraz in Canada, the USA and Ukraine, Severstal in the USA, Lukoil in Italy and Gazprom in Belarus. The biggest transnational corporations of Russian origin at the time also included Sistema, Sovkomflot, Norilsk

Nickel and Basic Element. By 2010 ODI by Russian firms exceeded $200 bn, and was going mainly to the CIS and EU countries.[6]

For the past 15 years Russia has targeted Ukraine for reabsorption into its traditional sphere of influence. There was an ongoing desire to preserve joint production in engineering, defence, aerospace and other high-technology sectors that survived the Soviet break-up. However, Russian capitalism was looking to new horizons as well, and Ukraine lay along its principal path of expansion into Central and Western Europe. It holds the downstream transit facilities and processing industries that Russian energy, minerals and chemical producers need. Russian producers made their first such cross-border acquisitions in 2000.[7] However, the gas and oil transit pipelines through Ukraine that link Russian suppliers to European consumers, the most valuable transit facility of them all, have remained steadfastly in state hands.

The Yanukovych presidency

The period of Viktor Yanukovych's presidency saw further popular alienation from the political order, the economy falter under the blows of the 2008 financial crisis, and the state face a zero-sum choice of accepting either Russia's or the West's terms of integration into their respective regional integration projects. The mixture of these three factors finally exploded in Kyiv in the winter of 2013–2014.

Yanukovych narrowly defeated Yulia Tymoshenko for the presidency in 2009 on a platform of political stability and the restoration of economic ties with Russia.[8] His predecessor Yushchenko

6   Alexey V. Kuznetsov, "Industrial and Geographical Diversification of Russian Foreign Direct Investments (April 5, 2010). Electronic Publications of Pan-European Institute; https://ssrn.com/abstract=2338170. Accessed 1 October 2015.

7   Marko Bojcun, "Trade, investment and debt: Ukraine's integration into world markets" in Neil Robinson, ed, *Reforging the Weakest Link: Global Political Economy and Post-Soviet Change in Russia, Ukraine and Belarus* (Aldershot: Ashgate, 2004), 46–60.

8   Marko Bojcun, "The International Economic Crisis and the 2010 Presidential Elections in Ukraine", *Journal of Communist Studies and Transition Politics*, 27:3–4 (September–December 2011), 496–519.

had fallen out bitterly with Tymoshenko as Prime Minister over policy towards Russia. Tymoshenko took the full force of the 2008 financial crisis. She negotiated for emergency funding with the IMF in 2009. Ukraine-Russia relations were dominated by disputes about the cost of Russian gas and its transit to Europe. The state corporation Naftogaz Ukrainy became more and more indebted to Gazprom, and the Russian government used the debt to pressure Ukraine on a variety of issues.

Yushchenko had tried to balance growing Russian economic penetration by opening up the country to Western investment. That influx ended spectacularly with the financial meltdown in 2008 that battered people's livelihoods and convinced enough voters, even in the nationalist west of the country, to give Yanukovych a chance to turn things around. The arrival of Armani-dressed oligarchs in limos with tinted windows and bodyguards inside to Yanukovych's inauguration in Kyiv in January 2010 gave everyone a taste of things to come.

Yanukovych perfected the scheme of taking bribes from all of the businesses his ministries permitted to trade. These appropriations made him a tycoon in his own right (he was nominally represented in the private sector by his son Andrii). Yanukovych created his inner circle, called the "Family", from the seven most powerful capitalists. He restored Dmytro Firtash, the gas trader, to financial health by giving him 12 billion cubic metres of Russian gas in settlement of a dispute that Firtash's firm Rosukrenergo had had with Naftogaz Ukrainy during Yushchenko and Tymoshenko's terms, when they tried to close him down. Rosukrenergo once again became the intermediary between Gazprom and Naftogaz Ukrainy in a scheme that allowed Russian and Ukrainian presidents and oligarchs to milk the interstate gas transit. Gazprom opened an $11 bn credit line for Firtash, which he used to build a monopoly stake in fertiliser processing in Ukraine, a port facility, a bank and the national television channel Inter.[9]

---

9   "Otochennia Putina dopomohla Firtashu zarobyty miliardy doliariv"; http://tsn.ua/politika/kogo-zdav-na-sudi-firtash-odkrovennya-yaki-mozhut-viklika ti-politichniy-zemletrus-v-ukrayini-425106.html. Accessed 1 August 2015.

Renat Akhmetov, the country's richest man, was also blessed when Yanukovych granted his firm DTEK a monopoly on electricity exports. Yanukovych ordered the state energy regulator to increase the tariffs local and regional authorities paid for DTEK's electricity from coal-burning stations, to levels comparable to those paid to state-operated nuclear power stations. Both Akhmetov and Firtash won tenders to privatise regional electricity distributors. Both placed their representatives into the state energy regulating commission to ensure that they continued to get high returns for their gas and electricity.[10]

In November 2012 President Yanukovych signed a Double Tax Treaty with the government of Cyprus to replace the Soviet-era treaty. Thus he preserved the channel used by the biggest corporations to expatriate their profits, either permanently or to recycle them back to Ukraine as foreign investments and loans that were subject to much lower levels of capital gains tax. Flight of capital to tax havens was taking place through various other channels used by Ukrainian and foreign firms alike. They consistently deprived the state budget of between $10 bn and $20 bn every year.[11]

As soon as he took office Yanukovych moved to strengthen presidential authority over the legislature, judiciary, the public procurator and the Kyiv city government. He appointed his own Cabinet of Ministers under Mykola Azarov, denying the legislature its constitutional prerogative. The rules were changed to make it easier for the Party of Regions to build voting majorities in the Verkhovna Rada. And in August 2012 the law by which the Rada was elected entirely on the basis of proportional representation of parties was replaced. Now half the seats would be chosen on the basis of proportional representation of those parties that gained more than 5 percent of all votes, and the other half by single mandate constituency elections. The new law gave the President's Party

---

10   Yatseniuk prosyt' kredytoriv dopomohty Ukraini; http://www.epravda.com. ua/news/2015/05/15/542594/ Accessed 5 May 2015.

11   T.A. Tyshchuk and O.V.Ivanov, "Shliakhy protydii prykhovanomu vidplyvu kapitalu z Ukrainy" National Institute of Strategic Studies, 2012; http://old2. niss.gov.ua/content/articles/files/Kapital_Tuschuk-72ec2.pdf. Accessed 1 December 2012.

of Regions a way to finance its own candidates disguised as independents to run in the single-mandate constituencies. It also provided the means to subvert the democratic oversight of local electoral committees and to deliver fraudulent vote counts to the Central Election Commission.

The October 2012 elections to Verkhovna Rada were the dirtiest in the history of independent Ukraine. They provided Yanukovych with a majority of deputies in the Rada, elected by proportional representation from the list of the Party of Regions and as nominally independent candidates standing in single-member constituencies.[12]

In addition to settling scores with potent rivals, the imprisonment of Yulia Tymoshenko and Yurii Lutsenko (former Minister of Interior) and their barring from public office for seven years served to intimidate the entire parliamentary and extra-parliamentary opposition. State security organs went after opposition candidates, independent analysts, university rectors and investigative journalists. A determined attempt was made—in the end unsuccessful—to muzzle the media by making slander of public officials a criminal offence. This broader offensive had the hallmarks of the drive to "sovereign democracy" made by Putin years before in neighbouring Russia.

The economy

Economic growth in the period 2000–2008 was driven by the influx of foreign direct investment into domestic retail markets and the commodities that dominated Ukraine's exports: raw and semi-processed minerals, chemicals and food products. When their hugely inflated prices finally collapsed in 2008, GDP dropped more than 15 percent in the following year, the second deepest fall in Eastern Europe after Latvia. The private sector was left holding debts equivalent in value to a year's GDP.[13] Commodity prices recovered

---

12 Serhii Rakhmanin, "Use vzhe vkradeno do nas". *Zerkalo tyzhnia*, 237, 19 October 2012.

13 "Ukraine—the spectre of default", *Economist Intelligence Unit – Business Eastern Europe*, 23 February 2009.

at the end of 2009, but in the longer term international demand did not. Ukraine's recorded annual GDP grew again, in 2011 by just over 5 percent, but then fell back and registered no growth at all in 2012 and 2013. In 2014 it began to contract as a result of the Russian seizure of Crimea and the war in the east of the country.

Trade

Ukraine's foreign trade was characterised by the following patterns:

- Trade with the EU single market and with Russia each accounted for one quarter of the value of its foreign trade.
- Ukraine incurred annual trade deficits in its trade with Russia as a result of its reliance on Russia's and Turkmenistan's oil and gas (transited through Russia).
- Ukraine incurred annual trade deficits with the EU as a result of the disparity between the capital content of goods it imported from the EU (machinery, consumer durables) and those it exported to the EU (primary and semi-processed goods).
- Ukraine covered its trade deficits with Russia and the EU by generating surpluses from trade with the East Asian, Middle Eastern and African countries.

External trade remained in balance or went into surplus as long as demand for the country's principal exports remained strong—that is, between 2000 and 2008. There-after, the trade deficit grew year on year, reaching $15 bn in 2012.[14]

In 2013 Russia began a trade war with Ukraine in response to the first easing of trade barriers between the EU and Ukraine ahead of the anticipated free trade area agreement between them. Russia claimed that EU exporters would use Ukraine to dump their products into the Russian market. It banned imports of Ukrainian dairy products, fruit, vegetables, meat, sunflower oil and alcohol.

---

14   Bohdan Danylyshyn, "Porady novomu uriadu"; http://www.epravda.com. ua/columns/2012/12/6/349303/. Accessed 6 December 2012.

Investment

Annual foreign direct investment leapt forward after the Orange revolution from $1.7 bn in 2004 to a peak of $9.2 bn in 2007. Ukraine was second only to China in these years in terms of per capita investment flowing into the country. For the first time much of this inflow came through the banking system, with many foreign banks setting up Ukrainian subsidiaries to provide both corporate lending and retail services. Most foreign direct investment went into export credits for agricultural and mining concerns, consumer lending, real estate and the domestic trade in imported luxury goods.[15]

The proportion of foreign capital held in Ukraine's banks grew from 13 percent to over 50 percent between 2004 and 2008. Between them the banks of six EU member states held 30 percent of the banking capital. Financial institutions based in Russia held another 10 percent. The European share was held overwhelmingly by large commercial banks, headed up by Raiffeisen of Austria, Unicredit and Intesa San Paolo of Italy, and BNP Paribas of France. The Russian share was distinguished by the predominance of state banks among their holders—VTB, Vneshekonombank, Sberbank, BM Bank and Prominvestbank, and by four other banks tied to the Kremlin.[16]

The international financial crisis in 2008 forced the rival centres of foreign capital to alter their positions in the Ukrainian market. Facing serious problems at home, the banks that had bought up the domestic networks of several Ukrainian banks were forced to sell. Ukrainian oligarchs, who had sold their banks at lucrative multiples of their book value, now bought them back at a good discount. Russian banks, on the other hand, were better protected from the financial crisis by ample credit from their own government's sovereign funds, so they strengthened their position in the Ukrainian banking system. On balance, however, the biggest initial winners were the Ukrainian private banks, which increased their share

---

15   Bojcun, "The International Economic Crisis".
16   *Ibid.*

of assets in the banking system from 40 to 51 percent between 2008 and 2012. The Ukrainian state banks Oshchadbank and Ukrexsimbank also increased their share from 11 to 15 percent over the same period.[17]

The overall share of banking capital owned by foreigners fell to 34 percent in 2014. The share of Russian capital rose to 12 percent, making it the largest bloc from any one country and double that of its closest rival, Cyprus, at 6 percent. Not to be over-looked is the fact that a considerable share of Cyprus-exported capital came originally from Russia. After 15 years of cross-border investment, Russian capital was deeply penetrated not only into Ukraine's banking services, but critically also in the processing and manufacturing sectors: petrochemicals, agrochemicals, food production, paper, construction materials, steel, non-ferrous metals, machinery and weapons manufacturing. It also had developed strong positions in mass media, telecommunications, insurance, business information and information technology.[18]

Debt

Ukraine's state debt (including state guaranteed debt of the private sector) grew only marginally between 2000 and 2007 to $18 bn, or 12 percent of its GDP. Thereafter it grew rapidly, peaking at $73 bn in 2013. The country's gross external debt, which included that of the private sector, was double that amount at $142.5 bn, equivalent to 78.3 percent of GDP in 2013.[19]

Tymoshenko's government negotiated a loan of $16.4 bn from the IMF, $10.6 bn of which were released by September 2009. Yanukovych's government led by Prime Minister Mykola Azarov that succeeded Tymoshenko's in 2010 was responsible for adding another $40 bn to the state debt over four years, including: $20 bn in treasury bills and Eurobonds; $6.85 bn in IMF Special Drawing Rights in August 2010 and April 2013; $6.6 bn borrowed from the

---

17   *Tyzhden'*, 18 February 2013.
18   Kuznetsov, "Industrial and geographical diversification".
19   Oleksandr Kravchuk, "Istoriia Formuvannia Borhovoi Zalezhnosti Ukrainy"; http://commons.com.ua/formuvannya-zalezhnosti/. Accessed 2 May 2015.

Chinese government in 2012; and $3 bn of the $15 bn originally offered by the Russian government in November 2013 to help persuade Yanukovych not to sign the Association and Free Trade Area Agreements with the EU. The Ukrainian government was additionally in arrears to Gazprom for several billions dollars' worth of gas.[20]

Debt repayment became an increasingly heavy burden on the state budget, at the end of 2014 accounting for 40 percent of total expenditures.[21] For both the West and Russia Ukraine's indebtedness provided a handy lever to influence its government. The IMF was the arbiter of its creditworthiness and gatekeeper to international capital markets. It tried to impose its conditions on the government to decrease state ownership of public utilities, and to withdraw subsidies on the cost of supplying them to households, communal services and businesses.

The Russian government used Ukraine's indebtedness and its dependence on Russian export markets to leverage the Kharkiv Accords in April 2010. The Accords extended the lease of Sevastopol and other Crimean ports to the Russian Navy until 2042 in exchange for cheaper gas. In June of that year the Verkhovna Rada excluded the goal of NATO membership from the country's national security strategy, thus restoring its non-aligned status. Yanukovych also agreed to start talks with Russia about merging the state utility Naftogaz Ukrainy with Gazprom and deepening co-operation between the countries' defence, aerospace and aeronautical industries.

---

20   "Ukrains'ka vlada ne hotova zarady kredytu ity na reformy"; http://dt.ua/ ECONOMICS/ukrayinska-vlada-ne-gotova-zaradi-kreditu-mvf-yti-na-reform i.html. .(accessed 13 February 2013);
"The hidden debts of Russia and Ukraine"; http://www.businessinsider.com/ the-hidden-debts-of-russia-and-ukraine-2014-3. Accessed 4 March 2014.
@Rosiia ne dopomahatyme Ukraini"; http://www. pravda.com.ua/news/20 14/01/29/7011938/. Accessed 1 February 2014.
Financial Times, 23 September 2013, 26 November 2013, 28 November 2013, 18 March 2015, 8 April 2015.
21   David Marples, "Poroshenko's choices"; https://www.opendemocracy.net/ en/odr/poroshenkos-choices/. Accessed 11 November 2014.

Labour migration

The movement of labour also reveals the pattern of Ukraine's incorporation into the international political economy. Since the collapse of the Soviet Union, Ukraine has exported its labour in two directions: workers living in the east of the country have gone largely into Russia, while those in the centre and west have gone into the EU countries. They number in the millions, and their outmigration has had a profound, if contradictory impact on the Ukrainian economy. It has lost skilled and well-educated people to countries where they are now employed as cheap, illegal or legally precarious labour. Communities depopulated by the outmigration have seen their social and family structures severely degraded. Migrant workers have been sending remittances from their earnings home that are estimated to exceed the combined foreign direct investment coming into Ukraine.[22] Without their remittances, the condition of the working class would be considerably worse than it is today. The overall impact of labour outmigration, however, has been negative as far as the reproductive capacity of Ukrainian society is concerned.

The zero-sum choice

Labour migration, trade, the repatriation of profits from foreign direct investment, debt repayments and capital flight are all tributaries for the extraction of wealth from the Ukrainian economy. The European Union and the Eurasian Economic Union are both regional integration projects designed to comprehensively regulate and channel such tributaries into their respective metropolitan cores. In 2013 the Ukrainian state found itself forced to choose between the EU on the one hand and Customs Union on the other. The Customs Union, formed in 2010 and made up of Russia, Belarus and Kazakhstan, was the precursor to the Eurasian Economic Union. The latter was launched in January 2015, together with Armenia as its fourth member. This was a zero-sum choice because

---

22   World Bank, *Migration and Remittances Fact Book* 2011.

there was no way for Ukraine to belong to both regional integration projects. The fact that its economy was closely tied to both the Russian and EU markets, asymmetrically but nevertheless in equally strong measure — through debt to the West, energy supplies from the East, and trade with both — was simply ignored by Russian and EU leaders.

The European Union and Ukraine had a Partnership and Cooperation Agreement since 1994. They had been negotiating since 2007 an Association Agreement and a common deep free-trade area based on the laws, state competition policy and production standards that are already enforced within the EU single market. These requirements, which the Verkhovna Rada was urgently adopting throughout 2013, would add considerable costs to the state and private sector in order to make Ukrainian goods acceptable in the EU market. Except for a transition period when EU food products and Ukrainian automobiles were protected from competition, the abolition of almost all tariff and non-tariff barriers to trade would in the long run expose several Ukrainian industries to sustained and ruinous competition from the EU side.[23]

Moreover, the EU's offer was "integration without the institutions": Ukraine was not offered membership in the EU nor even the prospect of membership, so it would remain excluded from the decision-making process that shapes the EU single market in which its own businesses and workers were going to compete. It was not an attractive proposition.

The Customs Union and its successor Eurasian Economic Union offered Ukraine something different. This integration project was far less developed than the European Union's. Russia accounted for 90 percent of the combined GDP of the Customs Union's members, which meant that Russia would dominate the Union whatever its formal governing structure. The Russian establishment saw in this project one of the important means to reclaim great power status. The news agency *Sputnik* hailed the launch of the Eurasian Economic Union in January 2015 as "the birth of a new giant".

---

23   "Five facts you need to know about the Ukraine-EU trade deal"; http://rt.com/business/168856-ukraine-europe-trade/;Accessed 27 June 2014.

Putin called it "a powerful supranational association capable of becoming one of the poles in the modern world and serving as an efficient bridge between Europe and the dynamic Asia-Pacific region".[24]

Yet such a bridge was hardly possible to build without Ukraine. Russian diplomacy focussed on this challenge, trying to coax it into the Union by promising generous energy subsidies if it joined and trade sanctions if it did not. Yet even under Yanukovych and in the worsened economic situation, the government continued to resist. There was a fundamental lack of trust between Kyiv and Moscow, at the heart of which was the refusal of the Russian state to acknowledge Ukraine's independence.

This refusal is rooted in a long history of Russian imperial domination of Ukraine. It is justified ideologically by the claim that the Ukrainian nation does not exist, that its people are simply the little brothers (*malorosy*) of the Russian nation. After gaining independence in 1991 Ukrainian leaders regularly faced jibes from their Russian counterparts about when they would finally come to their senses and stop playing their game of nation building. Putin expressed perfectly the paradox that Ukrainian statehood poses to Russia's leaders when he told George W. Bush in April 2008 at the NATO summit in Bucharest that Ukraine really was not a state, but if it tried to join NATO it would cease to exist as a state. It was also at this meeting that "Putin threatened to encourage the secession of the Black Sea peninsula of Crimea and eastern Ukraine".[25] It was therefore hardly surprising Kyiv baulked at pooling its sovereignty

---

24   Nadezhda Arbatova, "Three Faces of Russia's Neo-Eurasianism"; https://www.iiss.org/publications/survival/2019/survival-global-politics-and-strategy-december-2019january-2020/616-02-arbatova. Accessed January 2 2020.

25   "Putin hints at splitting up Ukraine"; http://www.themoscowtimes.com/news/article/putin-hints-at-splitting-up-ukraine/361701.html. Accessed 5 March 2015. See also Putin's address to the Russian Federal Assembly on 4 December 2014 when he justified the seizure of Crimea on the grounds that "Crimea, the ancient Korsun or Chersonesus, and Sevastopol have invaluable sacral importance for Russia, like the Temple Mount in Jerusalem for the followers of Islam and Judaism" http://en.kremlin.ru/events/president/news/47173

with Russia's in the Customs Union or the Eurasian Economic Union.

Despite the Kharkiv Accords lowering the price for Russian gas by $100 per thousand cubic metres, Ukraine continued to pay more than Germany and Italy, which are considerably further from Russian gas fields than Ukraine. Neighbouring Belarus enjoyed a lower price, but only after its president Alexander Lukashenko sold the country's gas transit pipelines to Gazprom. The Ukrainians were not ready to do that; instead, they began to diversify their sources of supply, reducing imports from Russia from 57 mcm in 2007 to 33 mcm in 2012 and 26 mcm in 2013.[26]

The Ukrainian government's inability to service its foreign debt brought matters to a head at the beginning of winter in 2013. Putin and Yanukovych held talks in Moscow on 22 November 2013 after which Yanukovych announced he would not sign the Association Agreement and the linked European Free Trade Agreement at the upcoming Summit of the EU Eastern Partnership in Vilnius. When the news reached Kyiv, several hundred people gathered on the Maidan to protest and demand Yanukovych sign the agreements.

In Vilnius on 29 November he said at his press conference: "We have big difficulties with Moscow. I have been alone for three and a half years in very unequal conditions with Russia".[27] He proposed as a way out of the situation that Moscow be involved in three-way negotiations with the EU and Ukraine. However, EU officials rejected his proposal.

Addressing the Eastern Partnership's plenary session Yanukovych insisted he was not rejecting the Agreements, but wanted further negotiations in order "to minimise the negative consequences of the initial period that will be felt by the most vulnerable groups of Ukrainians":

---

26   Arkady Moshes, "Will Ukraine Join (and Save) the Eurasian Customs Union?"; http://www.ponarseurasia.org/memo/will-ukraine-join-and-save-eurasian-customs-union. Accessed 20 June 2013.

27   The Guardian, 29 November 2013.

"Unfortunately Ukraine has been left facing serious financial and economic problems recently ... [we need] macro-financial assistance ... the restoration of co-operation with the IMF and WB ... a revision of trade restrictions on individual items ... participation of the EU and international financial institutions in the modernisation of the Ukrainian gas transit system ... as the key element ... to ensuring Ukraine's energy independence ... the elimination of contradictions and the settlement of problems in trade and economic co-operation with Russia and other members of the Customs Union related to the establishment of the free trade area between Ukraine and the EU".[28]

Yanukovych was being pressed to choose between Russia and the West, but he wanted co-operation with both sides to deal with the country's mounting problems.

The Maidan

By the time Yanukovych uttered these words, the protesters on Kyiv's Maidan had grown to several thousand. No-one was paying attention to the very real shortcomings of the Agreements, or that the EU was not prepared to offer more than ten million euros to help the government service a debt in the billions. The protesters simply saw in Yanukovych's refusal to sign the Agreements a rejection of the EU as a result of the pressure coming from Moscow. In the night of 29–30 November students camping on the Maidan were brutally beaten by riot police and dozens of them were imprisoned. Their treatment caused outrage in the capital and the numbers on the Maidan the following day swelled to tens of thousands.

Yanukovych went to Moscow again on 17 December. On that occasion the two sides agreed a loan of $15 bn to Ukraine, a lower price for natural gas and easing of some restrictions on cross-border trade in 2013–14. No agreement was reached concerning Ukraine's participation in the Customs Union. Putin insisted that it was not even an item of discussion at the talks.[29] If that was meant to placate

---

28   *Kyiv Post*, 29 November 2013.
29   Andrii Vyshynsky, "Yanukovych lih pid Moskvu"; http://www.epravda.com. ua/publications/2013/12/17/409320/. Accessed 17 December 2013.

the protesters then Putin and Yanukovych were poorly advised. That evening the crowds on the Maidan were bigger than ever, covering the entire square and spilling over into neighbouring streets.

Their demands grew in response to the government's hamfisted brutality against them. Initially they were limited to demanding that Yanukovych sign the Association Agreement and hold a public inquiry into the beating and imprisonment of the students. However, then the Party of Regions and the Communist Party in the Rada voted through laws on 16 January 2014 that criminalised public assembly and criticism of the government. Hundreds were arrested, charged and held in prison. The protesters put up barricades on Hrushevsky Street—which leads from the Maidan to the parliament—on 19 January. They now began to demand the release of all detained demonstrators, Yanukovych's resignation and immediate presidential elections. So began a month of violent confrontations between the riot police and the demonstrators.

The authorities escalated the conflict several times more: by recruiting thousands of thugs (*titushky*) from across the eastern and southern oblasts and deploying them against demonstrators in Kyiv; by kidnapping protesters right off the streets and from hospitals where they had been taken for medical attention, and in some cases torturing and murdering them; and finally by replacing rubber bullets and stun grenades with live ammunition.

As the confrontation in Kyiv grew to the brink of a shooting war, government buildings across the country came under siege. By the end of January protesters had seized Oblast State Administration buildings in ten regional capitals in western and central Ukraine.[30] In six other regional capitals they were surrounded by mass demonstrations, defended by Interior Ministry troops and gangs of *titushky*. These mobilisations spread to other cities in eastern and southern Ukraine where army barracks, offices of the Public Prosecutor and the State Security Service came under siege.[31]

---

30 Oblast State Administrations are institutions of direct presidential rule that override all elected local and regional governments.

31 "Khronika povstannia: 25 sichnia"; http://tyzhden.ua/News/100053. Accessed 26 January 2014. "Narodna Rada obrala prezydiu"; http://dt.ua/POLITI

From the beginning of February the government made preparations to introduce martial law in Kyiv. However, on 18 February
the State Security Service announced a more targeted "anti-terrorist
operation" to dismantle the barricades, reclaim the occupied buildings and disperse the Maidan.

The pivotal moment

On 19 February the fighting in Kyiv reached its peak: for the first
time demonstrators on the Maidan responded to the attacks by the
riot police with gunfire, and themselves came under sniper fire.
Seventy-seven people were shot dead, by far the single largest number of fatalities in a day.

A ceasefire ensued overnight and on 20 February President
Yanukovych entered into negotiations with leaders of the three opposition parties mediated by the foreign ministers of Germany, Poland and France. Russia's ambassador to Ukraine and later Putin's
special envoy were present at the negotiations. Agreement was
reached on the same day, signed by all present except Russia's representatives. It was not made public.

The Ukrainian signatories agreed: to restore the 2004 constitution within 48 hours, which would abolish the president's executive
powers to form the government; to restore the parliamentary republic; to form a coalition government of national unity within ten
days; by September to undertake a further constitutional reform of
the division of powers; to hold presidential elections immediately
afterwards, at latest by end of year 2014; to set up a commission of
Ukrainian and Council of Europe representatives to investigate the
violence and killings; to refrain from the introduction of martial
law; and to ensure the return of all illegally held arms to the authorities.[32]

CS/narodna-rada-obrala-prezidiyu-klichko-tyagnibok-i-yacenyuk-135971_.html.
Accessed 22 January 2014. "Na pivdni i shodi barykaduiut' ODA"; http://
www.pravda.com.ua/news/2014/01/30/7012104/. Accessed 30 January 2014.
32 "Avtobusy z VV proikhaly uriadovoho kvartalu"; http://ukr1.pravda.com.
ua/news/2014/02/21/7015500/. Accessed 21 February 2014.

This agreement was made public in the morning of 21 February. It was put to the Council (Rada) of the Maidan, who accepted it by 34 votes to 2. The opposition party leaders then put the agreement to the mass assembly of the Maidan, which rejected it and adopted a single demand instead: Yanukovych's immediate resignation. All this took place in the presence of embalmed bodies of demonstrators laid out on the stage before the assembly.[33]

During the day practically all Interior Ministry troops and Security Service left the government quarter in convoys that were escorted out of the city for their own safety by parliamentary deputies. Yanukovych's support crumbled further as 16 Party of Regions deputies in the parliament quit, so denying it and the Communists their majority. Some were reported leaving with their families for their home towns or out of the country altogether.

That evening President Yanukovych left the capital for his mansion compound at Mezhyhiria. He claimed later that his car was shot at as he left. At the compound his aides destroyed thousands of files, throwing some into the artificial lake from which they were later retrieved. The documents included detailed records of bribe taking over several years. They loaded all the valuables that two helicopters could carry and flew Yanukovych to Donetsk airport.

The parliament convened on 22 February and restored the parliamentary republic under the 2004 constitution. It resolved that Yanukovych had abandoned his office. Electing Oleksandr Turchynov as interim president, the parliament called new presidential elections for 25 May. It then started to elect a government from its own ranks.[34]

Outside the parliament building an angry mob attacked deputies from the Party of Regions and the Communist Party. Deputies from the Bat'kivshchyna Party and stewards from the Maidan shielded them from the mob and escorted them in and out of the building. On the same day the Communist Party headquarters in

---

33 "Liudy postavyly ul'tymatum"; http://www.pravda.com.ua/news/2014/02/21/7015590/. Accessed 21 February 2014.

34 "Rada skynula Yanukovycha"; http://www.pravda.com.ua/news/2014/02/22/7015777/. Accessed 22 February 2014.

Kyiv were ransacked, and that night a country house belonging to the son of Vasyl Symonenko, the Communist Party leader, was burned down.

Yanukovych responded to these developments, still from inside Ukraine, claiming he was the victim of a *coup d'état*, and that he would refuse to leave Ukraine or the presidency.[35] However, on 22 February he tried to fly out of Donetsk airport for Russia, but his helicopter was denied clearance by air traffic controllers. Days later he appeared in Crimea and from there he left by sea for Russia.

Finally, on 22 February members of the Party of Regions convened a meeting of several hundred people in Kharkiv that included deputies from the Crimean Autonomous Republic, Sevastopol City Council and several eastern and southern oblast councils. The meeting accused the parliament in Kyiv of dishonouring the 21 February accords and declared its decisions illegitimate in view of what it described as a climate of terror in the capital. The governments these deputies claimed to represent resolved to take constitutional order and power into their own hands.

Vadym Kolisnychenko, Party of Regions deputy and one of Yanukovych's close allies, rallied the delegates in the Kharkiv hall with cries of "For friendship with Russia — economic, spiritual, religious!" The delegates responded "Russia! Russia!"[36] The meeting clearly had a more far-reaching agenda than its resolutions revealed. It was launching the separatist movement across the eastern and southern oblasts.

On the same day Russian foreign minister Sergei Lavrov told US Secretary of State John Kerry that the Ukrainian opposition parties had broken the 21 February accords. While Russia demanded they return to the accords, it began preparing immediately to occupy and annex Crimea, and to promote the separatist movement in the eastern oblasts.

---

35   "Yanukovych: ya ne zberaiusia u vidstavku"; http://www.pravda.com.ua/news/2014/02/22/7015766/. Accessed 22 February 2014.

36   "Deputaty zi ziizdu u Kharkovi perebyraiut' vladu"; http://www.pravda.com.ua/news/2014/02/22/7015713/. Accessed 22 February 2014.

A coup?

Does the claim that Yanukovych was overthrown by a coup stand up to the available evidence? He had signed an accord that stripped him of executive powers and denied him the right to form the government. His Party of Regions could no longer muster a majority in the parliament. He would be investigated by a commission looking into the fatalities, disappearances and tortures. His continuation in office was rejected by the assembled thousands on the Maidan, and he fled Kyiv along with the Berkut, Alfa and Omega squads — special forces which had protected him — as they, too, headed for Crimea and the Donbas.

All three opposition parties stood by the accords and earnestly recommended them to the Maidan, as did the foreign ministers who mediated the talks. Yet after the troops and special forces left the government quarter and the now armed Maidan refused to move until Yanukovych stepped down, his position was indeed bleak, if not impossible. He lost his nerve and fled.

No doubt, members of his party and their Communist allies were also intimidated and in some cases terrorised by the angry mob and armed vigilantes. However, to their credit, the Maidan's stewards and members of the other opposition parties gave them protection as they continued to sit in parliament and vote in the new government. Except, of course, those deputies like Oleksandr Tsariov and Vadym Kolisnychenko who quit Kyiv immediately for Crimea, Kharkiv, Donetsk and Luhansk to organise the separatist movement.

Was it an American-inspired coup? Those convinced that the Americans were behind the Maidan and the overthrow of Yanukovych have pointed out that US politicians visited the Maidan, the US State Department pushed for Yatseniuk over Klychko as Prime Minister, that Victoria Nuland was recorded uttering "Fuck the EU" to the US ambassador in Kyiv, and that CIA director John Brennan visited Kyiv in April 2014. These acts hardly amount to a case that the USA inspired a coup to overthrow Yanukovych. Russian state actors had considerably more influence than their American counterparts over the unfolding events through their agents in the

SBU, diplomatic corps, armed forces general staff, interior ministry and the President's administration. Andrii Parubii, who commanded the Maidan's self-defence brigades and served later as Secretary of the National Security and Defense Council, recalls:

> We were working in a state where the SBU [State Security Service] and all the power ministries had been crammed full over two years with FSB agents [Russia's Federal Security Bureau] ... The power ministries in Crimea went over fully onto the side of the occupier ... A lot of weapons were removed. That is to say, formally we had our own power structures, but in reality they were working for our opponent.[37]

A fascist junta?

Another claim made soon after these events by Russia's leaders and repeated ever since by their Western supporters was that Kyiv after Yanukovych came to be ruled by a fascist junta. This claim does not stand up to the evidence either. Made up of 21 ministers, the new government was elected by an elected parliament. These ministers were put before an assembly of the Maidan for approval, which it gave with some reservations.

The UDAR party of Vitalii Klychko declined to take any portfolios, so the government was dominated by the Bat'kivshchyna party. Four of the government's ministers were from the far-right Svoboda party: Oleh Makhnitsky as Prosecutor General, Oleksandr Sych, deputy PM, Andrii Mokryk, environment minister and Ihor Shvaika, agriculture minister. In addition, Andrii Parubii, a Batkivshchyna deputy who in his youth was a founding member of the far-right Social National Party, was made head of the National Security and Defense Council. Dmytro Yarosh, leader of Right Sector, which played a big part in the Maidan's self-defence was offered the post of deputy to Parubii, which he declined.

There was justifiable concern that the far-right and fascist paramilitaries who had stood on the Maidan would either pose a threat to public order if they were not disbanded, or might merge with state structures. Members of these paramilitary groups turned

---

37 "Andrii Parubii: Koruptsia ne maie prizvyshch i imen"; http://www.prav da.com.ua/articles/2015/03/24/7062545/. Accessed 24 March 2015.

quickly towards the eastern oblasts after Yanukovych fell and the separatist movement emerged. For its part the government actively drew these militias into the eastern oblasts once the Anti-Terrorist Operation began. In May, the Maidan's self-defence forces were officially disbanded, but various groups continued to function either on their own or as recognised units of the army or interior ministry.

The presence and influence of fascists in Ukrainian politics, the volunteer battalions in the east and in the state structures was greatly exaggerated by Russian state actors to try and discredit the opposition to the Yanukovych regime and later those who replaced him in government.[38] After Russia intervened in the south and east, the far right lost its claim to the nationalist mantle as a sense of nationalist resistance spread across practically the entire Ukrainian political arena. In the May 2014 presidential elections won by Petro Poroshenko, the Svoboda candidate Oleh Tiahnybok took 1.2 percent and Right Sector's Dmytro Yarosh 0.7 percent of the votes. The September elections to the Verkhovna Rada saw Svoboda's share of the vote fall by more than half compared with the 2012 elections. They failed to clear the 5 percent hurdle needed to take any seats by proportional representation. Svoboda took six seats in constituency contests in Western Ukraine. Its three surviving ministers resigned from the Cabinet.[39]

The Ukrainian crisis internationalised

Russia turned the struggle for power inside Ukraine into an international crisis. As Yanukovych's position in Kyiv grew more tenuous, the Russian leadership deployed military forces to its border with Ukraine and reinforced its positions in the leased Crimean naval bases. Immediately after Yanukovych fled Kyiv, Russian forces

38   Anton Shekhovtsov, "The Spectre of Ukrainian Fascism: Information Wars, Political Manipulation and Reality"; http://euromaidanpress.com/2015/06/24/spectre-of-ukrainian-fascism-information-wars-political-manipulation-and-reality/. Accessed 1 July 2015.

39   Marko Bojcun, "Return of the Oligarchs: The October Parliamentary Elections"; https://ukrainesolidaritycampaign.org/2014/11/19/ukraine-return-of-the-oligarchs-the-october-parliamentary-elections/. Accessed 1 November 2014.

began taking control of the Crimean government, the peninsula's communications and the urban centres, laying siege to Ukrainian military bases there.

By seizing Crimea Russia violated the Budapest Declaration, which it signed along with the USA and the UK in 1994. In exchange for Ukraine giving up its nuclear weapons—which were sent to Russia, no less—the signatories had promised to respect Ukraine's territorial integrity and national sovereignty. Russia also violated the Treaty of Friendship, Co-operation and Partnership it had signed with Ukraine in 1998. It violated the UN Charter by changing international borders by force, offering as its only defence the fact that the Western powers had done the same by upholding the separation of the Kosovan statelet from Serbia. Putin acknowledged much later that he ordered the occupation and annexation of Crimea.[40] In addition, the Russian FSB agent Igor Girkin-Strelkov, who served in Crimea at the time before being dispatched to the Donbas, described on the Neiromir TV channel how Russian armed forces, and not the local authorities, organised the so-called referendum.[41]

Putin's plans were far more ambitious than what he actually achieved. Eight oblasts were targeted for separation from Ukraine. If successful, this would have given Russia a land bridge from its western border through to Crimea and across to Transnistria, thereby cutting Ukraine off completely from the Black Sea.[42] In the end, Russian and Russia-backed Ukrainian forces took only parts of two oblasts, Donetsk and Luhansk. Although initially constituting about 4 percent of the territory of Ukraine in 2014, and 5 percent after the separatist offensive in January 2015, they accounted for a quarter of its GDP and around 30 percent of export earnings.

---

40   "Putin reveals secrets of Russia's Crimea takeover plot"; http://www.bbc.co.uk/news/world-europe-31796226. Accessed 9 March 2015.
41   "I. Strelkov vs. N. Starikov"; https://www.youtube.com/watch?v=G04tXnvKx8Y. Accessed 22 January 2015.
42   See the English translation of the full text of the Kremlin policy paper that set out these plans, originally published by *Novaia gazeta* on 24 February 2015, http://www.unian.info/politics/1048525-novaya-gazetas-kremlin-papers-article-full-text-in-english.html. Accessed 25 February 2015.

The separatist movement was launched by members of Yanu-kovych's Party of Regions when it became clear that their power in Kyiv was broken. Renat Akhmetov, a prime beneficiary of Yanu-kovych's patronage whose businesses are concentrated in the Don-bas, provided the initial finance for its armed detachments.[43] The separatists' declared aim was to protect the region's Russian speak-ers from Ukrainian "fascists and banderites" allegedly coming from Kyiv to ethnically cleanse them. However, their real aim was to pre-vent the spread of the Maidan into the east where the oligarchs' in-dustrial assets and power were concentrated. The ousted fragment of the oligarchic regime clung to this separatist platform in the east and started to rock it so as to upend the Kyiv government.

The separatists were reinforced by Russian nationalists, fas-cists, mercenaries and soldiers "on leave" from across the Russian border. Russian nationals took over the leadership of the Donetsk People's Republic (Aleksandr Borodai) and its Sloviansk military head-quarters (Igor Girkin-Streltsov), side lining the original Ukrainian leader (Pavel Gubarev, member of the neo-Nazi Russian National Unity).[44] As the Kyiv government stepped up its military campaign against these militias and their declared republics, Russia increased both the calibre and supply of personnel and weaponry to them. The so-called Donetsk and Luhansk People's Republics did establish a certain social base and a professional cadre drawn from the region itself, but their military, diplomatic and financial capac-ities were almost entirely dependent on the Kremlin.

Russia's principal motive in seizing Crimea and backing the separatist movement in the east was not to gain territory, but above all to suppress the Maidan and to restore Russia's influence over the government in Kyiv that Yanukovych had previously guaran-teed. The Maidan threatened Russia's interests not only in Ukraine: it showed that oligarchic-capitalist states in the region could be overthrown by a sustained popular uprising.

---

43   "Nariad muchenika primeriat' ne khochu"; http://www.rg.ru/2014/05/12/gubarev.html. Accessed 5 December 2014.

44   See Zbigniew Marcin Kowalewski, "Russian White Guards in the Donbas", https://peopleandnature.wordpress.com/2014/07/06/ukraine-russian-white-guards-in-the-Donbas/. Accessed 10 July 2014.

Russia aimed to prevent Ukraine's further incorporation into the Atlantic alliance through an association agreement or a free-trade regime with the EU or a path to NATO membership. It was alarmed at the economic consequences for itself of an EU-Ukraine free-trade regime and at the possibility that the EU association agreement might become a back door for Ukraine to get into NATO. It sought guarantees for Russian capitalists' access to Ukraine's markets and their protection from competition by EU investors and producers. It wanted a government in Kyiv that would instead align its economic and security policies with Russian regional and global strategies, and that would eventually join the Eurasian Economic Union and a Russia-led security alliance.

Russia's timing and calculations

Why did Russia choose this moment to seize Crimea and intervene into the eastern oblasts? Russia was weaker militarily than the USA, but only in an abstract comparative sense. In the real disposition of their forces Russia was stronger than NATO in its own near abroad. Its immediate neighbours were militarily weak and NATO was unable to project and sustain its power in the region. It could not fulfil its commitments to mutual defence of members in Eastern Europe for strictly logistical reasons — it had no forward bases there of any significance and could not establish them quickly. As the Estonian defence minister Sven Mikser put it on 24 June 2015, "Putin believes that he enjoys regional superiority".[45]

Most important to Putin's calculations were the political divisions between the USA and its European allies over relations with Russia. According to a survey conducted by the Pew Research Center, the leaders of Germany, France and Italy were not prepared to come to the defence of East European member states like Latvia, Lithuania or Estonia if they were attacked by Russia.[46] And there

---

45   "Baltic states to receive heavy military equipment from the US"; http://www.thenews.pl/1/10/Artykul/211359,Baltic-states-to-receive-heavy-military-equipment-from-US. Accessed 23 June 2015.

46   *Financial Times*, 24 June 2015.

was a growing resistance among the American public to more military campaigns abroad that placed real restraints on the American administration.

All of these factors emboldened Russia to intervene in Ukraine at the moment of opportunity, for which it had been preparing. Russia was rebuilding its military capabilities and placing them forward across its own borders. After the Soviet Union's collapse, the Russian Federation held onto military bases in Belarus, Transnistria in Moldova, Kyrgyzstan, Tajikistan and Kazakhstan. After Putin became president, they were augmented with new bases and additional forces at existing ones in Belarus, Armenia, Georgia and Ukraine. In 2014, after annexing Crimea, Moscow annulled its previous agreements with Ukraine on its bases at Sevastopol, Kerch and other Crimean locations. In January 2015 the Russian defence ministry issued a new military doctrine and announced plans to spend 20 tr roubles ($310 bn) by 2020 to upgrade its military capabilities in Crimea, Kaliningrad and the Arctic.[47]

Into the arms of the Western powers

If Putin's aim was to dissuade the Ukrainian state from seeking closer ties with NATO then his actions had the opposite effect. The Verkhovna Rada revoked the country's non-aligned status and urged the government to seek NATO membership again. The government sought lethal military equipment from NATO, which was refused. The attitude of the population towards NATO membership also made a historic shift from a majority consistently opposed since 1991 to a majority in favour. Throughout this period the official position of NATO states, including the USA, was no more than stating that Ukraine had a right to seek NATO membership and to actively discourage any such application. This was their response in a period when Russia stepped up deliveries of heavy weapons to the separatists, including the BUK missiles that shot

---

47   "Russia to boost military capabilities in Crimea"; http://rt.com/news/222371-russian-defense-plan-2015/. Accessed 16 January 2015. As a percentage of GDP, Russian defence spending grew from 3.9 percent in 2010 to 4.2 percent in 2013. Over the same period the USA's defence spending fell from 4.6 to 3.8 percent.

down Malaysian passenger airliner MH17, and sent in its own trainers and political advisors, helping them to halt the Ukrainian offensive in the summer of 2014, return to the offensive themselves and take more territory and population. Poroshenko walked away from the NATO summit in Wales in August 2014 without the weapons he had asked for. Then he was obliged by his Western allies to send ex-President Kuchma to negotiate the Minsk Accords in September with the leaders of the separatist republics, by which they were recognised as parties to an interstate agreement.

So what is the evidence that in 2013 and 2014 it was NATO encroaching further into Russia's traditional sphere of influence that provoked Putin to react by intervening militarily into Ukraine? The available evidence suggests otherwise: Putin was the proactive side in the confrontation that ensued. He calculated correctly that NATO would not respond in kind to Russia's attack on Ukraine if that attack was decisive and rapidly attained its objectives.

In part, that is what happened, at least with regard to the Crimea. The Western powers took it as a fait accompli. However, the ongoing crisis did not play out like the Russia-Georgia shooting war that lasted for only four days in August 2008. Putin miscalculated on the readiness of Ukrainian government forces to resist the separatist insurgency in Donetsk and Luhansk oblasts and to suppress his efforts to widen it to the other oblasts. Putin had planned a rapid advance deep into the country, seeking to envelop eight eastern and southern oblasts (Kharkiv, Kherson, Mykolaiv, Odesa, Zaporizhzhia, Dnipropetrovsk, as well as Donetsk and Luhansk) and thereby acquire an unassailable position from which to dictate his terms to the Kyiv government. He failed to achieve that position and the pro-Russia separatist forces were contained in the eastern reaches of Donetsk and Luhansk oblasts. The Russians' advantages in speed and geographic proximity diminished as the conflict dragged on, leaving them with superiority only in firepower. The war of movement became a war of position, and the longer it dragged on the more it encouraged NATO member states in the region to seek reinforcements of their own borders with Russia from their Western allies.

The balance of power

Framing the Ukrainian crisis is the changing balance of power between Russia, the USA and Germany as the leading EU state. Russia's economic and military expansion places it on a collision course with US hegemony over Western and Central Europe. This collision is all the more destabilising the weaker the USA's capacity to project its own power into Eastern Europe becomes.

As noted above, Russian capital is investing and diversifying its portfolios in Western and Central Europe, and its government has long sought and secured bilateral co-operation with separate EU member states. It has done so deliberately to avoid negotiating with the EU as their collective representative. Germany is the most important such partner for Russia. It has the biggest investment in Russia of any country in the world, and Germany has admitted significant Russian inward investment in return. Corresponding to that mutual economic relationship there was a political axis of EU (Berlin)-Kyiv-Moscow in the making when the Ukrainian crisis broke open. The imposition of Western sanctions against Russia has created huge uncertainty as to its future.

This axis passes through a specific faction of the ruling class in Ukraine grouped around the tycoon and key Russian point of contact Dmytro Firtash, his ally Serhii Liovochkin, former head of Yanukovych's presidential administration, and the Opposition Bloc in the Ukrainian parliament. This group is trying to build an EU–Kyiv–Moscow axis to compete with the existing Washington–Kyiv–Moscow axis. Its international platform to build this axis is the Agency for Modernisation of Ukraine, created in Vienna in March 2015. Its European participants include a range of prominent public figures.[48] Its two main pillars of support in Ukraine are the Employ-

---

48   Prof. Rainer Lindner, head of the German-Ukrainian Forum; Karl-Georg Wellmann, Bundestag Member; Bernard-Henry Lévy, French public activist; Lord Risby, British MP; Karl-Georg Wellmann, Bundestag member; Gunther Verheugen, European Commissioner for the EU in 1999–2004; Peer Steinbrück, ar-

ers Federation, headed by Firtash himself, whose members' businesses accounted for 70 percent of the country's GDP in 2014, and the leadership of the Federation of Trade Unions. The faction of Firtash, Liovochkin and the Opposition Bloc has been preparing to challenge the current government. The likelihood that they will do so depends on at least two things: whether Poroshenko and Yatseniuk succeed in crushing Firtash first by destroying his business empire (as part of the current campaign to "de-oligarchise" the state), and whether the Western powers and Russia agree between themselves that the current Ukrainian leadership needs replacing in order to impose a settlement to the war on all sides.

The second political axis passing through the Ukrainian ruling class is a Washington–Kyiv–Moscow axis, which in Kyiv passes through the Poroshenko–Yatseniuk faction. This faction has been trying hard to discipline the biggest oligarchs Renat Akhmetov, Ihor Kolomoisky and Dmytro Firtash to its pro-Western course. However, all three oligarchs have powerful interests in maintaining ties with both Russia and the EU states, and this political axis does not have as powerful an economic chain at its foundation as the EU (Germany)–Kyiv–Moscow one has because the USA does not have a vital economic relationship with either Russia or Ukraine. Rather, its main underlying motive is to demarcate and discipline the European region over which the USA exercises hegemony. The war between Russia and Ukraine has become the issue through which Washington tries to contain German ambitions and marshals all of its European allies to oppose Russia, rather than allowing them to

---

chitect of the Euro protection programme during the 2008 economic crisis; Laurence Parisot, ex-President of the French Employers Association; Lord Mandelson, formerly European Commissioner for Trade; Rupert Scholtz; Włodzimierz Cimoszewicz, the Prime Minister of Poland in 1996–1997; Lord McDonald, Prosecutor General of England and Wales in 2003–2008; and Bernard Kouchner, ex-Foreign Minister of France and founder of the international organization Medecins sans Frontières. "Agency for modernisation of Ukraine founded in Vienna"; http://www.fru.org.ua/en/events/international-events /u-vidni-predstavnyky-frantsii-nimechchyny-ta-velykobrytanii-stvoryly-ahen tstvo-z-modernizatsii-ukrainy-iake-cherez-200-dniv-predstavyt-chitkyi-plan-v yvedennia-ukrainy-iz-kryzy. Accessed 9 March 2015.

work out deals with Russia behind the USA's back. The USA's approach is fundamentally different from Germany's, which is to get Russia to uphold a common rules-based regional order that is also economically productive for both of them. Has the Ukrainian crisis, then, become a lightning rod for the further bifurcation of the Western alliance that places Germany on a tightrope between the USA and Russia?

Conclusions

I have not ventured into the period since the start of the war in the east. It has been marked by many thousands dead and injured in the fighting, more civilians than soldiers, a humanitarian crisis in the occupied territories, an exodus of a million now internally and externally displaced people, a deepening economic and social crisis throughout the country, the imposition of Western sanctions against Russia, rising nationalisms in Russia and Ukraine, military exercises and mobilisations by Russia and NATO across Eastern Europe. They amount to further escalation and widening of the conflict.

In this article I have tried to show it is not enough to examine the actions of the big powers in order to understand how this crisis began. Its tap root grows out of the historical experience of Ukrainian society and their state. This is the first and necessary condition for the activation of all the other roots. So too will the solution to the crisis grow out of Ukraine. It will have to confront the failure of the contemporary ruling class to fulfil the popular expectations arising from the attainment of independence in 1991 for prosperity, social justice, democracy and national self-determination. While the first three of these expectations were denied by the Ukrainian ruling class, the present war with Russia shows that this same class is also incapable of defending its country's national independence. The current situation powerfully echoes the two previous attempts in history—in 1648 and 1917—when a new social class tried and failed to build an independent state centred on Kyiv and the Dnipro River basin. Will the same happen again? Will Ukraine be reduced again to territory contested by the Great Powers?

The social forces mobilised by the Maidan in 2013–2014 also failed, in their case to offer up an alternative, revolutionary leadership and a way out of the crisis. This particular failure belongs to the Ukrainian and the international left as much as it does to anyone else. Until the left gets involved with these social forces on the ground the nationalist right will continue to dominate the political terrain on which the Ukrainian question is contested.

What happens inside Ukraine is far too often deemed irrelevant or of secondary importance by people on the left who proffer their own solutions to the present crisis. I can understand why John Mearsheimer does not even want to know about the internal situation. What states do to each other is all that matters to realists like him. However, when Professor Stephen Cohen and Jeremy Corbyn MP take the position that the USA is primarily responsible for the crisis and that Russia's claims to Ukraine as its "traditional" and "historic" sphere of influence are justified, they do exactly the same thing as Mearsheimer: they see the solution to the crisis in restoring a balance between the Great Powers. They admit no role in it for the Ukrainian people. This is not simply a failure of analysis, but a failure to uphold these people's democratic right to national self-determination. That leaves them and many avowedly left-wing organisations and individuals standing in the camp of Russian imperialism.

Russia, the USA and the West European states all bear responsibility for their parts in this crisis. I have tried to show here that the political economy of Ukraine is stretched across a re-knitted transnational capitalist economy in which Russia on the one hand and the Western powers on the other are vying to draw Ukraine's ruling class, national market and productive assets into their respective integration projects. Despite trying for a quarter-century, the Ukrainian state has been unable to gain membership in the political and military-security institutions of the Western, Euro-Atlantic project. Over the same period it has been refusing to join equivalent institutions of the Russia-led project.

My findings draw attention to the revival of Russian imperialism since 2000, the divisions in the Western alliance over policy towards Russia, and the diminished capacity of the USA to project its own power into the region. These three factors steadily altered the balance of power in Eastern Europe between these competing regional integration projects. The collapse of the Yanukovych regime gave Russia's leaders the opportunity to exploit the changing balance, return to the initiative and try to draw Ukraine back into its own sphere. Russia militarised and internationalised the crisis. It provoked the Western powers to respond with economic sanctions and strengthening the capacity of NATO member states bordering Russia and Ukraine. Both the Western powers and Russia have pressed the Ukrainian leadership to engage with the separatist movement and seek a negotiated solution with them. The harder it is pressed, the less room exists for its manoeuvre between them.

Whether it is Russia or the Western powers who claim Ukraine as part of their own sphere, this can only be an imperialist claim. One or another faction of the Ukrainian ruling class may submit to such a claim, or even to a joint Russian-Western tutelage over the country. Sooner or later their common class interests will lead them to it, but it will not be accepted by the Ukrainian people, nor should it be by those who want to support them.

Index

SOVIET AND POST-SOVIET POLITICS AND SOCIETY

Li Bennich-Björkman, Sergiy Kurbatov (Eds.)

WHEN THE FUTURE CAME

The Collapse of the USSR and the Emergence of National Memory in Post-Soviet History Textbooks

ibidem

Editor: Andreas Umland

Founded in 2004 and refereed since 2007, SPPS makes available, to the academic community and general public, affordable English-, German- and Russian-language scholarly studies of various empirical aspects of the recent history and current affairs of the former Soviet bloc from the late Tsarist period to today. It publishes approximately 15–20 volumes per year, and focuses on issues in transitions to and from democracy such as economic crisis, identity formation, civil society development, and constitutional reform in CEE and the NIS. SPPS also aims to highlight so far understudied themes in East European studies such as right-wing radicalism, religious life, higher education, or human rights protection.

JOURNAL OF SOVIET AND POST-SOVIET POLITICS AND SOCIETY

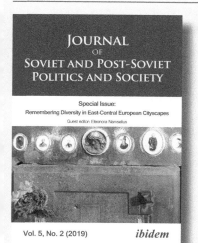

Editor: Julie Fedor

Review Editor: Gergana Dimova

The *Journal of Soviet and Post-Soviet Politics and Society* is a new bi-annual journal that was launched in April 2015 as a companion journal to the *Soviet and Post-Soviet Politics and Society* book series (founded 2004 and edited by Andreas Umland, Dr. phil., PhD). Like the book series, the journal will provide an interdisciplinary forum for new original research on the Soviet and post-Soviet world. The journal aims to become known for publishing creative, intelligent, and lively writing tackling and illuminating significant issues and capable of engaging wider educated audiences beyond the academy.

ibidem
Press

UKRAINIAN VOICES

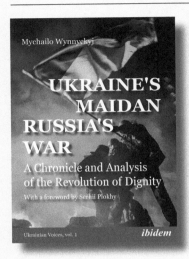

Collected by Andreas Umland

The book series *Ukrainian Voices* publishes English- and German-language monographs, edited volumes, document collections and anthologies of articles authored and composed by Ukrainian politicians, intellectuals, activists, officials, researchers, entrepreneurs, artists, and diplomats. The series' aim is to introduce Western and other audiences to Ukrainian explorations and interpretations of historic and current domestic as well as international affairs. The purpose of these books is to make non-Ukrainian readers familiar with how some prominent Ukrainians approach, research and assess their country's development and position in the world.

FORUM FÜR OSTEUROPÄISCHE IDEEN- UND ZEITGESCHICHTE

Editors: Leonid Luks, Gunter Dehnert, Nikolaus Lobkowicz, Alexei Rybakow, Andreas Umland

FORUM features interdisciplinary discussions by political scientists—literary, legal, and economic scholars—and philosophers on the history of ideas, and it reviews books on Central and Eastern European history. Through the translation and publication of documents and contributions from Russian, Polish, and Czech researchers, the journal offers Western readers critical insight into scientific discourses across Eastern Europe.

ibidem Press

European Studies in the Caucasus

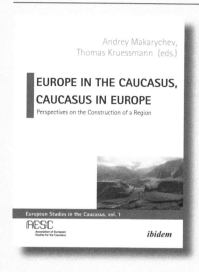

Editor: Thomas Krüssmann

The book series *European Studies in the Caucasus* offers innovative perspectives on regional studies of the Caucasus. By embracing the South Caucasus as well as Turkey and Russia as the major regional powers, it moves away from a traditional viewpoint of European Studies that considers the countries of the region as objects of Europeanization.

Journal of Romanian Studies

Editors: Lavinia Stan, Margaret Beissinger

Review Editor: Radu Cinpoes

The *Journal of Romanian Studies*, jointly developed by The Society for Romanian Studies and ***ibidem*** Press, is a biannual, peer-reviewed, and interdisciplinary journal. It examines critical issues in Romanian studies, linking work in that field to wider theoretical debates and issues of current relevance, and serving as a forum for junior and senior scholars. The journal also presents articles that connect Romania and Moldova comparatively with other states and their ethnic majorities and minorities, and with other groups by investigating the challenges of migration and globalization and the impact of the European Union.

www.ibidem.eu | facebook.com/ibidem.Verlag

ibidem
Press

Balkan Politics and Society

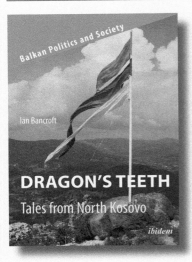

Editors: Jelena Džankić, Soeren Keil

The book series *Balkan Politics and Society* (BPS), launching in 2018, focuses on original empirical research on understudied aspects of the multifaceted historical, political, and cultural trajectories of the Balkan region.

In Statu Nascendi

Editor: Piotr Pietrzak

In Statu Nascendi is a new peer-reviewed journal that aspires to be a world-class scholarly platform encompassing original academic research dedicated to the circle of Political Philosophy, Cultural Studies, Theory of International Relations, Foreign Policy, and the political Decision-making process. The journal investigates specific issues through a socio-cultural, philosophical, and anthropological approach to raise a new type of civic awareness about the complexity of contemporary crisis, instabilities, and warfare situations, where the "stage-of-becoming" plays a vital role.

ibidem
Press